Writing N

ONE WEEK LOAN

Studies in Mathematics Education Series

Series Editor: Paul Ernest, University of Exeter, UK

The Philosophy of Mathematics Education
Paul Ernest

Understanding in Mathematics
Anna Sierpinska

Mathematics Education and Philosophy
Paul Ernest

Constructing Mathematical Knowledge
Edited by Paul Ernest

Investigating Mathematics Teaching
Barbara Jaworski

Radical Contructivism
Ernst von Glasersfeld

The Sociology of Mathematics Education
Paul Dowling

Counting Girls Out: Girls and Mathematics
Valerie Walkerdine

Writing Mathematically: The Discourse of Investigation
Candia Morgan

Studies in Mathematics Education Series: 9

Writing Mathematically
The Discourse of Investigation

Candia Morgan

UK   Falmer Press, 1 Gunpowder Square, London, EC4A 3DE
USA   Falmer Press, Taylor & Francis Inc., 1900 Frost Road, Suite 101,
            Bristol, PA 19007

First published in 1998

A catalogue record for this book is available from the British Library

ISBN 0 7507 0811 5 cased
ISBN 0 7507 0810 7 paper

**Library of Congress Cataloging-in-Publication Data are available on
request**

Jacket design by Caroline Archer

Typeset in 10/12pt Times by
Graphicraft Typesetters Limited, Hong Kong

*Printed in Great Britain by Biddles Ltd., Guildford and King's Lynn on
paper which has a specified pH value on final paper manufacture of not
less than 7.5 and is therefore 'acid free'.*

Contents

Contents

List of Figures and Table

Acknowledgments

This work would not have been possible without the encouragement, support and criticism of many colleagues both collectively and individually. The mathematics education community in the United Kingdom, through the agency in particular of the British Society for Research into Learning Mathematics and the group for Research into Social Perspectives in Mathematics Education, has provided a forum within which I have been able to try out and refine my ideas. While those who have contributed to the final shape of this book are too numerous to mention, I would like especially to thank Steve Lerman, who made me start writing and gave me confidence in the early stages; Celia Hoyles, whose high expectations have helped me to be both self-critical and determined; and the series editor, Paul Ernest, for his critical appreciation.

The students and teachers who appear (although their names are changed) in these pages gave generously of their work and time. It is clear that the discourses within which they were participants created tensions and contradictions for them. Any criticisms I may make, explicitly or implicitly, of the outcomes of the students' or teachers' practices should be seen as criticisms of the systems and structures within which they were situated rather than of the individuals themselves.

I would like to thank London Examinations, a division of Edexcel Foundation for kind permission to reproduce Figure 8.1.

Preface by Series Editor

Mathematics education is established world-wide as a major area of study, with numerous dedicated journals and conferences serving ever-growing national and international communities of scholars. As it develops, research in mathematics education is becoming more theoretically orientated. Although originally rooted in mathematics and psychology, vigorous new perspectives are pervading it from disciplines and fields as diverse as philosophy, logic, sociology, anthropology, history, women's studies, cognitive science, linguistics, semiotics, hermeneutics, post-structuralism and post-modernism. These new research perspectives are providing fresh lenses through which teachers and researchers can view the theory and practice of mathematics teaching and learning.

The series Studies in Mathematics Education aims to encourage the development and dissemination of theoretical perspectives in mathematics education as well as their critical scrutiny. It is a series of research contributions to the field based on disciplined perspectives that link theory with practice. This series is founded on the philosophy that theory is the practitioner's most powerful tool in understanding and changing practice. Whether the practice concerns the teaching and learning of mathematics, teacher education, or educational research, the series offers new perspectives to help clarify issues, pose and solve problems and stimulate debate. It aims to have a major impact on the development of mathematics education as a field of study in the twenty-first century.

One of the major areas of growth in mathematics education research concerns the interactions between language, linguistics and mathematics. Although it has long been recognized that symbols and symbolization and, hence, language, play a uniquely privileged role in mathematics and its teaching and learning, the systematic application of linguistics and discourse theory to the field has been slow to develop. I would like to speculate that this may be due to two factors. First of all, thinking about mathematics has until recently been dominated by an absolutist epistemology which suggests that the role of language in mathematics is merely to describe the superhuman realm of 'mathematical reality'. Furthermore, the correct use of language in mathematics is for the same reason understood to be determined by the immutable canons of logic. Secondly, the dominance of mathematics education by traditional psychological theories has also meant that mathematical thought and cognitions have been foregrounded at the expense of mathematical talk and writing. Indeed, as Candia Morgan says here, there is a widespread, associated and problematic myth of transparency which assumes that talk and text provide a non-distorting window into the mind of the speaker/writer.

However, there are a number of emerging changes of perspective which have brought these assumptions into question. The scientific research paradigm with its absolutist epistemology is no longer dominant in mathematics education research. It is now merely one of a number of legitimate alternatives. Language, text, discourse and their relationship with the social context have now become central areas of investigation in mathematics education research. Fully developed disciplinary perspectives and theories are being imported from linguistics and discourse theory for use in mathematics education. In part, this has been driven by methodological necessity, as an increasing range of empirical research studies analyse transcripts of speech, discourse, and writings collected during their inquiries. However, the present work goes beyond this utilitarian need and provides an overview of language and linguistics as applied in mathematics education research, as well as developing its own unique perspective and investigation. This is because the language of mathematics and the discourse of open-ended investigatory work are themselves the objects of study. It is also a reflection of the developing maturity of the field of study, out of which confident and definitive works like the present one can emerge.

Candia Morgan draws upon the social semiotics of Halliday and the critical discourse analysis of Fairclough, Hodge and Kress as a basis for her theorization. She provides a state of the art survey of international research into language and mathematics. Although this is intended as a backdrop to her own inquiry into one of the most interesting uses of writing in mathematics, many researchers and students will find this in itself, with its three hundred and fifty bibliographic references, an invaluable foundation for their own further researches in the area. However, her unique contribution lies in developing and applying her own theoretical perspective. Candia Morgan investigates both secondary school children's writing, and also how it is 'read' by teachers. She investigates the latter from the perspective of how their readings are used as a basis for institutionalized assessment, focusing on reports of open-ended problem solving tasks ('investigational work'). Clearly the use of writing within the educational system is a vital dimension to consider, and yet it has been hitherto much neglected. Some aspects of her analysis are both powerful and startling, such as how teachers infer pupil ability from a few key features of their texts. All in all, this volume exemplifies perfectly the series philosophy of linking theory with practice, with the result that both are enriched.

Paul Ernest
University of Exeter
December 1997

Chapter 1

Introduction

As a mathematics teacher in a London secondary school in the late 1980s I became involved in the implementation of the curriculum development of 'coursework' as a component of the General Certificate of Secondary Education (GCSE) examination.[1] This innovation involved students throughout the school, but particularly in the two years leading up to the GCSE (ages 14–16), in writing substantial reports of their work on mathematical investigations. In most cases this meant that students were given a situation to explore mathematically, searching for relationships and generalizations; they were to be assessed not so much on the basis of the results of their investigation as on the quality of the mathematical processes (e.g. working systematically, conjecturing, generalizing, explaining, communicating) that they demonstrated. I was pleased that the students' work on more open and extended mathematical tasks was to be valued by the public examination system in this way and that the importance of problem-solving processes was also to be recognized. Simultaneously, however, like many mathematics teachers, I was unhappy with the quality of the written work that my students produced. It was often the case that the quality of the activity that had taken place in the classroom and the observations and reasoning that a student had displayed to me in discussion were not represented in the written report or were expressed so poorly that it was difficult to make sense of them. At the same time, I was forced to admit that, although I felt able to write competently myself, I did not have the knowledge about language or the skills in teaching writing that would enable me to help my students to communicate their mathematical activity more effectively in writing. This was the starting point for my study of mathematical writing and for the work that is contained in this volume.

The writing done in secondary school mathematics classrooms has, until recently, been extremely restricted. While students have sometimes recorded page after page of repetitive symbolic manipulations, their writing of verbal language has generally consisted of little more than a few isolated words. Some short passages, such as definitions or word problems, might be copied from the board or from a textbook, but little of any length or requiring original composition has been required. A survey of written work across the curriculum in Scottish secondary schools (Spencer et al., 1983), for example, revealed no examples of more extended writing in mathematics. This contrasts with the sort of written texts that more mature mathematicians compose. Research mathematicians and those mathematicians employed in industry or by government are expected to produce coherent, sometimes lengthy documents that incorporate both symbolic and 'natural' language.

1

This difference in the types of text produced reflects, in part at least, differences in the types of mathematical activity undertaken by school students and by 'real' mathematicians, differences in the purposes for which the writing is done and in the audiences to whom it is addressed. On the whole, students have worked only on relatively short, routine problems for which little elaboration or explanation is required. Their writing has been addressed only to their teacher (who is expected to know the content already — better than the student does), usually with the main purpose of checking the correctness of the result of the manipulation. In contrast, 'real' mathematicians tend to work on relatively substantial and often original problems. Their anticipated audiences are expected to be genuinely interested in knowing the results and to need to be persuaded of the correctness of the results.

Recent curriculum development movements, however, have prompted a move away from the type of school curriculum described above. For example, in the United States the internationally influential National Council of Teachers of Mathematics (NCTM) (1989) has argued with the publication of its 'Standards' for a curriculum that is based on a notion of mathematics

> as more than a collection of concepts and skills to be mastered; it includes methods of investigating and reasoning, means of communication, and notions of context. (p. 5)

and for teaching that includes the use of exploration and project work. The international concern with the use of 'open-ended' tasks may be seen in the existence since 1994 of a discussion group at PME[2] conferences involving teachers and researchers from many countries (Pehkonen, 1997). In the United Kingdom, one of the original aims of the 'investigations' movement (which will be described in more detail in Chapter 5) was to enable all students to experience doing mathematics like a 'real' mathematician, working on non-routine, possibly substantial or original problems. Such changes to the types of activity undertaken in the mathematics classroom are inevitably accompanied by changes in the sorts of linguistic activity, including writing, that students need to use to communicate about what they have done; linguistic activity has both increased and changed its character and purposes.

There has been some interest in recent years, particularly in the United States and Australia, in developing the use of writing within the mathematics classroom. This is largely based on the premise that writing is an activity that is in itself conducive to learning. The current position of writing in mathematics classrooms is described in Chapter 3. With a few exceptions (e.g. Driscoll and Powell, 1992; Morgan, 1994), however, little attention has been paid to the form of the writing produced by students or to helping them to learn to write more effectively. The focus of researchers and curriculum developers has been on the mathematical learning taking place rather than on the writing itself. It has largely been assumed that students will learn to write through experience and that they will develop appropriate[3] forms of language 'naturally'. Where writing plays a central and continuous role in classroom communication this assumption may have some basis; in the vast majority of mathematics classrooms, however, it is unlikely that enough time will be devoted to writing activities for this sort of learning through 'immersion' to take place. Certainly, the writing of investigation reports for GCSE coursework, although important because of the weight of the examination system, tends to be isolated from other parts of the curriculum and is often the only extended mathematical writing that students engage in. It would seem, therefore, that there is a case for developing means of supporting students as they learn to write in mathematical ways; this is discussed further in Chapter 4.

An immediate issue that arises with any attempt to support students learning to write mathematically is the question of what 'writing mathematically' is actually like. Researchers in mathematics education have increasingly paid attention to the role of language in the learning of mathematics; indeed, the theme of the PME conference in 1996 was 'mathematics and language'. Most attention, however, has been paid to the difficulties children may have in making sense of mathematical language or the benefits that may arise from engaging in talking or writing in the classroom rather than addressing the nature of mathematical language itself. Indeed, attempts to describe what distinguishes mathematical language have tended to be rather naive, focusing on obvious surface characteristics such as symbolism and vocabulary and failing to consider higher level[4] structures. Moreover, it has largely been assumed that there is a unity across mathematical texts[5] that makes it possible to talk of 'the language of mathematics'. This unity is an illusion. We would probably recognize a primary school text book, a secondary student's investigation report and a research mathematician's paper published in an academic journal as all being mathematical texts. The language in which they are written, however, has extremely little in common.

As I attempted to find a way of characterizing mathematical writing that would take account of this diversity and provide a useful means of communicating with others, including mathematics teachers and students, about the texts and the writing activities that occur in mathematics classrooms, I found two concepts enormously useful in providing me with ways of thinking (and writing) about language. Firstly, the concept of a mathematics 'register', introduced by Halliday (1974) and elaborated in a mathematics education context by Pimm (1987), expands the view of what is special about the language used in mathematical settings to include consideration of grammatical structures and forms of argumentation as well as symbolism and specialist vocabulary. At the same time, by defining the mathematics register as the linguistic means developed for expressing mathematical meanings it is possible to take account of and describe the diversity of mathematical texts.

The concept of 'register' thus provides a more theoretically developed means of looking at language in diverse mathematical contexts but nevertheless does not by itself provide a means of saying whether a particular text is appropriate to a particular purpose. In order to address my concern with effective communication of mathematical activity it has been necessary for me not only to review existing descriptions of mathematical language (see Chapter 2) but also to develop a means of analysing mathematical texts that would both take account of and account for the wide variation in the forms of language used in different mathematical and social settings. 'Effective' or 'appropriate' writing is necessarily 'effective' or 'appropriate' in relation to the purposes for which it is written and read and the perceptions of those who make use of the writing. This brings me to the second important concept that forms a framework for my thinking about linguistic activity and mathematics education in general: the concept of 'discourse'.

An orientation towards the study of language as *discourse* does not allow one to see language as a neutral and transparent means of communication but as a means by which meanings are constructed within social and institutional practices. As Macdonell (1986) puts it:

> meanings are to be found only in the concrete forms of differing social and institutional practices: there can be no meaning in 'language'. (p. 12)

Discourse comprises not only texts[6] but the wider set of social and linguistic practices within which the texts are situated. Discourse refers to 'the social process in which texts are embedded, while text is the concrete object produced in discourse' (Hodge and Kress, 1988, p. 6). Studying language as discourse, therefore, involves studying not only the lexis, grammar and organization of particular texts, but also the concepts and categories that participants in the discourse have available to construct meanings and the possible positions that participants may adopt as they compose or receive texts. Interpreting a particular text necessitates knowing who composed it and who is intended to receive it, as well as the kinds of interpretations that are possible within the discourse. Thus, for example, within the traditional mathematics classroom a correctly worked solution of an equation might be interpreted variously as: an exemplar to be copied, illustrating a method to be followed (composed by the teacher or other 'authority', written on the board or in the textbook); a demonstration of the author's competence (composed by a 'successful' student as part of a homework task or in a test); evidence that the author has 'cheated' (composed by a 'poor' student in conjunction with other texts suggesting a lack of competence). The concepts 'example', 'competence', 'cheating' and the positions of 'teacher', 'successful student' and 'poor student' are all part of the discourse of school mathematics.

I have sought to devize a method for analysing mathematical texts that adopts this discursive orientation, taking into account the concepts and positions available within the discourses in which writers and readers are participants. I use the plural 'discourses' not only to suggest that the analytic method is applicable to texts produced in a wide range of mathematical settings but also to indicate the complexity of single settings. Discourses are not isolated but may overlap and compete. In the case of investigative mathematics in secondary schools, the participants may be positioned variously[7] within the discourses of 'investigation', of the more traditional 'school mathematics', and of 'assessment'. The adoption by a participant of different positions within these discourses may lead to different and possibly contradictory meanings being constructed from the same text.

Within mathematics education, use has been made of analysis of discourse to address the ways in which some groups of students are disadvantaged by the positions available to them in classroom practices (McBride, 1989) and in text books (McBride, 1994) and the idea of multiple discourses has been used to identify diversity in mathematical practices (Richards, 1991) and in types of language use in mathematics classrooms (Mousley and Marks, 1991). These approaches have not, however, provided knowledge about how language is used within the discourses of mathematics education at a level of detail that would be enough to help students and teachers to take control of the language and manipulate it in order to adopt powerful positions within these discourses. They thus do not address my concern with the disempowerment of those students who lack the control over language needed to write reports on their mathematical investigations in ways that will be judged to be effective and appropriate. Such a level of detailed knowledge requires analysis of the texts themselves and of how the forms of language in the texts function in the construction of meanings. The method of text analysis described in Chapter 6 and applied to a set of student texts in Chapter 7 makes use of Halliday's (1985) Functional Grammar and the ideas of Critical Discourse Analysis (Fairclough, 1989; 1995; Hodge and Kress, 1993), focusing on what may be achieved by choosing to use one form of language rather than another. This makes it possible to consider the effectiveness and appropriateness of a given text in relation to a given purpose and a particular audience.

My interest in mathematical language is not solely theoretical. As has been described above, it arose from a very practical concern with my students' ability to communicate their mathematical activity effectively in a context in which they would be assessed on the basis of their written products. In educational contexts, it is very often (perhaps almost always) the case that students' achievement is assessed through the medium of spoken or written language. There is currently an international interest in the development of means of assessment that represent more completely the aims of the curriculum. In mathematics this has been seen in a move away from multiple-choice format tests and timed examinations consisting of routine questions towards more varied forms of assessment. For example, the Australian state of Victoria's Certificate of Education requirements now involve senior secondary students in extended mathematics projects including independent investigation and 'challenging' problem solving (Stephens and Money, 1993), while several states in the US have changed their mathematics assessments to include open-ended questions in their tests (California Assessment Program) or even to use portfolio assessment (Vermont) (Dossey and Swafford, 1993). Most of these developments, like GCSE coursework in England and Wales, involve increasing dependence on students' production of texts (mostly, but not exclusively, written texts) of various types and lengths, including some extended writing. It is, therefore, relevant to consider the ways in which teachers or other assessors make sense of students' linguistic production and the ways in which the language used by students may affect judgments that are made about their achievement.

A review of existing research on assessment practices (discussed in Chapter 8) revealed very little information on how teachers make sense of and judge students' mathematical writing. Without knowledge of this, however, it is impossible to say whether a student's text is appropriately or effectively written. The concepts of appropriateness and effectiveness are only meaningful within a given social setting; what is appropriate and effective in a primary school text book may be entirely inappropriate and ineffective in a secondary school text book, a piece of coursework, an academic research paper, etc. In an attempt to address this, therefore, I needed to look at the assessment context in which students' texts are produced and consumed. Chapter 9 to 11 describe my exploration of the ways in which mathematics teachers make sense of and judge their students' writing. By listening to teachers reading and assessing a set of coursework texts, I have attempted to identify those features of the writing that they pay attention to and the forms that influence their judgments of the value of the piece of work and the achievement of the student. This allows me to draw some conclusions about what may be appropriate and effective mathematical writing in the particular context of reports of investigations. It also raises a number of issues about the relationship between this form of assessment and the curriculum development it is intended to support. In particular, there are some tensions and contradictions within teachers' practices that may jeopardize curriculum aims related to encouraging creativity and the use of open-ended problems.

There are thus two interrelated themes that I attempt to address in this book: mathematical language in secondary school mathematics (in particular written language), and the assessment of students' mathematical activity, particularly within the context of curriculum developments that seek to broaden students' mathematical experiences and to value independence and creativity rather than rule following. My original concern with my students' apparent failure to communicate their mathematical activity effectively in writing, together with concern about the ways in which teachers may make sense of student texts, lead me to consider in Chapter 12 how both students and teachers of mathematics may come to be more aware of how mathematical language works and, consequently, more able to make powerful use of it themselves.

Notes

1 The General Certificate of Secondary Education (GCSE), a national qualification for students in England and Wales at age 16+, was examined for the first time in 1988. A proportion of the marks for the examination (varying from 20 per cent to 100 per cent, but since 1995 restricted in mathematics to 20 per cent) may be gained by the presentation of work completed during the last two years of the course rather than a terminal examination. This component is called 'coursework' and in most cases consists of a small number of extended tasks undertaken by students during class time and for homework. The course-work component is normally assessed by the student's own teacher and moderated both within the school and externally by the examining board. The traditional timed examination component is marked by an external examiner employed by the examining board.

2 The annual conference of the International Group for the Psychology of Mathematics Education.

3 Here and elsewhere, when I use the terms *appropriate* and *effective* to describe writing, I do not intend to suggest that these have any absolute meaning. Rather, they must

always be seen as relative to the particular context. Thus, a text may be 'appropriate' if it matches the expectations of those empowered to make judgments within a given practice. It may be 'effective' if it succeeds in performing the functions intended by its author.

4 'Higher level' is not intended to imply greater difficulty or a higher cognitive level. In linguistic terms, the word is at a higher level than the phoneme, the clause is at a higher level than the word, the paragraph or the complete text are again at higher levels, each level consisting of groupings of items from the level below.

5 *Texts*, here and elsewhere, may be either written or oral.

6 The term *text* will be used to refer to a piece of written or spoken language that has 'a socially ascribed unity' (Hodge and Kress, 1988, p. 6) such as an article, a conversation, a piece of coursework, an interview, a diary entry, a note to the milkman. The term *discourse* is sometimes used to label such socially coherent pieces of language by those linguists and others who are concerned with the study of language at this level as opposed to at the level of the sentence or below (e.g. Sinclair and Coulthard, 1975). I am using *discourse* in a stronger sense.

7 The idea of multiple positioning in relation to mathematics education has been used notably by Walkerdine (1988) and Evans (1994).

Chapter 2

'The Language of Mathematics' — Characteristics of Written Mathematical Texts

To attempt to describe 'the language of mathematics' is to ascribe a unity to the field that is justified only in the broadest terms. Just as there are a number of varying social practices that may be labelled as mathematics (including academic mathematics, school mathematics, recreational mathematics, etc.) there are a variety of genres of text that may be called mathematical (e.g. research paper, textbook, examination question and answer, puzzle, etc.). Within any mathematical practice some texts will be considered to be appropriate to the practice and others will not. There are clearly some features of the genre of academic mathematics research papers that we would be surprised to see appearing in, for example, a child's report of their investigative work or in a book of mathematical puzzles. It seems likely, however, that any text that is commonly identifiable as mathematical will share at least some linguistic characteristics[1] with other texts that are also considered to be mathematical. This is not necessarily to say that there are core characteristics common to all mathematical texts but that there are likely to be areas of 'overlap' that contribute to our ability to identify a particular text as mathematical.[2]

In the case of texts written by school students as part of their mathematical studies, any such texts are produced within the discourse of school mathematics and as such are likely to be influenced by the characteristics of other mathematical texts experienced by students and their teachers both in the school and beyond. In later chapters, I shall be looking specifically at texts written by students as reports of their mathematical investigative work. As well as considering how this genre relates to other forms of school mathematical writing, its relationship to types of writing produced by professional mathematicians is of interest, particularly in the light of claims that involvement in investigative work is similar to the activity of research in mathematics (see Chapter 5). In this chapter, I seek to establish a background of knowledge of those characteristics of those mathematical texts written by 'experts', that is, by professional mathematicians and by the authors of mathematics text books. This knowledge is necessarily limited to a relatively small selection of genres, although it may be possible to make some general statements about characteristics common to a range of mathematical genres. The characteristics of texts produced by school students will be considered in the next chapter.

The linguistic features that contribute to a text's acceptance within a particular mathematical context include its vocabulary and symbolic context, its grammatical structure and the forms of argumentation used. A number of authors have provided descriptions of general features of mathematical texts. Notably, Halliday's contribution to the 1974 UNESCO symposium on Linguistics and Mathematics Education introduced the use of the concept of a mathematical 'register'[3] to discussions about language in the mathematics education context and provided an overview of some of the grammatical characteristics of such a register. This has been elaborated from a mathematics education perspective by Pimm (1987). The nature of a mathematical register is discussed in the next section. I then turn to the two types of mathematical text whose features have been considered in more specific terms: the academic text and the school mathematics text book (although neither of these types of text are entirely homogeneous).

In contrast to the relatively small amount of research concerned with explicitly mathematical texts, there is a greater amount that addresses the nature of scientific writing. Although there are many differences between the disciplines, some aspects of the research in scientific writing are relevant. Many of the concerns of teachers of science and of English for Science and Technology (EST) about the difficulties that learners at many different levels of education (including both native and non-native speakers) have with reading and writing scientific texts are similar to the concerns of mathematics educators. To name but a few, the features of scientific and mathematical texts which appear to cause concern in both disciplines include: specialist and semi-specialist vocabulary; use of symbolism; an abstract, impersonal style; the construction of academic argument. While there are differences between the forms of language used in the two subject areas (as indeed there are between different areas within science and technology) it is likely that some of the features of scientific texts are similar to those of some mathematical texts and that examination of the field will yield results and methods that may prove to be of use in the study of mathematical writing. I shall, therefore, refer to examples of research on writing in science where these appear relevant.

The Mathematical Register in General

As has been argued above, there is some difficulty in producing a comprehensive definition and description of what constitutes 'mathematical language'. Nevertheless, many authors discussing this topic have treated it as an identifiable entity and have described general characteristics of mathematical language without distinguishing between different types of text. Such general characteristics are likely to contribute towards making a text containing them likely to be seen as 'mathematics' (though they are likely to be neither necessary nor sufficient for such an identification).

Some attempts to characterize mathematical language have focused almost entirely on its symbolic system (e.g. Ervinck, 1992) or on the specialist vocabulary used to name specifically mathematical objects and concepts (e.g. Otterburn and

Nicholson, 1976), usually from the point of view that these aspects cause difficulties for students. Apart from the recognition that some symbols and terms are used either exclusively or in unusual ways in mathematical contexts, I do not intend to attempt a full characterization of the nature of mathematical lexis; discussion of its form and derivation may be found in Halliday (1974) and Pimm (1987). While symbolism and specialist vocabulary are perhaps the most obviously visible aspects of many mathematical texts, they are clearly inadequate to provide a full description of the nature of mathematical texts. Mathematical texts do not on the whole consist only of strings of symbols or of naming things; rather, they are, like other academic texts, rhetorical in nature, addressing and attempting to persuade a reader (Ernest, 1993a; Hansen, 1988). It is, therefore, necessary to look beyond the level of vocabulary at the syntax of the text and at the structures which serve to construct mathematical arguments.

Discussions of mathematical language often attempt to describe it as a set of additions to some more basic or 'natural' form of language. Kane, for example, describes 'mathematical English' as a mixture of 'ordinary English' and 'various brands of highly stylized formal symbol systems' (1968, p. 296). This definition is not, however, entirely adequate, as Kane himself demonstrates when he attempts to elaborate it. The non-symbolic 'ordinary' component also has specifically mathematical aspects which bring into question its 'ordinary' nature: 'For example, phrases such as "if and only if, if . . . then, A or B" are direct translations from the sentential calculus' (ibid.). This demonstrates some of the difficulties brought about by considering mathematical language as formed by an augmentation of a basic form of 'ordinary' or 'natural' language. The 'ordinary' component must itself be transformed in order to express mathematical meanings. As well as specialist vocabulary this may involve the creation of new grammatical structures or 'the bringing into prominence of structures which already existed but were rather specialized or rare . . . like . . . "the sum of the series to n terms"' (Halliday, 1974, p. 67). While such developments are also characteristic of the development of the language of other specialist domains, Pimm (1987) suggests that the extent to which this occurs in mathematics is such as to be qualitatively different.

In addition to specialist vocabulary and structures, other features that have been identified as characteristic of much mathematical text include its 'density and conciseness . . . which tend to concentrate the reader's attention on the correctness of what was written rather than on its richness of meaning' (Austin and Howson, 1979, p. 174). Halliday and Martin (1993) point out that scientific texts in general have a high 'lexical density', that is, a high ratio of 'content' words to 'grammatical' words (p. 76).

It must, however, be recognized that there is substantial diversity between the forms of language that are used in different mathematical contexts, and it is not clear that the idea of a single mathematical register is sufficient to cope with the variation of functions and meanings to be found, for example, in a primary school text book and in an academic research paper. Not only does the subject matter vary but the modes of argument used in different domains of mathematical activity are likely to differ substantially. Considering the relationships between the academic discipline of mathematics and school mathematics, Richards (1991), for example, identifies at least four 'distinct domains of discourse' associated with mathematics:

1 Research Math — the spoken mathematics of the professional mathematician . . .
2 Inquiry Math — mathematics as it is used by mathematically literate adults . . .
3 Journal Math — the language of mathematical publications and papers . . .
4 School Math — the discourse of the standard classroom in which mathematics is taught. (pp. 15–16)

He draws parallels between the assumptions and methodologies to be found in the 'Research' and 'Inquiry' domains and between those of 'Journal Math' and 'School Math'. In particular, he identifies the modes of argument as distinguishing between the domains, claiming that the former use the 'logic of discovery' while the latter depend on 'reconstructed logic'. These different modes of argument will clearly be accompanied by different linguistic structures.

Rather than attempting to characterize a unified field of mathematical language, I feel it is more appropriate to consider mathematical English in the way that Halliday and Martin (1993) define scientific English — as a semiotic space with diatypic variation and diachronic evolution (i.e. varying both between a number of different practices and over time) which is: 'by and large . . . a recognizable category, and any speaker of English for whom it falls within the domain of experience knows it when he sees it or hears it' (p. 54). A text may thus be identified as mathematical if it is identified as such by a reader whose experience qualifies them to make such a judgment.[4] While the presence of symbols, specialist vocabulary and grammatical structures and a high level of density and conciseness may serve to make it likely that a text will be identified as mathematical by such a reader, to be judged a 'good' or 'appropriate' text within a particular mathematical practice the text is likely to have to conform to a number of other characteristics.

Academic Mathematics Texts

Given the claim made by the advocates of investigative work in school mathematics that the processes involved in investigative activity are similar to those used by professional mathematicians (see Chapter 5), the academic research report may be seen as the 'adult' equivalent of the investigation report. This is not a claim that the two types of report resemble each other closely, merely that it is of interest to compare and contrast them.

While the literature reveals relatively little analysis of mathematical academic writing, mathematicians have offered advice to each other about the forms their writing might take, focusing in particular on reading difficulties for both novices and experts perceived to be caused by the excessive use of symbols, the construction of proofs and an impersonal style. A formal, impersonal style, including an absence of reference to human activity, is one aspect that mathematical writing appears to share with many other academic areas, in particular with writing in the sciences. In this section, the nature of academic mathematics texts is considered, taking into account the views of mathematicians themselves and research concerned with scientific academic texts in general. Examples from one academic mathematics text (Dye, 1991) will be used to illustrate the ways in which some of the characteristics are manifested in a mathematical context.[5]

The Professional's 'Common Sense' View: Mathematics is Its Symbol System

For students and new entrants to the scientific and technical academy and professions there is a considerable body of publications providing advice on how to write in scientific and technical genres. In mathematics the field is less substantial; it is possible that this difference is in part due to the smaller lay readership for technical and academic mathematical texts but it may also be due to a common perception among mathematicians that the only significantly meaningful part of a mathematics text resides in the symbol system. Since producing 'correct mathematics' may be seen as equivalent to producing a correct sequence of symbols, the mathematical writer's task is merely to record the content without any need to pay separate attention to the form of the language in which it is recorded. Tobias (1989) characterizes the mathematicians' and mathematics teachers' attitude that 'spoken language' or any non-symbolic elaboration that provides context 'is a temporary scaffolding to be discarded as soon as the new code is mastered' (p. 49). This identification of mathematics with its symbol system is even perpetuated by some of those who advocate using writing as a way of learning mathematics. One 'writing to learn' activity suggested by Kenyon (1989) instructs the student to 'Write out the solution in words (no mathematics)' (p. 79). While the wording of this instruction may be merely intended to make the teacher's expectations clear to the student, it nevertheless emphasizes the symbolic nature of mathematics itself and its apparent independence from linguistic expression and from context.

The frequently stated aphorism that 'mathematics is a language' is associated with this identification of mathematics with its symbol system (Rotman, 1993). To take an extreme example, Ervynck's (1992) paper entitled *Mathematics as a Foreign Language* deals almost exclusively with the nature of mathematical symbols and their internal syntax. The only non-symbolic elements recognized are the words *let, thus, so, hence,* and *obviously* and phrases such as *after a short calculation the reader will come to the following result* which Ervynck describes merely as 'connectives' linking the deductive development together (p. 226), implying that they have no fundamental effect on the meaning of the text.

Nevertheless, some mathematicians, expressing concern about the production of effective mathematical texts, have published guidelines and advice which recognize that some 'natural language' is required to supplement the symbols (e.g. Gillman, 1987; Knuth, Larrabee and Roberts, 1989; Steenrod, Halmos, Schiffer and Dieudonné, 1973). Even the advice to authors submitting research articles to the journal of the London Mathematical Society requires that no page should be entirely without words (cited by Pimm, 1987, p. 121). The reasons given by these authors for including non-symbolic elements in mathematical texts, however, suggest that they are merely to make the text easier to read, particularly to an audience beyond the very small group of colleagues working in the same field, rather than to contribute to its meaning. Similarly, Roe (1977) argues that 'these verbal realizations . . . may in some cases be semantically empty' (p. 11). His analysis of the ways in which mathematical symbolism may be integrated into a scientific text presents a view of science and mathematics as potentially independent of human activity. By describing devices such as the use of *we* or words such as *surprisingly* or *useful* as 'meta-statements' whose function is to humanize rather than to inform, Roe implies that it is possible to separate the content of science from the processes of discovery or manipulation and from the form in which it is communicated. Mathematics educators, writing from a psychological point of view, tend to recognize that the symbolic system is embedded in 'natural language' (e.g. Ernest, 1987; Kaput, 1987) although this does not necessarily mean that their discussion of mathematical language takes this into account. For example, Ernest's analysis of the 'meaning' of mathematical expressions deals only with the syntax of the symbolic system.

In contrast, Rotman (1988) argues that 'understanding' and 'conviction' of the strength of a mathematical argument formed by manipulation of symbols is only achieved through the natural language within which it is embedded. It is not clear, however, whether this natural language must be physically present in the written text or whether it is only implicitly present and is constructed or reconstructed by the reader. Rotman's argument arises from a philosophical position that views the activity of mathematicians as socially constructed rather than as the discovery of platonic truths. Indeed, in a later book (Rotman, 1993) he describes the belief that 'mathematics is a language' as arising from a platonist view of mathematics. Certainly Layzer's (1989) claim for the universal communication of mathematics makes no concessions to cultural relativist views of mathematics.

> We can never hope to understand Euripedes' plays in the way they were understood by their original audiences, but Euclid's *Elements* speak to us as clearly as it did to his contemporaries. Chinese poetry is untranslatable; but T.D. Lee's lectures on particle physics and quantum field theory, originally given in Chinese, lose nothing in translation to English. (p. 126)

A detailed examination of the lexis and syntax of the symbol system itself is beyond the scope of this study; analyses may be found in, for example, Ervinck (1992) and Roe (1977). Recently, there has also been increasing interest in semiotic aspects of mathematical symbolism both in advanced mathematics (Rotman, 1993) and in school level mathematics (see, for example, Vile and Lerman, 1996). However, although much of school mathematics may consist of the repetitive manipulation of symbols (Ernest, 1993b), the range of symbols used by any but the most advanced school students is restricted almost entirely to those of arithmetic and elementary algebra and, in particular, the quantity and scope of symbolic activity involved in most investigative work is extremely limited. While this means that, in reading texts produced by school students, making sense of the symbolic content of a text may not be of major importance, nevertheless, the extent of the identification of mathematics with its symbol system is very likely to be significant in its effect on readers' interpretations of the texts — even to the extent that the presence or absence of symbolism may determine whether or not a student's text is considered to be 'mathematical' at all.

Formality and the Place of Human Beings in the Text

It is accepted as common knowledge that both scientific and mathematical texts are impersonal and formal. Clearly, the symbolic content discussed above contributes to this, but there are also a number of relevant characteristics of the 'natural' language. There has been little detailed consideration of this aspect of mathematical texts, though Chapman (1997) identifies high modality (i.e. a high degree of certainty and an absence of such human frailties as doubt or expressions of attitude) as a feature of what she sees as 'more mathematical language' in the classroom. 'Formality' has, however, been an area of substantial study in scientific writing. Strube's (1989) attempt to define what constitutes a formal style with specific reference to physics textbooks identifies a major aspect as compliance with conventions and rules that 'give writing authority and objective validity in its own sphere' (p. 292). Some of the rules Strube identifies seem to apply more widely to academic writing in many fields, in particular the use of a *distant authorial voice*, manifested in the use of the passive voice and the absence of direct reference to the author (apart from an impersonal 'we') or the reader.

One source of the 'distant authorial voice' is the use of nominal rather than verbal expressions. Halliday (1966; 1974) notes the extensive use of nominalizations in both scientific and mathematical texts. In particular, long nominal constructions are very common in mathematics; Halliday and Martin (1993) illustrate the phenomenon with the example *solving the open sentence over D*. This form of grammatical metaphor, by transforming an action into an object, clearly contributes to the 'formality' of the text by obscuring any human agency involved in the action. At the same time, however, 'packaging a complex phenomenon into a single semiotic entity' (Halliday and Martin, 1993, p. 60) also contributes to the kinds of meanings that can be expressed in the text; the nominal expression can itself become an actor in the text and can be the cause or effect of other phenomena. Thus Dye (1991) uses statements such as:

> The **demand that the first vertex of (13) is polar to the other two** *gives*
> $Aj + Bj^2 - Cj^3 = Aj^2 - Bj^3 + Cj = 0.$

in which the use of nominalization alienates the reader from the source of the 'demand'. The necessity is represented as an abstract entity whose independent existence has material consequences. Nominalizations also play a significant role in the specifically mathematical meanings available. For example, nouns constructed from verbs such as *stabilizer*, *permutation*, and *discriminant* are used extensively within Dye's paper. The ability to represent processes as objects and hence to operate on the process-objects themselves is part of the power of mathematics; at the same time, it increases the impersonal effect, strengthening the impression that it is these process-objects that are the active participants in mathematics rather than the human mathematicians.

It is clear that an impersonal style is an accepted convention in much academic writing, particularly in the sciences, and analysis of the linguistic features contributing to this style (e.g. passive voice, use of personal pronouns and choice of tenses) is a major focus of research in this area. In spite of the common perception that the impersonal is the rule, however, there is some evidence to suggest that it is by no means universal and that there are, in fact, systematic, purposeful ways in which personal forms are used within formal academic writing. Sutton (1989) suggests that the extent of the use of passive or active constructions in scientific writing may vary according to individual taste or contemporary fashion, but there is also evidence of more systematic variation between different genres (e.g. text book, popular article, research article) and between different branches of science. Tarone et al. (1981) point out that most quantitative studies showing extensive use of the passive do not differentiate between texts in different genres or in different fields of scientific endeavour. Their own study showed that the authors of astrophysics research papers used the passive voice where established, standard procedures had been followed but used *we* + active voice 'to indicate points in the logical development of the argument where they have made a unique procedural choice' (p. 195). Thus, while the passive might be seen to be the default form of expression for describing methods used, at critical points in the development of their work the authors claim personal responsibility. Similar observations about the presence of the author are made by Bazerman (1981) who notes in his analysis of a scientific paper that:

> all the uses of the first person are to indicate intellectual activities: statement making . . . making assumptions . . . criticizing statements . . . and placing knowledge claims within other intellectual frameworks. . . . The object is taken as given, independent of perception and knowing; all the human action is only in the process of coming to know the object — that is, in constructing, criticizing, and manipulating claims. (p. 367)

A factor that Tarone et al. consider to be important for the validity of their interpretation of the rhetorical functions of active and passive voice constructions is the fact that their research team included both linguists and an astrophysicist. Judgments about the functions of parts of the text could thus be made from a position of knowledge of the content and accepted forms of argument within the field. The difference between the quantitative findings of this and other studies of passive voice use, however, illustrates the danger of assuming that features of one type of scientific writing will also occur in other fields or genres, although Swales (1985) points out that the context of such decisions is likely to be relevant to understanding choices of voice in other fields.

In specifically mathematical contexts, the extensive use of the personal pronoun *we* by teachers in the mathematics classroom has been discussed by Pimm (1984; 1987) and Rounds (1987). Its use in written mathematical texts has not been addressed to the same extent, but Gillman's (1987) advice to mathematical writers that *we* means 'you and the reader' (p. 11) appears oversimplistic in the light of the evidence of how the pronoun is used in other forms of academic writing. It seems likely that academic mathematics texts would to some extent resemble those in the sciences in their use of passive constructions and personal pronouns. This may be illustrated by some examples from Dye (1991) in which the passive is used to refer to previously established results:

> *It was shown in [5] that $PO_3(9)$ acts on a set of 12 hexagons . . .*

while the first person plural (apparently referring to the single author) is used to state new definitions:

> *For us, a hexagon is a set of six points, no three collinear, in PG(2, K): we call the six points the vertices of the hexagon, and their 15 joins in pairs its edges.*

and in other contexts, such as 'Operating by V we see that . . .', may indeed comply with Gillman's advice to include the reader.

A human presence does, however, intrude into mathematical text in a way that is not so characteristic of academic writing in other sciences through the use of imperatives, conjuring up a human actor. Thus, the reader of higher mathematics texts is likely to be frequently enjoined to *suppose*, *let*, or *define*. The imperative is also a characteristic component of school text books, although the nature of the relationship between author and reader thus constructed is rather different. Rather than being addressed as a 'thinker' and invited to join the author and 'institute and inhabit a common world' (Rotman, 1988, p. 9) the school student is more likely to be ordered to perform some material action — to *add*, *measure*, *differentiate*, or *solve*.

Forms of Mathematical Argument

In attempting to discover the characteristics of mathematical texts, it is necessary to go beyond the level of looking at individual symbols, words or even more complex phrases or statements. The higher level structure of extended sections of texts, in particular the ways in which arguments are constructed, also differs between different domains. As Hansen's (1988) and Bazerman's (1981) comparative studies of academic writing produced within different disciplines point out, the forms of argument used relate to the standards and the epistemologies of the disciplines concerned. In academic mathematics high value is place on deductive reasoning as a means of both 'discovering' knowledge and providing its warrant. The linguistic structure of mathematical texts is thus likely to reflect this.

One aspect of such higher level structures that has been looked at in mathematical texts is the formal mathematical proof. Not only is this a standard component of most formal mathematical texts above school level (and some school texts as well) but it is also commonly perceived that even advanced students have considerable difficulty making sense of written proofs and constructing their own. This has prompted some researchers to attempt to analyse the structure of proofs and even to recommend alternative ways of writing them that might be more accessible.[6] Alibert and Thomas (1991) remark on the linear nature of the traditional presentation of proofs. This is, however, questioned by other analyses which reveal references backwards to previously established results (Roe, 1977) and structuring using both linguistic and paralinguistic[7] signals (Konior, 1993). For example, Konior identifies examples of such signals, serving a function as 'delimitators', marking the beginning ('It remains to show that . . .') and end ('Whence formula (36) follows') of phases in the argument. He remarks that expert readers will make use of these signals to structure their reading of the whole text, but that beginning readers may not appreciate the function of such phrases. Equally it may be supposed that beginning writers may not know how to make use of them effectively.

A characteristic of the proofs contained in Dye (1991) is the occurrence of strings of statements thematizing[8] both the fact that an act of reasoning is occurring (i.e. starting with words such as *hence* or *but*) and the previously established facts which act as the bases for the deductions:

> *But by (4), ... Hence, by (16), B = C. Then, by (4), (15),*
> $A = C(j^2 - j) = C.$ *Hence, . . .*

There may, however, be differences between the forms of argument used in different domains within mathematics. Knuth's (1985) analysis of a set of texts from various fields suggests that a number of different forms of reasoning were being used. Although Knuth does not make explicit reference to linguistic features of these forms of reasoning, it seems likely that there would be identifiable differences between them.

The literature on academic writing in science describes conditional structures used to indicate causality (Horsella and Sindermann, 1992), a prevalence of inanimate and abstract grammatical subjects for active verbs in the expression of causality and explanation (Master, 1991), and frequent use of marked themes providing a contextual framework (Gosden, 1992). The fundamental differences between the bases upon which arguments may be made and validated in science and in mathematics, however, suggest that there are likely to be corresponding differences between the forms of language used to express them.

The characteristics of academic mathematical texts discussed above form part of the background to the consideration of mathematical writing in school. While school students themselves are unlikely to come across such texts, they do form part of the experience of mathematics teachers and textbook writers and, as such, influence the texts encountered by students in school and the values placed by teachers on various forms of writing. In the next section of this chapter, I will consider the language of school mathematics text books.

School Mathematics Texts

Most of those authors who have examined the language of school mathematics text books have focused on the difficulties that students may have in 'getting the meaning off the page' (Shuard and Rothery, 1984, p. 1).[9] They have identified difficulties associated with the use of graphical elements, the different status of different sections of text, the layout of the page, as well as vocabulary and symbolism, any of which may contribute to a student's inability to make sense of the mathematics. My concern here, however, is not with the student-reader's understanding of the mathematical meanings intended by a text book's author but with the characteristics of the genre of mathematics text book. While Hubbard (1992), for example, may criticize the conciseness and formality of much text book language because of the difficulties that they may cause student-readers, these characteristics nevertheless form part of the experience of many students and must contribute to their own development of mathematical writing. Indeed, Hubbards' own students 'reverted to the standard textbook style' (p. 87) when writing themselves rather than using the 'humanistic' style she had introduced them to. Text books form a very large part of most school students' (and their teachers') experience of mathematical text and characteristics of their language are likely, therefore, to influence student writing and teachers' readings of student writing.

Like academic texts, school texts contain a symbolic element, although the range of symbols is likely to be more limited. In addition, most school mathematics texts contain a substantial graphic element, including 'tables, graphs, diagrams, plans and maps, pictorial illustrations' (Shuard and Rothery, 1984, p. 45). The extent to which these elements may be considered to be 'mathematical', however, is likely to vary. Indeed, Shuard and Rothery themselves make a distinction between those graphic elements that may be considered 'essential' to the meaning of the text and those which are merely 'decorative' (p. 47). While it is clear that even the 'decorative' elements do contribute to the meanings that readers may construct from the text,[10] this distinction suggests that teacher-readers are unlikely to recognize as mathematical those graphic features which they see as serving decorative function.

The density and conciseness identified by, among others, Austin and Howson (1979) as characteristic of mathematical text might lead one to suppose that there would be little redundancy (an aspect of a text that makes it easier for the reader to predict what the rest of the text will be). Indeed, this is explicitly claimed by Woodrow (1982) for the symbolic aspects of mathematical text. As Kane (1968) points out, however, because of the conventional and repetitive structure of some parts of school texts this is not always the case. Kane provides the example of a calculation for which 'its total redundancy is high enough that some readers need only the first few symbols in order to predict the whole passage' (p. 297). A repetitive structure is characteristic of some parts of school mathematics texts, in particular those parts which Shuard and Rothery (1984) label 'examples and exercises'; the extent of this type of structure is probably not found in other genres.

Ernest's (1993a) 'criteria of rhetorical style which apply to school mathematics':

- Use a restricted technical language and standard notation
- Use spare, minimal overall forms of expression
- Use certain forms of spatial organization of symbols, figures and text on the page
- Avoid deixis (pronouns or spatio-temporal locators)
- Employ standard methods of computation, transformation or proof (p. 8)

he claims, serve to 'depersonalize' the discourse. They disguise the dialogical nature of mathematics itself (Ernest, 1994) and the extent to which the student-reader must be involved in the text. Characteristic features that contribute to this involvement are the plethora of questions and instructions. Questions and instructions apparently intended to involve the student as an active participant occur not only in those sections of text books providing practice exercises or testing student knowledge but also in sections which are attempting to impart new knowledge (Shuard and Rothery, 1984). This includes the use of rhetorical questions and, in some types of texts, series of exercises intended to lead to the 'discovery' of a new fact or generalization (van Dormolen, 1986). Indeed,

> very few examples of exposition by straight explanation are to be found other than in advanced texts. (Shuard and Rothery, 1984, p. 11)

Such dominance of instructions for student action, together with a proliferation of worked examples, clearly contributes to a procedural emphasis in much of school mathematics. It also constructs a particular pedagogic relationship between the text (or its author — and the teacher who instructs the student to read the text) and the student.

Even within the domain of secondary school text books there are major differences in the forms of language used, varying with the age of the students, with their supposed 'ability' (Dowling, 1991), and with the specific type of pedagogic relationship between author and reader (Fauvel, 1991; van Dormolen, 1986). Indeed, one of the problems in producing this description of the language of school mathematics texts is the fact that most analyses have either focused on extremely limited samples of texts or, apart for some discussion of symbolism and vocabulary, have focused on differences between texts and what makes a particular text easy or hard to read rather than on what differences there might be between mathematics texts and those of other subjects. I cannot claim to have completely characterized the genre of school mathematics texts but merely to have identified a number of its features.

School mathematics texts have on the whole very different functions from those of students' own mathematical writing, especially their reports of investigative work. They are likely to differ in the subject matter they address, the manner in which they address it, and in the relationship between author and reader. There will inevitably be limitations to the similarity between the language of text books and that produced by students. Nevertheless, since the text book is the dominant model of mathematical writing available to school students, it is of interest to consider the extent to which students adopt text book language in their own writing.

In this chapter, I have surveyed some of the features of 'official' mathematical writing — that which is written by those who may be considered authoritatively entitled to call what they write 'mathematical': the professional mathematicians and mathematics teachers. Students, of course, are less authoritative writers and the extent to which what they write is labelled 'mathematical' is likely to depend on the extent to which it meets the expectations of their teachers. Moreover, the writing that they are expected to do in the classroom must serve different functions from those served by the writing of 'experts' and, hence, is likely to have some rather different features. In the next chapter, I will turn to the writing produced by school students.

Notes

1   Linguistic characteristics are not, however, sufficient to identify a text as mathematical. Austin (1981), in his deliberate play on the formal structure of academic mathematics, provides a good example of a text which conforms to the linguistic norms of such academic writing in the domain of mathematics but which fails to be mathematical because it lacks essential intertextual links to other mathematical texts that would allow the reader to construct mathematical meaning from it. Its standing as a joke (or a meta-mathematical comment) depends on this tension between its form and its content; it is this which marks it as not-mathematics. It appears that other academic disciplines have given rise to similar jokes or meta-comments. Gilbert and Mulkay (1984), discussing humour among scientists, provide an example of the circulation of a spoof research paper featuring the formal characteristics of such papers but purporting to report a fictitious experiment which yielded no results and indeed could not have yielded any.

2   An interesting discussion of differences in usage of mathematical vocabulary and symbolism between different countries may be found in Hirigoyen (1997). These differences (e.g. using a comma rather than a decimal point; using 'billion' to mean 10^9 or 10^{12}) are *dialectical* rather than *generic*. It is simple to effect a direct translation between such dialectical forms without significantly altering the functions of the text (except in so far as it would be recognized as being written by, say, a French or an American mathematician). Such dialectical variations will not be considered in this chapter as my concern is with the ways in which characteristics of mathematical text vary and serve different functions in different settings.

3   Halliday (1974) defines 'register' as:

> a set of meanings that is appropriate to a particular function of language, together with the words and structures which express these meanings . . . including the styles of meaning and modes of argument. (p. 65)

4   This formulation is not unambiguous as the nature of the experiences and the interests of different readers may give rise to contestation. For example, while the majority of the population might identify any texts produced within school mathematics at primary or secondary level as mathematical, some professional mathematicians might deny them such a status.

5   I cannot claim that this particular paper is representative or even typical of such texts in general or even of texts within the author's own specialist domain of mathematics. Nevertheless, having reviewed a range of research papers from authors working in

many areas of pure and applied mathematics (Burton and Morgan, forthcoming), I feel that I can assert that I could have found similarly appropriate illustrations in the vast majority of these.

6   It is interesting to note that, while Leron's (1983) suggestion of a 'structured' way of writing proofs was generally positively received as a 'good idea' by those who were concerned with student difficulties, it has had virtually no effect on the writing of those who produce academic texts (often the same individuals).

7   Including 'type face, section, different indentations, different ways of numbering cases and distribution of the text on the page' (Konior, 1993, p. 252).

8   In English, the 'theme' of a statement is positioned at its beginning (Halliday, 1985). The theme usually coincides with the subject of the statement and where it does not, as in the cases quoted in which 'hence', 'then' or 'but' are thematized, this draws particular attention to the 'marked' theme.

9   I would agree with Wing's (1985) criticism of this view of 'meaning' residing in the text rather than in interaction between text and reader.

10 See Kress and van Leeuwen (1990) for discussion of the contribution of illustrations to the meanings of a social studies text book.

Chapter 3

Writing in the Mathematics Classroom

Recent years have seen increasing interest in communication in the mathematics classroom; this is evident in the professional literature, in mathematics education research, and in curriculum documents such as the National Curriculum for England and Wales (DfE, 1995) and the NCTM 'Standards' in the United States (1989). In particular, in accord with trends towards constructivist views of learning, students have started to be seen as producers of mathematical language rather than merely as consumers. Attention has thus moved on from the difficulties that students may encounter in attempting to read mathematical texts or to understand what is said to them by their teacher, towards consideration of the roles that talking and writing may play in students' mathematical experience.

There have been many advocates of talking as a means of learning mathematics and many suggestions have been provided of ways for teachers to encourage talk in their classrooms (e.g. Brissenden, 1988; Mathematical Association, 1987); indeed 'discussion' was one of the six ways of working prescribed by the Cockcroft report (Cockcroft, 1982), a government-sponsored report that has had enormous influence on the subsequent development of the mathematics curriculum in the United Kingdom and elsewhere. The place of writing, however, is rather less established. There are advocates of 'Writing-to-Learn' mathematics, primarily in the US and Australia; their impact, however, has been relatively limited. In the United Kingdom recent curriculum developments related to the introduction of investigative work into mathematics classrooms have focused attention on students' writing in two ways. Firstly, some of those advocating investigative ways of working have simultaneously advocated writing as part of the investigative process, claiming that writing can actually help students in their learning of mathematics, in particular in supporting moves towards the symbolization of generalizations, but also in supporting reflection and the development of problem solving processes. Secondly, the introduction of assessment by coursework at GCSE, including the assessment of reports of investigative work, has ensured that the great majority of mathematics students and teachers in secondary schools have had to be involved in the production of extended writing, in many cases for the first time.

There are, of course, many different kinds of writing. In the previous chapter some of the characteristics of academic and text book mathematical writing were considered, but these are not necessarily the characteristics of the genres of writing that students produce in the mathematics classroom. Later chapters will explore in detail the forms of writing expected of students in their investigation reports. In this chapter I attempt to describe the experience of writing that students are likely to have in the traditional mathematics classroom and the forms of writing they are likely to use. I then review the arguments for engaging students in Writing-to-Learn in mathematics, in particular I shall consider those arguments that relate most strongly to writing as part of investigative work. I then look at what is known about the characteristics of student writing produced in those few 'Writing-to-Learn' experiments that have considered the written products as well as the learning processes, and in more structured research settings.

Student Writing in the Traditional Mathematics Classroom[1]

Before the general introduction of assessment by coursework brought about by the advent of GCSE, major studies of the writing taking place in different curriculum areas in secondary schools in the United Kingdom found very little writing taking place in mathematics classrooms. In England and Wales, Britton et al. (1975) comment only that they found too little writing in mathematics for it to be analysed separately, while the only mention of mathematics made by Martin et al. (1976) is an anecdote about a boy writing a poem (about the death of a friend) during a mathematics lesson. Similarly in Scotland, Rogers and MacDonald (1985) reported that in some cases no data was collected for mathematics because no written work had been done during the period of the investigation. Spencer et al. (1983), in contrast, found that large numbers of pupils had produced some written work in mathematics during the week of their survey. However, the amounts written by individual pupils were very small; moreover, only 10 per cent of pupils had written anything in their own words (while 72 per cent had copied work) and these had only written an average of 6.2 lines of writing, none producing 'extended' writing over a page in length. (The difference between the results of these studies may probably be accounted for by the use of different definitions of 'writing'. Mathematics students may cover pages of their exercise books without completing a single 'ordinary English' sentence — is this 'writing'?) Similarly, the National Writing Project (1986) reports a Sheffield-based survey of all the writing done within a week by first year secondary students in three comprehensive schools, remarking that 'the writing in Science and Mathematics is likely to be totally teacher determined' (p. 6). Both the quantity and the quality of writing in school mathematics must thus be questioned. These studies, of course, took place before the wide spread introduction of coursework for public examination which must have substantially increased the amount of writing done in secondary mathematics classrooms, at least at some points during the year. Nevertheless, they indicate the traditional background of a lack of independent mathematical writing into which reports of investigative activity have been introduced.

Two more recent surveys in secondary schools in the United States (Davison and Pearce, 1988) and Australia (Swinson and Partridge, 1992a) again suggest that, in spite of the greater influence of the Writing-to-Learn movement in the professional literature in these two countries, neither the quantity nor the quality of writing use in the mathematics classroom was substantial (quality being defined as the types of writing activities that, it is claimed by Swinson and Partridge, 'will promote cognitive growth'). Davison and Pearce (1988), for example, report that the most common type of writing activity used was the copying or transcribing of information, while 87 per cent of the teachers surveyed reported no 'creative' use of language 'to explore and convey mathematically related information' (p. 10). Swinson and Partridge found less than 10 per cent of teachers using any writing activity on a weekly basis, while the most commonly used writing activities were copying or rewriting and summarizing information. Studying the use of language in mathematics in a small number of Australian primary and secondary schools from the point of view of the development of mathematical literacy, Marks and Mousley (1990) also found a limited range of types of writing. Some of the teachers in-volved were committed to the idea of increasing opportunities for students to use language in the classroom 'in order to develop and communicate their understandings in the light of their personal experiences' (p. 123). However, the activities they employed only encouraged writing in a 'recount' genre and did not provide students with a wider experience of mathematical writing.

The limited nature of the secondary school student's experience of producing written text in the traditional mathematics classroom is reflected in the lack of attention to this in the literature. Even Pimm's (1987) extensive discussion of the language of the mathematics classroom restricts its consideration of students' writ-ten production almost exclusively to the recording of generalizations and the nature of mathematical symbolism. Nevertheless, it represents a broader view of students' legitimate mathematical writing activity than that characterized by, for example, Laborde (1990) and Bauersfeld (1992)[2] as being entirely circumscribed by the technical format prescribed by text book or teacher. This lack of attention to the form of students' written production may be related both to the limited and tightly prescribed nature of much of school mathematics and to the identification of math-ematics with its symbol system discussed in the previous chapter. If it is assumed that the meaning resides only in the symbols, then only the 'correctness' of the symbolic formulation needs to be considered; non-symbolic aspects are merely ritual or are relevant only in the affective domain.

Ernest (1993a) is unusual in considering the rhetoric of the traditional, repet-itive type of school mathematics writing, pointing out that, while the text may appear to present the processes gone through in achieving the answer, this rhetoric is in fact only a 'rational reconstruction' (p. 9). In his analysis of a single example of the production of a solution and written answer to a trigonometry problem (Ernest, 1993b), he identifies a number of features of the student's writing process which relate to what he calls 'the rhetorical requirements of classroom written mathematical language' (p. 242), including a transformational sequence leading to a labelled answer. The writing considered in Ernest's study seems typical of much of the day-to-day written exercises done in traditional classrooms. Even when students are asked to write other types of texts, in the absence of other models and experience it seems likely that they will be influenced by their knowledge of the expectations of writing related to other aspects of school mathematics.

'Writing-to-Learn' Mathematics

Over the last two decades there has been a development from the idea of 'Writing across the Curriculum', which focused on the development of writing through its use in various curriculum areas (as represented in the UK by e.g. Britton et al. (1975) and Spencer et al. (1983)), towards the idea that writing is a useful intellectual tool for helping learning in all areas of the curriculum. Curriculum development in mathematics based on this idea has been most apparent in the United States although it has also been present to a lesser extent in Australia and, through the National Writing Project, in England and Wales. Its theoretical justification derives largely from Emig (1983) who draws on, among others, Vygotsky and Bruner to support her claims that the process of writing shares the characteristics of successful learning:

- writing is *integrative* in that it involves hand, eye and brain and simultaneously deploys Bruner's enactive, iconic and symbolic ways of representing reality;
- writing provides immediate *feedback and reinforcement* which are 'the central requirement for reformulation and reinterpretation' (p. 127) of learning;
- writing is *connective* as it involves the deliberate construction of semantic connections;
- writing is *self-rhythmed* because it connects past, present and future through analysis and synthesis.

From this basis it is argued that writing supports learning, although Emig does not specify what is being learnt or which forms of writing might be most supportive.

This lack of specificity has, unfortunately, not been addressed adequately by many of those who have been involved in curriculum development based on the idea of Writing-to-Learn. Langer and Applebee (1987) criticize the literature as generally superficial and anecdotal, claiming that it does not seriously address the issue of how writing helps learning. Their own study (of social studies teachers and students) indicated that different types of writing led to different types of learning: note-taking and comprehension questions leading to knowledge of a body of facts, while analytic essay writing led to knowledge of relationships and concepts. This obvious interdependence between the type of writing task and the type of learning that might ensue is considered to some extent in the literature of Writing-to-Learn in mathematics, but the claims for enhanced learning are largely made without concrete evidence.

Some of those arguing for the use of writing in mathematics classrooms have seen a special relationship between writing and mathematics. Emig's (1983) definition of 'clear writing' as:

> that which signals without ambiguity the nature of conceptual relationships, whether they be coordinate, subordinate, superordinate, causal, or something other. (p. 127)

suggests a concern with precision and with relationships that parallels that in mathematics. The means of achieving such clear writing are not, however, elaborated, meaning that writing certainly cannot be seen as a panacea for the achievement of conceptual clarity.

Claims of Benefits from Writing-to-Learn Mathematics

Cognitive gains through the opportunities that writing provides for making connections between new and old learning and for organizing thought have been claimed for: writing about problem solving (Kenyon, 1989); writing about applications of mathematics (Stempien, 1990); writing summaries of work done (Mett, 1989; Meyer, 1991); responses to regular 'writing prompts' asking for reflection on or explanation of a recently taught topic (Miller, 1992b; Wilde, 1991). Similarly, broad claims are made that writing about solutions to problems enhances students' problem solving processes (Bell and Bell, 1985; Elsholz and Elsholz, 1989; Kenyon, 1989). A more narrow claim is made by Mett (1989) that writing definitions helps students to understand the need for precision in their formulation and Borasi (1992) provides rather more detailed evidence of development in high school students' understanding of the nature of definition through an experimental learning programme which included writing. The writing of word problems has been found to help students to focus on the meanings of key words and on the relations between the words and the associated equations (Abel and Abel, 1988; Johnson, 1983; Wilde, 1991), while Ford (1990) claims additionally that this enables them to solve harder word problems than they would otherwise have been capable of. In discussing investigational work with primary children, Brown (1990) suggests that, by translating other forms of representation into written description, 'the child will reflect on the rules and relations inherent' in each of the other forms and will develop 'an active relationship to the mathematics they are doing' (p. 17).

In addition to claims for the cognitive effects of writing, a major purpose for Writing-to-Learn activities, especially among those teaching US college students who are non-mathematics specialists and who may have anxiety about mathematics, is to improve the students' affective response to mathematics and hence remove one of the obstacles to their learning. Journals, autobiographical writing or fictional stories in which feelings about doing mathematics are explored may be seen to have a therapeutic effect (Borasi and Rose, 1989; Brandau, 1988; Stempien and Borasi, 1985; Tobias, 1989) or to play a role in 'empowering' students by legitimizing their feelings and actively engaging them in reflecting on their own learning (Mett, 1989; Oaks and Rose, 1992; Powell and López, 1989). A similar role is suggested by a National Writing Project (1987) report of journal writing in a Welsh primary classroom. The use of writing about feelings (Oaks and Rose, 1992) and about aspects of mathematics such as beliefs about the nature of mathematical discovery (Borasi and Rose, 1989; Stempien, 1990), are also suggested to help change students' perceptions of mathematics and to move them away from the idea that mathematics is always about getting a single right answer, while writing reports or diaries of problem solving is claimed to help students towards a greater awareness of the nature of mathematical thinking (Berlinghoff, 1989; O'Shea, 1991). A more general claim is made by Birken (1989) that writing activities are less threatening than traditional mathematical teaching techniques for those with 'math-anxiety' or lower levels of skill. Similar claims of increased confidence are reported for the writing of algorithms in words (Lesnak, 1989), creating word problems in the primary school (Ford, 1990) and collaborative analysis of problems (LeGere, 1991).

Writing-to-Learn and the Mathematics Curriculum

Many of those reporting on the effects of the introduction of writing activities into mathematics education clearly maintain traditional views of the curriculum, of the nature of mathematical knowledge and of student learning. This may be seen, for example, in the focus on improving student performance on 'word problems' by a number of the US authors mentioned above. Writing activities are presented as an addition to the teacher's repertoire rather than representing a radically new approach to teaching and learning. Miller (1991; 1992a; 1992b), for example, worked with high school teachers in the United States and in Australia who included five minutes of writing in response to a 'prompt' at the beginning of every lesson. The main effect noted by Miller was increased teacher awareness of the students' state of understanding of the topic. The ways in which this is said to influence teachers' practice, however, — reteaching a topic; delaying an assessment because of a lack of understanding apparent in the writing; planning a revision lesson; discussing particular misconceptions with individuals (Miller, 1992a) — do not suggest that any fundamental change is proposed in their conception of the curriculum or of the nature of student learning. Similar claims of improved teacher assessment of student understanding are made by many of those reporting their own classroom use of a variety of different types of writing activities with students at all stages of education (including Borasi and Rose, 1989; McIntosh, 1991; Meyer, 1991; Richards, 1990; Wilde, 1991). There is, however, no indication of how these teachers formed their assessments or, in particular, what features of the students' writing contributed to the teachers' judgments about 'understanding'. There is a general assumption that the interpretation of writing produced by students is unproblematic.

A traditional approach is also seen in research studies such as those by P.E. Johnson (1990), L.A. Johnson (1991) and Paik and Norris (1984), all of which found significantly higher results on traditional tests and examinations for groups of university students who had engaged in journal or essay writing compared to control groups who had followed the usual non-writing curriculum. Davison and Pearce (1988) and Swinson and Partridge (1992b) take a similarly static view of the curriculum when reporting that high school students who had been given writing activities performed equally or less well than those who had not, although Davison and Pearce are also concerned with affective gains. These studies are based on an assumption that all students are learning the same things, although possibly at different rates and more or less effectively; there is no suggestion that the introduction of writing activities might fundamentally alter the nature of the curriculum.

In contrast, Powell and Borasi and their collaborators see the incorporation of writing into the mathematics classroom as just one part of a change to a different approach to teaching and learning. Powell et al. (Hoffman and Powell, 1989; Hoffman and Powell, 1992; Powell and López, 1989; Powell and Ramnauth, 1992), working with adult students from disadvantaged sections of society, draw on Freire to criticize traditional 'chalk and talk' methods of teaching for focusing on the subject matter rather than on the learner and see writing as a way of developing 'critical thinking' and hence contributing to student empowerment:

> As writing requires an active rather than a passive involvement of learners, this project aimed to empower students in two ways; (i) to promote students' awareness of and facility in the use of writing as a vehicle of learning, and (ii) to put students at the centre and in control of their own learning by engaging them in reflection and critical reflection on mathematical experiences. (Powell and López, 1989, p. 162)

The forms of writing used were thus predominantly expressive, with a focus on student reflection. These included 'free writing', in which students were given time during class to write without the expectation that the teacher would read the writing produced, and journals or 'multiple entry logs' (Powell and Ramnauth, 1992) which might be used to form a dialogue between student and teacher, the teacher's entries being used to encourage further student reflection rather than to evaluate student achievement. Borasi and Rose (1989) also used journals as a means of encouraging students to reflect on their mathematical experiences but, in more recent work (e.g. Borasi, 1992; Borasi and Siegel, 1994), Borasi and her collaborators do not see reflection as the only, or even the most important, purpose for writing in mathematics. A fuller exposition of the philosophy underlying their use of writing and reading in mathematics classrooms at all levels is found in Borasi and Siegel (1994). They argue for an 'inquiry' model of education which is contrasted to the traditional 'transmission' model in the assumptions it makes about the nature of knowledge, of learning and of teaching. Social interaction between learners, teacher and a wider mathematical community is a fundamental part of this model and a wide variety of reading and writing activities, including transactional writing, play a part in this interaction. Reading and writing are thus not seen as an addition to the curriculum but are a naturally integrated part of it.

Writing-to-Learn and Investigation

Probably the most fully developed argument for the place of writing in investigative work is made by Mason et al. (1985) who recommend that recording of the problem solving process and subsequent 'writing up' for another person to read both play a role in developing mathematical thinking about the problem and its solution. They propose a set of self-monitoring prompts to writing during problem solving which provide 'a framework for organizing, recording, and creating mathematical experiences' (p. 22), while, by producing a report for someone else, 'you are also brought into close contact with the key events' (p. 40), and are assisted in reflecting, checking and extending your understanding of the problem and its implications. While Mason et al.'s book was addressed to the independent student of mathematics rather than being an explicit comment on the mathematics curriculum, current coursework expectations also recommend that students should write down their actions and observations as they work on the investigations. In becoming a formal expectation, however, this has become an assessment tool rather than an aid to the problem solving process itself.

One of the most important objectives for students and teachers working on the most common types of investigation is to form a generalization and, eventually, to express this generalization in a symbolic algebraic form. James and Mason (1982), using examples of children working on such investigations, suggest that children should be encouraged to describe patterns in their own words rather than being expected prematurely to use algebraic symbols to express their generalizations. The struggle to do this is seen as a crucial factor in gaining insight into the situation being described. The sequence of 'seeing-saying-recording' (where 'saying' is taken to mean writing in a verbal form without using algebraic symbols) has become an established part of teachers' pedagogic knowledge about the teaching and learning of algebra, enshrined in curricular materials (e.g. the DIME Pre-Algebra Project), in official curriculum documents (e.g. HMI, 1987), and in the literature related to investigations (see Chapter 5). Some versions of the National Curriculum and the GCSE examination boards' assessment criteria have used this developmental sequence explicitly as a means of distinguishing between students at different levels of attainment. The Southern Examining Group (SEG, 1992), for example, described the work of GCSE candidates at different grade levels:

E   Attempt to make generalizations;
D   Attempt to make generalizations and, with guidance, express them in words;
C   Make generalizations and express them in words and, with guidance, in symbols;
B   Make generalizations and express them in symbols;
A   Make generalizations in symbols.

The use of writing has come to be seen both as a part of the process of forming a particular algebraic generalization and as a stage in the development of algebraic thinking.

The pedagogic rationale for including writing as part of the investigative process arises within a perspective that sees the role of 'investigation' in the curriculum as a way of learning mathematics. As will be seen in Chapter 5, however, an alternative position views 'investigations' as a means of assessing part of the mathematics curriculum. This alternative position is associated with a different view of the relationship of the written report of the investigative work to the problem solving process itself. The discourse of examination appears to identify writing only with its communicative function. It merely records what has been done rather than playing any fundamental part in shaping the problem solving or students' learning.

Given the amount of writing that school students in the UK must now do in producing their coursework, it is perhaps surprising to find so little attention paid to the possible benefits accompanying it. One explanation of this difference in level of interest in Writing-to-Learn between the US and Australia and the UK may be the source and direction of the curriculum developments that have taken place. The developments reported in US and Australian classrooms are, on the whole, initiatives by individual teachers, schools or colleges who are clearly committed to the idea that writing activities will help them to achieve their personal aims for their own students; moreover, the types of writing activities introduced have been designed or chosen by the teachers themselves and have, therefore, been compatible with their existing classroom practice and their beliefs about teaching and learning. In the UK, on the other hand, the introduction of examination by coursework, although welcomed by many teachers, has been imposed at a national level, allowing individual teachers little flexibility or power to determine its form. The main focus of the curriculum innovation, moreover, has been on introducing investigative ways of working; the writing of reports of such work has been a by-product of the development, necessary in order to manage the assessment process, rather than a good thing in its own right.

The Forms of Writing Used by Students

For most of those teachers and researchers involved in Writing-to-Learn, both the act of writing and the process of interpreting and judging students' writing appear to be unproblematic. When teachers read student texts, however, there are likely to be unspoken (and probably unconscious) assumptions about which forms of language are 'appropriate' and which are taken as signs of more or less 'advanced' thinking. As Kress (1990) argues, unless these assumptions are made explicit, some students are likely to be disadvantaged because their lack of facility with language is interpreted as lack in the subject content involved. One of my main motivations in studying mathematical language is to add to our knowledge of what forms of language are likely to be valued and how these are likely to be interpreted in order to provide teachers and students with the tools needed to improve their mutual written communication.

In spite of the substantial amount of work describing the use of writing in the mathematics classroom, there has been relatively little analysis of the texts themselves. The writing is described largely in general terms as, for example, 'expressive' or 'transactional' (many of the Writing-to-Learn advocates have adopted Britton et al's (1975) descriptors) but these categories are applied to the type of task set by the teacher rather than to the type of text produced by the students. Where those involved in the Writing-to-Learn movement have developed analyses of student texts, this has normally been for the purpose of attempting to evaluate the introduction of writing into the classroom; the method of analysis has, therefore, been closely related to the specific aims of the curriculum development. Another strand of research (mainly in France) that has involved linguistic analysis of student texts has attempted to probe cognitive aspects through experimental situations involving writing activities.

Analysis of Student Texts Produced in Writing-to-Learn

A substantial, longitudinal study by Waywood and Clarke looked at the writing produced in a curriculum development involving mathematical journals in an Australian secondary school. Their analysis of the language used in the journals relates to their general pedagogic aim of encouraging reflection and to their further aims of changing students' perceptions of the nature of mathematical activity and, in particular, developing students' problem solving strategies, e.g. 'question-asking' (Clarke, Waywood, and Stephens, 1993). As part of the incorporation of journal writing into the school curriculum, the students' journals were read and graded by their teachers. Waywood and Clarke make some use of teacher assessments to validate their analyses.

At the broadest level of analysis, three types of text produced within the journals are identified and labelled 'recount', 'summary' and 'dialogue'. These categories are defined by the organization of the text and it is hypothesized that each corresponds to a particular stance towards learning: the recount is claimed to represent passive observation of objective knowledge; the summary reflects a utilitarian stance towards knowledge; the dialogue 'signals a creative stance towards knowledge' (Waywood, 1992b, p. 36). In relation to the aims of the development, the three types of text are seen, both by the researchers and by the teachers involved in assessing the students' work, as a hierarchy with the dialogue being the most highly valued form. The finding that the dialogue was valued most highly by the teachers in Waywood and Clarke's study is particularly interesting. In spite of the researchers' association of type of text with orientation towards mathematical knowledge, they present no evidence of whether the teachers involved shared this interpretation or of the reasons for the value they placed on dialogue.

As well as using the textual form as evidence of students' thinking, Waywood is concerned with the interaction between students' language skills and the mathematical content of their writing. He attempts to separate the significant mathematical learning factors that he sees in students' journal writing from their language proficiency. For example, the volume of writing produced (which may be taken as a crude indicator of language proficiency) is claimed not to interact with the type of text produced (Waywood, 1992b). Two case studies that are presented in some detail support this relative independence between language proficiency and journal quality. They describe one girl who gained A's in English but whose journal contained relatively low level types of questions; and a second who, although she produced writing which 'because [she] is an ESL student . . . is awkward and in some cases opaque' (Waywood, 1994, p. 333), nevertheless posed more sophisticated questions which suggested that she was attempting to integrate her learning of mathematics with her previous knowledge. On the other hand, a quantitative analysis of lexical items appearing in the journals (Waywood, 1992a) is used to construct a factor, labelled as 'engagement' in the mathematical activity and derived from both the volume of writing produced and the deployment of vocabulary, which is positively associated with teacher assessment of the journals. Such a quantitative analysis, while pointing to the possible significance of measurable linguistic differences between students' texts, nevertheless does not provide insight into the nature of these differences at a level that might be used to help students to produce 'better' texts. Nor does it provide insight into how such differences may have influenced the ways in which the teacher-readers of the texts formed their assessments.

In another study of journal writing, Powell et al. report their use with 'underprepared' US college students, the aim being that the writing activity should promote 'student reflection and empowerment' (Hoffman and Powell, 1989, p. 55) and support mathematical thinking. In relation to these aims, student texts are categorized by their position in relation to three intersecting axes: non-personal ↔ personal, non-reflective ↔ reflective, affective ↔ cognitive (Hoffman and Powell, 1992), with a claim that personal, reflective writing is that which best addresses the aims of the writing activity. While the affective ↔ cognitive axis is clearly related to the subject matter of the writing, both of the other axes appear also to be related to the forms of language used. For example, although the linguistic signals that they are using to locate texts on each of these axes are not made explicit, Powell and López's (1989) description of a student's progression along the non-personal ↔ personal dimension identifies one characteristic of non-personal journal writing as a 'general narrative' (p. 168) which reports what was done in the class in general rather than the student's individual involvement.

Shield and Swinson (1994) report a more narrowly focused study of the types of writing produced in response to a demand for 'expository' writing: writing a letter to a friend about mathematics they had learnt recently. A method for analysing the student texts, incorporating both qualitative and quantitative aspects, was developed (Shield, 1994) based on van Dormolen's (1986) textual analysis categories with the aim of identifying the degree of elaboration ('linking and integration of information being learned' (Shield and Swinson, 1994, p. 273)) apparent in the texts. The method of analysis, developed originally to describe the language of mathematics text books, may be applied appropriately to these students' 'letters' as they, like text books, seek to provide an exposition of a mathematical topic; its use of categories specific to such texts, however, makes it unsuitable for application to other forms of writing which do not share this characteristic. The design of the study was based on the hypothesis that writing should help children to organize their thoughts and integrate their learning. The form of writing asked for, however, prompted predominantly procedural responses with very little elaboration. Shield and Swinson suggest that this result is likely to be caused by the overwhelmingly procedural view of mathematics found in much school mathematics teaching and text books. While this is certainly an important factor to consider, the nature of the writing activity itself must also be taken into account. It cannot be naively assumed that every type of writing is equally likely to achieve the desired learning results. Nor can it be assumed that students share a teacher's or a researcher's view of the nature of the writing task they are undertaking.

A rare example of close attention being paid to the writing produced by students during investigative work is provided by Billington and Evans (1987). Their analysis of primary school children's solutions to the 'Handshakes' problem[3] is illustrated with multiple extracts of written work displaying a wide variety of styles. There is generally an assumption that the production and reading of the texts is unproblematic and that the students' cognitive processes are represented transparently by the texts. The authors do, however, remark on the differences between two of the texts in a way that illuminates some of the features of the writing that are influencing their judgments. While one of the students, Daniel, had introduced the problem using impersonal language, the other, Martha, had presented it as a concrete situation involving named individuals. Billington and Evans comment that Daniel's description of the problem was 'sophisticated', establishing the relevant parameters clearly, while Martha 'found it necessary to weave a story around the problem and to use real characters' (p. 14). These judgments are using the form of the writing as evidence of the children's skills in problem representation and solution. There is no suggestion that Martha might be taught that stories and 'real characters' are not generally considered an appropriate part of mathematical discourse or even that she might benefit from considering Daniel's more abstract formulation; her text is presented as a necessary consequence of her 'level of knowing'.

Analysis of Student Writing as a Tool in Cognitive Research

The assumption of a close identification between thought and language is an essential component to research which seeks to use texts (whether written or oral) produced by students as evidence of their thinking. In much research in mathematics education it is assumed that there is a simple transparent relationship between the student's intention, the text she[4] produces and the researcher's interpretation of that text; there has, therefore, been little systematic consideration of the forms of language used in student texts and the relationships these may have with the student's thinking. The main exceptions to this have been in the area of logical reasoning and proof, perhaps because this is an aspect of school mathematics which is difficult to express entirely in symbolic form.[5] The following examples indicate the ways in which linguistic features of texts, especially features which indicate the author's personal involvement, may be interpreted by those involved in mathematics education as signals of particular types of cognitive activity.

Duval (1989) reports on a teaching experiment with 13–14-year-old students focusing on identifying the status rather than the meaning of propositions within proofs. Texts containing geometric proofs produced by the same student before and after the teaching are analysed. Although no model texts had been provided to the students during the teaching programme, there are major differences between the two texts. In particular, while the 'before' text consisted almost entirely of a list of symbolic statements, the 'after' text is a fully connected piece of prose with a small amount of symbolism integrated into it. The main points that Duval makes in interpreting these differences are about the status accorded to the various propositions made within the two texts. Whereas in the first text, observations, hypotheses, conclusions, etc. are not distinguished, in the second, each is signalled clearly. Conclusions, for example, are introduced by modal expressions of personal certitude ('Je suis sure que . . .', 'donc maintenant je sais que . . .' (p. 232)). These are interpreted as evidence not only that the student is focusing on the logical status of the propositions but also that he is personally involved in the process of logical reasoning to the extent that he is genuinely convinced by it.

In contrast to Duval's identification of personal involvement as a sign of a more sophisticated understanding of the process of proof, Balacheff (1987) characterizes the language required for 'intellectual' as opposed to 'pragmatic' proofs as decontextualized, depersonalized and detemporalized (p. 159). He points out that the personal language used by children writing pragmatic proofs focuses on the particulars of what they did rather than on what is the case in general, independent of that action. While it might appear that Balacheff's insistence on the symbolic and the impersonal is in opposition to Duval's interpretation of personal language as a sign of a higher level of engagement with proof, an examination of the types of personal processes involved suggests that the two positions are compatible. Whereas Balacheff's examples show the student writers to be performing material actions such as calculating and drawing examples, Duval's are performing mental actions, reflecting on their state of knowledge rather than on describing a series of events.

The use of personal pronouns is also used as an analytic tool by Coquin-Viennot in her (1989) study of written explanations produced by 8–11-year-old children and by adult students. The degree of personal implication in the texts produced varied with the social setting of the task (school or non-school), with the way in which the problem was posed (personal 'Which would you choose . . .' or impersonal 'Which should one choose . . .') and with the age of the writer. Coquin-Viennot suggests that the differences between different social settings might be explained by the subjects choosing to use different forms of language appropriate to those settings. She claims that the other variables and other evidence related to the types of justifications given favour an alternative explanation in terms of the subjects' cognitive representation of the problem as 'mathematical' or 'spontaneous'. The interaction between the language used, the social setting and the representation of the problem remains to be fully explored.

Although the primary purpose of the studies described above was not to describe the forms of language used by students in writing about mathematics, their descriptions of students' writing and their use of linguistic features as signals of particular types of mathematical thinking help to identify features of student's writing that may be interpreted as significant by readers. In particular, the explicit presence of the writer in the text is clearly influential in the way in which the readings of the text and of various aspects of the writer's understanding and competence are constructed.

From 'Writing-to-Learn' to 'Learning-to-Write'

The introduction of writing activities into the mathematics classroom has been accompanied by a number of claims for its potential cognitive and affective benefits. There is some evidence suggesting specific gains for some types of activity; overall, however, the evidence is limited and largely anecdotal. The claims by a number of authors that teachers find the writing produced by students to be a useful tool for gaining better insight into their understanding of mathematics are not accompanied by any explicit statement of how such assessment takes place. There is an underlying 'common-sense' assumption that the writing provides a transparent representation of the students' intentions and hence of their understandings. Such an assumption of transparency is not justified in the light of current theories of communication; moreover, students' lack of experience and facility with mathematical forms of written language must throw additional doubt on simplistic claims about the value of writing as an assessment tool. While a classroom setting is likely to include opportunities for judgments to be mediated in practice through other means of communication and other forms of evidence, the assessment of written work in isolation from the context of its production (as in the case of the assessment of coursework for examination purposes) makes greater demands on the reader-assessor's interpretative resources. In later chapters, I seek to throw some light on the ways in which teachers read and interpret students' writing in order to make judgments about their mathematical competence.

In order that teachers should be able to help their students develop forms of written language that are acceptable within a particular context, the teachers must themselves have explicit knowledge of the ways in which written mathematical language may be used within the relevant genre. Spencer (1983), reporting on writing across a number of school curriculum areas, found that most teachers of a range of subjects 'thought of 'specialized subject language' as vocabulary rather than style' (p. 28); such a level of awareness of language is clearly inadequate to help students acquire the skills required for extended writing. The few analyses, reported in this chapter, of the forms of writing used by students in mathematics provide indications of some of the properties that such writing may have and of how these properties may be interpreted by readers. They are, however, very limited in scope and in the amount of detailed information they provide. In particular, it must be borne in mind that each analysis provides information related only to the specific form of writing activity used in that study. In some cases, the interpretation by the researchers of features of the writing provides some indication of the assessments and interpretations that may be made by teachers reading students' texts,[6] although a different context may lead to different interpretations.

From what we have seen in this chapter, it seems that:

- 'Dialogue' may be valued more highly than 'recount' as an indication of a more sophisticated way of thinking.
- Making agency explicit may be valued as it can appear to present a clearer picture of what has been done, particularly in a context in which students' individual work is to be assessed. This may, however, conflict with traditional conventions of 'sophisticated' academic writing which make substantial use of nominalizations and the passive voice.
- The value and interpretation placed on the use of the first person appears to vary with the role that the author is constructing for herself in the text and with the researcher's (or teacher's) perception of the purposes of the writing. While the 'personal' in journal writing is valued as a sign of ownership and

empowerment by Powell et al., this again conflicts with conventions of academic writing. The comparison between the work of Duval and Balacheff suggests that, while personal involvement in material processes may have a low value placed upon it and be interpreted as a sign of a student's focus on the specific and the concrete rather than on the general, the use of the first person to display mental processes may be taken as a sign of engagement in the process of logical reasoning. Clearly the use of the first person influences the way in which the text is read; the specific nature of this influence, however, must depend both on the nature of the general context of the writing activity and on the specific context within the text itself.

In the next chapter, I provide an overview of what is known about how students may learn to write in ways that their mathematics teachers value.

Notes

1   What I refer to as the 'traditional' mathematics classroom is likely to be most familiar to those readers in the United Kingdom and other English speaking countries and in those countries that have been strongly influenced by the imperialism of English education. I am aware that there are major differences in the 'traditional' education of other cultural heritages; see, for example, (Schmidt et al., 1996) and (Leung, forthcoming).

2   These authors presumably base their characterization on their experience of practices in, respectively, France and Germany. It is likely, of course, that there are differences in what is considered legitimate student writing within school practices in the UK and in other countries, particularly non-English speaking countries.

3   The 'Handshakes' problem is widely used in both upper primary and lower secondary mathematics classrooms in the UK. Although it may be posed in various ways its general statement is: If each person in the room shakes hands with every other person in the room, how many handshakes will there be?

4   Of course, I am aware that not all students are female. Given the lack of acceptable gender-neutral pronouns, I will generally use *she* and *her* where generic referents for students, teachers, mathematicians etc. are needed. In Deborah Cameron's (1992) words:

> If there are any men reading who feel uneasy about being excluded, or not addressed, they may care to consider that women get this feeling within minutes of opening the vast majority of books, and to reflect on the effect it has. (p. vii)

5   Although Balacheff (1987) identifies use of a strictly symbolic language as the highest level of proof, he admits that in practice there is normally recourse to a mixture of 'natural' and symbolic language.

6   I am making the assumption that researchers in mathematics education and mathematics teachers share many of the resources for interpreting such texts. Indeed, most of those involved in research on 'writing-to-learn' are analysing texts produced by their own students or are collaborating closely with teachers. Clarke et al.'s (1993) use of teachers' assessments to validate their own judgements of student texts suggests that, at least at a surface level, the values of researchers and teachers coincide. Clearly, however, there are also likely to be differences in their orientations to the texts which may lead to differences in interpretations.

Chapter 4

Learning to Write Mathematically

Although the process of writing in the mathematics classroom may be justified by reference to its learning benefits for students, its products, the written texts, are also used as an assessment tool. In particular, a primary function of the written report of investigative work in the UK is to provide a means by which students' achievement may be assessed. It is, therefore, of importance to the student that the quality and style of their writing should be such that their teacher-readers will evaluate their achievement highly. However, it is not necessarily the case that all students will develop the linguistic skills needed to produce such highly valued writing within the particular genre without help.

As was seen in Chapter 3, studies have consistently revealed very limited writing to be taking place in mathematics classrooms. Even since the introduction of coursework, a high stakes examination involving extended writing, there has been remarkably little attention paid in the UK to writing in mathematics. More-over, in spite of general agreement that students' mathematical writing is generally poor, few attempts to improve it have been reported. The National Writing Project, which coincided with the beginning of GCSE, identified the writing of coursework reports in mathematics as one of the areas in which work needed to be done (White, 1991). Although a small number of reports of work related to mathematics are to be found in the project newsletters, there is no evidence, for example in professional journals, that the project succeeded in disseminating its work more widely among mathematics teachers. In spite of increasing interest in the role and development of oral language in mathematics education, little attention has been paid to the role of writing. A review of perspectives and current issues related to language in mathematics education (Durkin and Shire, 1991), containing papers by a selection of mainly UK authors, is typical. Students' production of written language is dealt with in the context of the writing of numerals (Sinclair, 1991) and the problems encountered by dyslexic children (Thomson, 1991), but the only mention of more extended writing is made by Pimm (1991) whose contribution suggests briefly that 'oral reporting back' on investigative work can help in preparing for 'coursework write-ups' (p. 22).

Nevertheless, it appears to be widely recognized that some students are not successful at producing extended writing and that the requirement to write may prevent them from doing the mathematics, or at least prevent them from being assessed to have done the mathematics (e.g. Ball and Ball, 1990). A particular difficulty with non-narrative writing is noted by Waywood (1992b) in the context of journal writing. He identifies 'dialogue' as an effective form of writing in which the writer takes account of alternative points of view in order to construct an argument, yet:

> What is often seen in journals is the start of a dialogue which is cut off in mid-flight because the students haven't the control over language, or their thinking, or the material, to carry the dialogue through. (p. 38)

Waywood's difficulty in identifying which of the suggested factors is lacking indicates the difficulty of making a clear distinction between the form and the content of a text. If texts are to be used to assess mathematical problem solving, it is of importance to the students that they should not be judged to lack control of their thinking or of the material because of their lack of control over the language. The purpose of this chapter is to consider ways in which students may learn and be helped to learn to have such control over written mathematical language.

Natural Development or Deliberate Teaching?

Even where attention has been paid to the use of writing to learn mathematics there is relatively little work, particularly concerning students below college level, considering how students may learn to write mathematically. General exhortations to include opportunities for writing in the curriculum tend to assume that the means of communication will develop naturally. Thus, the influential NCTM Standards (NCTM, 1989), while discussing in some detail the power of language as a tool for learning, merely suggests that its development:

> is best accomplished in problem situations in which students have an opportunity to read, write, and discuss ideas in which the use of the language of mathematics becomes natural. (p. 6)

This assumption of natural language development is common to many descriptions of programmes, particularly those involving younger children, which claim to develop mathematical communication (e.g. Carton, 1990; Greenes, Schulman, and Spungin, 1992; Mumme and Shepherd, 1990; Wilde, 1991). McIntosh (1991) even seeks to encourage mathematics teachers to include Writing-to-Learn among their teaching techniques by stating categorically 'We don't need to teach writing' (p. 423).

Much of the Writing-to-Learn movement in all areas of the curriculum makes use of Britton's (1975) theory of language development which prioritizes expressive forms of writing in the early stages of learning, claiming that other forms will develop from these.

> what children write in the early stages should be a form of written-down expressive speech, and what they read should also be, generally speaking, expressive. As

their writing and reading progress side by side, they will move from this starting point into the three broadly differentiated kinds of writing . . . Thus in developmental terms, the expressive is a kind of matrix from which differentiated forms of mature writing are developed. (pp. 82–3)

This developmental view of writing appears to have been interpreted in practice to mean that the development is natural and spontaneous. In consequence, little attention has been paid to the various conventional forms of mathematical writing or to the ways in which students may be helped to attain them. This approach to learning and language development has been criticized by, among others, Williams (1977) and Sheeran and Barnes (1991) who (although from different perspectives) argue that the distinctive forms of language used in different disciplines are closely linked to the distinctive ways of looking at the world and structuring knowledge that are characteristic of those disciplines. Sheeran and Barnes, for example, examine cases of expressive writing in science which fail to construct a scientific view of the world and thus do not address the curricular aims of the writing task. If students are to be required to produce writing in mathematics, it cannot be assumed that they will naturally develop forms which are conventionally appropriate. Nor, indeed, can it be assumed that expressive forms of writing, such as stories, journals or 'free-writing', will enable mathematical ways of thinking.

Where there is discussion of how teachers might help school students to develop their use of mathematical language the method is usually aligned explicitly or implicitly with Graves' (1983) model of 'process' learning of writing, involving the first steps of prewriting, drafting and revising, often after peer or teacher review of a first draft. The use of peer reading of student writing[1] and 'conferencing' as part of the drafting and revising process is found in a number of studies (Duncan, 1989; Gopen and Smith, 1989; Havens, 1989; Hoffman and Powell, 1992; Keith, 1989; National Writing Project, 1989) which claim consequent improvements in the quality of mathematical writing produced. Another technique that is suggested to help students to develop their writing processes is the modelling of writing behaviour by the mathematics teacher; this may merely involve the teacher writing at the same time as the students (Wilde, 1991) or, as Richards (1990) recommends, participating more directly in the students' writing process through thinking aloud or scribing for children.

Marks and Mousley (1990; Mousley and Marks, 1991) criticize this 'process' approach for the limited experience of different genres of mathematical writing that it is likely to provide for children. They refer to critics of the way in which 'process writing' has been implemented in language education, who have observed that it gives rise to predominantly narrative writing, and claim that 'Writing is an *unnatural* act: it needs to be learned' (Reid, cited in Marks and Mousley, 1990, p. 134). In order to develop mathematical literacy, children need to learn a wide range of the types of writing used in mathematics:

Events are recounted (narrative genre), methods described (procedural genre), the nature of individual things and classes of things explicated (description and report genres), judgments outlined (explanatory genre), and arguments developed (expository genre). (p. 119)

The authors suggest some ways in which such genres might be developed in primary or secondary mathematics classrooms and recommend that students should be led 'to development of an explicit understanding of the role of language in specific mathematical contexts' (p. 133) through critical reading of alternative models of writing by adults, including their teacher, and by their fellow students.

One specialized genre of mathematical writing (not now commonly found in UK classrooms) is the formal 'two column' geometry proof. In general, studies of the learning of proof have focused on students' understanding of the nature of proof itself rather than on their learning of its written form. However, studies by Sekiguchi in classrooms in the US (1992) and in Japan (1994) have looked at students learning to produce such proofs from the point of view that they are learning to participate in a new form of discourse. Sekiguchi (1994) argues that learning to prove:

involves an introduction of a new mathematical language system, qualitatively different from previous systems. It required the students to follow and internalize new ways of interpreting, arguing, and writing mathematics. (p. 239)

He describes the standard use of 'fill-in-the-blanks' exercises in a Japanese classroom which, he suggests, act as scaffolding for the students as they learn to write their own proofs, although he warns that inappropriate over-use may be unhelpful for some students. Sekiguchi's perspective on learning formal proof as learning to participate in a new discourse could usefully be extended to look at other aspects of learning in mathematics classrooms.

The most deliberate attention to teaching students to acquire mathematical writing skills has been at college level in the United States. This appears to be largely motivated by general university requirements for all students. Snow (1989), for example, describes a programme which arose from a college-level requirement for every student 'to demonstrate writing proficiency within the student's particular major' (p. 193). Although some authors (e.g. Gopen and Smith, 1989; Paik and Norris, 1984) simultaneously use the rhetoric of Writing-to-Learn, there is greater concern with the students' need as future professionals for technical writing skills. The descriptions provided of the methods used to help students to achieve better mathematical writing range from drafting and revising with teacher comments (Paik and Norris, 1984; Snow, 1989) to Price's (1989) provision of fully detailed 'guidelines' with rules for good writing such as 'Write in sentences', 'Respect the equal sign', 'Avoid pronouns' (p. 394). All these authors claim major improvements in student writing during their teaching programmes although little evidence is generally offered.

One aspect of mathematical writing which has received some attention in the UK is that of the use of algebraic symbolism, although the focus has normally been on the development of algebraic thinking rather than on the notation itself. James and Mason's (1982) sequence of seeing-saying-recording, discussed in the previous chapter, may be seen as an approach that, while valuing children's own forms of writing, simultaneously sees them as leading, with teacher support, to conventional mathematical forms. It includes a role for the teacher in assisting the development of more conventional forms by intervening 'to plant the seeds of helpful language patterns and recording devices' (p. 256).

In the UK, the introduction of investigations and examination by coursework has involved school students in generating substantial amounts of writing. Although only anecdotal evidence is available, it appears to be widely recognized that many students find such writing difficult and consequently may be handicapped in the assessment process; for example, Ball and Ball (1990) remark that:

> Students who are not good at writing are likely to feel threatened by having to produce coursework, and might therefore not be able to communicate their grasp of a subject. (p. 10)

This concern has not, however, been substantially addressed. Where classroom experiences of investigative work have been described or analysed, writing appears merely as a background activity that does not require specific attention. Other authors, concerned with the difficulty that students have in writing a complete record of their investigative processes for assessment purposes, merely advocate that the importance of the written record should be lessened and other means of communication valued more (e.g. Bloomfield, 1987; MacNamara and Roper, 1992a; 1992b). The concern that students' writing skills may not be adequate to represent their problem solving activity has not been accompanied by any attempt to enhance the writing itself.

Evidence of Development in Mathematical Writing

Waywood (1994) and Powell et al. (Powell and López, 1989; Powell and Ramnauth, 1992) report 'improvements' in student writing in long term programmes involving mathematics journal writing. (Some of the forms of writing identified in these programmes were discussed in the previous chapter.) Waywood reports development in the qualities of questions posed by an individual student over a period of years while Powell and López (1989) claim that, over time, students' journal entries become both more personal and more reflective. General improvements in the use of written language are also identified, Powell and Ramnauth (1992) commenting on an increase in 'control' of the language of mathematics and on the use of 'bolder and more confident' language. The authors provide examples to illustrate these developments, but, while it is clear from a non-analytic reading that there are major differences in both content and style between the several extracts from individual students, it is less clear how the authors are identifying and categorizing these differences. The finding by these authors that the quality of students' writing (as defined by the teachers and researchers involved) developed over time points to the possibility that, with extensive experience and feedback from teachers and from peers, students come to learn the features of the genre that will be valued by their teachers. This seems likely, however, to be a lengthy process, making considerable demands on the time and commitment of the teachers and students involved.

Driscoll and Powell (1992) describe writing arising from more discrete writing activities in which students wrote in small groups. Whereas the first drafts included features such as the use of additional personal knowledge and personal involvement in the text, the final text produced by the group is described as:

> clear direct and concise . . . without personal references . . . resembles the level of abstractness and precision that opinion would have us believe is the interpretive starting point of readers' response to transactional text. (p. 262)

It would appear that such peer group feedback and editing provided these mature students with a context which prompted them to use some of the characteristic features of formal mathematical texts.

While any development in the cases discussed above seems to arise from the sort of feedback and editing associated with the 'process' approach to writing, few programmes have paid deliberate attention to 'appropriate' forms of language. One exception is Gopen and Smith's (1989) work with undergraduate students writing reports of computer-based investigations. Although one of the aims of introducing writing into their mathematics course was to improve the students' learning, Gopen and Smith also paid attention to the communicative effectiveness of the texts produced. Using a theory of 'reader expectation', which identifies the quality of writing with the amount of 'energy' available to the reader to determine the writer's intentions, given the amount required to determine the structure of the text, Gopen and Smith used questions such as 'What actions are taking place?'; 'What is new and important?'; 'Who is the agent?' to interrogate and evaluate students' texts and to provide the students themselves with a means of interrogating and revising their own texts. These questions, by paying attention to the transitivity system (the actions and actors) and the thematic structure (identifying what is new), address the way in which the nature of mathematical activity is constructed within the text as well as the type of argument that is constructed. However, Gopen and Smith use these analytic tools in a normative rather than a descriptive way. For example, their theoretical position leads them to value more highly those texts in which the agency is clear. They mention in particular their dislike of the use of nominalizations and their wish to see the student-author's actions made explicit through the use of personal pronouns. It is not certain that similar qualities will be valued by other teachers, particularly where the context of the writing is different. While the questions used to direct students' attention to significant aspects of their writing may have been effective in developing their grasp of the desired genre, the authors' claim about the general efficacy of their theory must be treated with caution, particularly given the conflict between some of their preferences and the characteristics of much academic mathematics writing.

'Audience' as an Influence on the Development of Effective Writing

Major studies of school writing across the curriculum, both in Britain (Britton et al., 1975; Martin et al., 1976; Spencer et al., 1983; White, 1991) and in the United States (Applebee, 1981; 1984), have expressed concern about the fact that they have found the vast majority of writing done by students in secondary schools to be addressed to an audience consisting of the teacher, mostly in the role of examiner. It has been suggested that this is one of the roots of students' difficulties and lack of motivation in their development as writers.[2] In particular, while the student's teacher is the actual reader of the text produced, consideration of the teacher's own state of knowledge about the subject matter may not help the student to produce writing that will be evaluated as effective. It is sometimes suggested that students may be helped to write more effectively by addressing imaginary audiences such as 'your friend in Australia' (School Mathematics Project, 1989, p. 8) or someone who 'is intelligent but knows nothing about your assignment' (Bull, 1990, p. 105).[3] It is this suggestion that I examine in this section.

In their discussions of the audiences for school writing, Britton et al. (1975) categorize the various audiences that children may write for in school in terms of the relationship expressed in the writing between the writer and the reader:

- self;
- teacher (subdivided into: child to trusted adult; pupil to teacher, general; pupil to teacher, particular relationship; pupil to examiner);
- wider audience, known (subdivided into: expert to known layman; child to peer group; group member to working group);
- unknown audience;
- virtual named audience;
- no discernible audience.

These categories, however, while providing a useful framework for thinking about school writing, are not as straightforward as they might seem; there are problems both in the application and in the theoretical basis of the concept of *audience*[4] used in these studies. Both the studies mentioned and most others concerned with audience in education have adopted an apparently naive view of audience which fails to take into account the dichotomy between the audience *addressed* by writers, the 'actual readers external to their texts', and the audience that writers *invoke* 'within their texts, teaching their readers through textual cues how to relate to and read a given text' (Willey, 1990, p. 26). Studies of the practices of writers suggest that they may create an imaginary reader (Odell, 1985) or manipulate their relationship with their reader by deliberately breaking the usual conventions of the discourse (Faigley, 1985).

The Teacher-Reader

The audience for the vast majority of school writing may be the student's teacher, but Purves (1984) identifies a multiplicity of reading roles that a teacher may adopt, ranging from 'common reader' through, among others, 'proof reader', 'gatekeeper', 'critic' and 'diagnostician'. The student-writer:

> must learn to deal with all these kinds of readers, know something of what the concerns of each might be, and know that a writing is not simply to or for *an* audience, but that the text is read variously by different people for different purposes, but also variously by the same reader.

While Purves suggests that any or even all of these roles may be adopted in reading a single text, most studies of school writing have focused primarily on the teacher's role as a judge of student writing. A crucial problem with writing that is addressed to a teacher-as-examiner is that the teacher-as-examiner is 'not personally involved in the topic' (Redd-Boyd and Slater, 1989). She is an 'overhearer' (Bell, 1984) rather than the rhetorical audience of the text; her role is to judge whether correct information has been included and whether the writing is persuasive, rather than to be informed or persuaded herself. As Kinneavy (1971) points out, this is an artificial context for writing where the student is expected to write informatively to a reader who is already completely informed about the topic. This may cause difficulties for writers in deciding what and how to write. It also may not be the best context for developing writing or subject skills. As Applebee (1984) says, 'the teacher-as-examiner can be a very undemanding audience' (p. 3) because she is looking for 'evidence' within the text and may construct the 'argument' for herself. Thus, in some cases, such a teacher may read a text which contains specific desired pieces of information without noticing that it lacks textual or logical coherence. Spencer et al. (1983) report an 'intelligent' pupil who, although she produced high quality writing for English, wrote 'scrappy, unparagraphed History essays, which were in effect lists of poorly linked pieces of information written out as prose'.

> She told us in her interview that she obtained high marks in History for getting the facts right and did not need to bother with the problem of writing more cohesively.
> (p. 127)

This student was clearly aware of her audience and adapted her writing to suit her reader's requirements; such adaptation does not necessarily produce forms of writing that would be considered of high quality.

Even writing that is produced for a teacher audience may be qualitatively changed by altering the teacher's role as reader from teacher-as-examiner to teacher-as-part-of-an-instructional-dialogue (using Applebee's (1981) adaptation of Britton's categories). Langer (1984) found that children who addressed the teacher-as-part-of-an-instructional-dialogue were more 'fluent' than those who addressed the teacher-as-examiner. This finding is ambiguous, however, as Langer suggests that the difference may be a developmental one indicating that those children who 'choose' to write to the teacher-as-part-of-an-instructional-dialogue need further teaching in order to learn how to start to address a teacher-as-examiner audience. Furthermore, it is not clear that the 'fluency' did not itself contribute to the way in which the audience was categorized.

Specifying Non-teacher Audiences

It is often suggested that writing for a 'real' audience is more motivating for children than writing for a teacher. Moreover, Tomlinson (1990) argues that interacting with 'intimate' readers actually helps writers develop the ability to write effectively for wider audiences:

> it is only *because* we have these irritatingly idiosyncratic *individual readers* that we can ever learn to *generalize about readers*, to fictionalize our audiences effectively (original italics)

While Tomlinson's discussion focuses on the influences of the variety of audiences for writers of academic papers, her emphasis on the importance of discourse communities in which writers and readers interact and negotiate their meanings also has relevance in other contexts.

The main feature of the school writing tasks that Applebee (1984) categorizes as for a 'wider audience' is that they instruct the student writer to address an audience other than the teacher; this audience may be real or imaginary, specific or general but in almost all cases the child knows that the teacher will still be the most important (and often the only) reader. In fact, Spencer et al. (1983) found that many children did not consider that being assigned an imaginary audience was helpful, suggesting that they recognized that the teacher was the main addressee. Butt (1991) suggests an alternative interpretation of this, based on his attempt to introduce 'audience-centred' writing tasks into geography classes:

> It was obvious that some children would have been much happier writing for the normal restricted audience of the teacher assessor as this required far less thought, originality and effort. (p. 76)

As Long (1990) points out, the writing teacher's advice 'don't forget your audience' is superfluous because students are always aware of their audience — the teacher. Indeed, Gilbert's (1989) case studies of high school writers showed that following such teacher advice rigidly was not necessarily the best way to get good marks; the most successful student 'deliberately ignored' some instructions, predicting instead what the teacher *really* wanted.

Herrington's (1985) study of writing in undergraduate chemical engineering courses, in which hypothetical audiences were specified, showed not only that perceptions about the identity of the audience differed between teachers and students but also that perceptions of the characteristics of the audience differed, particularly perceptions of the amount of knowledge about the subject matter. Differences in perceptions about the amount of information that needs to be included are likely to lead to negative evaluations of student writing by the teacher, both where the teacher perceives the amount of information included to be too little and where it is perceived to be too much. Herrington argues that it might be more helpful to students to be honest about the purposes of school writing rather than to provide mixed messages about imaginary audiences.

The complexity of the relationship between student-writer, teacher-reader and assigned audience is also demonstrated by studies considering the effects of assigning audiences on the writing produced (e.g. Crowhurst and Piché, 1979; Donin, Bracewell, Frederiksen and Dillinger, 1992; Hays, Durham, Brandt and Raitz, 1990; Prentice, 1980; Quick, 1983; Redd-Boyd and Slater, 1989; Rubin and Piché, 1979). Factors which may play a part in the amount of adaptation made for a specified audience include the students' level of socio-cognitive development (Hays et al., 1990), their knowledge of the subject matter (Prentice, 1980), their relationship with the supposed audience (Butt, 1991; Prentice, 1980), as well as the extent to which they genuinely adopt the assigned audience (Redd-Boyd and Slater, 1989).

There is some evidence that intervening to prompt students to consider their audience can help to improve the quality of their writing (Roen and Willey, 1988; Rubin and O'Leary, 1990; Scardamalia, Bereiter, and Goelman, 1982), although this improvement may be primarily due to the act of revising a first draft rather than to more specific attention to audience characteristics. Actual interaction with a reader also appears likely to lead to adaptation of the writing (Prentice, 1980). Interestingly, there seems to have been relatively little research into this interaction, perhaps because of the difficulty of studying such potentially complex and time consuming situations.

Audiences for Mathematical Writing — Some Examples

Some curriculum developments attempting to specify non-teacher audiences for mathematical writing have been described, including the use of 'letters' (Havens, 1989; McIntosh, 1991) and 'explanations' (Hurwitz, 1990; Miller, 1992b) addressed to imaginary audiences. Such specification of imaginary audiences may be intended to improve student motivation or to attempt to influence the content or the form of what is written. Havens, for example, claims that a non-teacher audience forces students 'to be more thorough in their explanations', while Hurwitz (1990) states that imagining 'that they are explaining the subject to someone with little or no background in the specific topic' helps students to 'understand the amount of specificity they will need in their explanations' (p. 702).

When considering the writing which results from such contexts in the light of the discussion above, however, it seems likely that students will still perceive their primary audience to be the teacher and that this perception will influence both the content and the form of their writing. A study by Schubauer-Leoni et al. (1989) showed that, when in a classroom context, children still used the conventions of formal mathematical notation when asked by the teacher to write 'so that the other children would understand' or when asked to write by and for a non-teacher adult, although outside the classroom context 'their written solutions are more hetero-geneous in nature using natural language, illustrative drawings etc.' (p. 675). Merely assigning an imaginary audience is by itself unlikely to make significant changes in children's perceptions of writing tasks, in the content they choose to include, or in the forms they choose to use. It would seem that the institutional setting is likely to have a stronger influence than any exhortation to imagine a non-teacher audience. Even where 'real' non-teacher audiences are involved, the evidence of studies such as Redd-Boyd and Slater (1989) suggests that many students will not necessarily change their perceptions of their readers, particularly where the writing context is such that there is not a close relationship between the writer and the potential reader(s). Contexts suggested by curriculum developers such as writing mathematical contributions for a school newspaper (McIntosh, 1991) or writing problems for younger children (Carton, 1990) may not, in themselves, have significant effects on children's writing. Where there is contact between the writer and readers during the writing process, however, the findings on the effects of intervention make it appear more likely that the quality of the writing may be affected. Examples of classroom activities which involve such communication include children reading and discussing each other's journals (McIntosh, 1991), peer-editing of written work (Penniman, 1991), and collaborative problem solving and sharing of solutions between children in different schools via electronic mail (Barclay, 1990; Hatfield and Bitter, 1991).

Most of the mathematics educators whose work has been mentioned so far have been primarily concerned with 'Writing-to-Learn' mathematics. This is reflected in their emphasis on the possible gains in reflection and understanding that are claimed to arise from such communicative contexts. From a different point of view, Bolon (1990; 1991) suggests engaging children in writing for audiences of their peers with the aim of helping them to learn to write mathematically. Her 'Jeux de Communication', recommended to student teachers as a way of introducing conventional geometrical vocabulary while enriching mathematics pedagogy (1990, p. 1), involve writing and then reading and editing 'telephone messages' to instruct other pupils how to draw geometric figures. The 'telephone message' metaphor is apparently intended to indicate only that no drawing is to be used, rather than to call up the kind of language that might be used during a telephone conversation. Such 'telephone messages' are also used in spoken form, where the desired precision of mathematical language may be developed through the negotiation of meaning between the participants that is possible in oral dialogue. Specifying an audience in order to construct such messages in written form may be seen as an attempt to overcome the lack of such negotiation of meaning between participants by stimulating the writer to shift between writer- and reader-roles in order to undertake negotiation of meaning within herself. What might constitute a context in which this can effectively take place remains to be investigated. The evidence of Guillerault and Laborde (1982; 1986) suggests that children 'decoding' such messages by producing the figure described do not recognize ambiguities in the texts that had been identified by the researchers but are able to interpret them by using the context, often in the way intended by the writer. Thus calling up a hypothetical reader or even a real peer-group reader seems unlikely to help the writer to identify what might conventionally be considered to be ambiguities.

Borasi and Siegel (1994) argue strongly that reading and writing should be integrated into purposeful mathematical activity. They describe the work done by children during a project focused on the national census which involved them in communication with an audience of their peers and in reflection on the content and form of their writing. During one part of the extended project, for example, having conducted a questionnaire, the children became aware that some of their audience had been unable to understand the questions in the way intended. The claim that 'writing was never done just for the teacher nor was evaluation its main purpose' (p. 41) is made, however, entirely from the perspective of the teacher with the assumption that the task set to the students defined their activity. While it may be true that:

> Whenever students write and share that writing not only with the teacher but also with peers, new channels of communication are automatically opened, thus breaking the traditional pattern of classroom discourse in which communication is channelled through, and therefore controlled by, the teacher. (p. 45)

there is no evidence presented of the students' views of the nature of the activity or of their audience which might support Borasi and Siegel's claim or provide some idea of the nature of the changes that might be effected in the 'pattern of classroom discourse'. While writing in mathematics that is set within such communicative contexts appears to have the potential to provide children with opportunities to consider what content and form they should use to communicate with a particular audience, one must be careful about the claims that are made about the 'reality' of the audience, remembering that the discourse of the school context may still be more 'real' to the writers themselves.

In an earlier study (Morgan, 1992a; 1992b) I attempted to look at the ways in which pre-GCSE students (aged 13–14 years) perceived their audience and adapted their writing of reports of investigative work when placed in a situation in which their readers were to be their own peer group, including known individuals in their own class. The students produced reports of their work, a selection of which were published in a class magazine edited by a group of students chosen from within the class. The rough work and final reports, the deliberations of the editorial group and interviews with students after the publication of the magazine were used to explore the students' beliefs about the characteristics of effective writing in this context and the extent to which the students had adopted and adapted to the audience of their peers. The 'real audience' setting appeared to be motivating and meaningful for at least some students and there was some spontaneous use of other students as readers during the revision process.

There was considerable variation in style between the texts produced by different groups of students and it appeared that most student-writers produced texts which contained the features that they themselves found most important, although there was some evidence of students being influenced by feedback from their peers, suggesting that their initially naive view of audience might be affected by greater experience of interaction with readers. On the other hand, some students were unable to accept the assigned audience at all, one girl expressing her astonishment when her work appeared in the published magazine:

> *I thought it wouldn't be in the magazine because we were a bit noisy and ... and ours weren't very good at the beginning until we writ it out all neat. Cos it was messy and horrible and everything.*

Her previous experience in the classroom apparently led her to believe that her deviant behaviour would cause her work to be devalued and to distrust the assurance that only the final 'neat' version of her work would be considered. An important finding was that students appeared to experience tensions between their own preferences when reading a text (for example, a preference for colourful illustrations), their awareness of the audience that had been specified and their knowledge of the expectations of texts produced in standard school mathematics settings (for example, awareness of the value normally placed on 'lots of content'). It is clear that the invocation of a non-teacher audience, whether imaginary or 'real', to help students improve their writing in the mathematics classroom is not a simple matter and is unlikely to be fully effective if it takes place in isolation.

In this chapter a general lack of attention to the form of writing in mathematics classrooms has been identified. It has been argued that an assumption that mathematical forms of writing will develop naturally is unwarranted and that there are problems related to the question of 'audience' in school writing, both when the audience is unambiguously the teacher and when a non-teacher audience is specified. It seems that deliberate attention to forms of language may be a more effective way of supporting learners. It is thus crucial to identify those forms which may be considered 'appropriate' within a given genre of mathematical writing. This is the task that I attempt to undertake in later chapters of this book for the particular genre of reports of investigations.

Notes

1 The use of peer reading during the drafting and revising process is also related to the idea that having a real audience will improve the quality of writing. The issue of audience is discussed below.

2 The National Writing Project, however, recognized the necessity of writing for a teacher-examiner audience, reflecting recent reactions against the 'personal growth' approach to writing represented in the earlier studies and criticizing this approach for creating a bias towards narrative or informative genres (White, 1991, p. 72).

3 Bull (1990) is a guide for students doing coursework. It is discussed in more detail in Chapter 5.

4 Rather than using italics or inverted commas every time I use the word 'audience', I would ask the reader to bear in mind throughout that this concept is not unproblematic.

The Public Discourse of 'Investigation'

So far I have attempted a general review of the place of writing in mathematics and mathematics classrooms. In the rest of this volume I now turn to a specific examination of the writing that students in UK secondary schools undertake in response to 'investigation' tasks. In order to understand the texts they produce and interpret the significance of the features of their writing it is necessary to establish a background of knowledge about the discourse within which they are produced.

What is mathematical 'investigation'? There are two common ways of approaching such a question: explicit definition by articulating a statement of the form 'Investigation is . . .' and implicit definition through exemplification. As we shall see later in this chapter, a range of explicit definitions have been attempted, some of which are similar but many of which give rise to contradictions or tensions. Problems also arise in attempting to exemplify, as apparently very different types of tasks have been offered to teachers and students under the label 'investigation', including, for example:

> Investigate sums of consecutive integers.

and

> A single straight line cuts a circle into, at most, 2 regions. Two straight lines cut a circle into, at most, 3 regions.
> (a)   Investigate what happens when you use 3 lines.
> (b)   Draw up a table showing the maximum number of regions that can be obtained using 1, 2, 3, 4, . . . straight lines.
> (c)   Try to find a rule which connects the maximum number of regions and the number of lines.

The two examples I have given here differ in a number of ways (though only some of the possible ways), reflecting some of the contradictions and tensions within the discourse of 'investigation' that will be identified and explored in this chapter. I do not intend to attempt to enumerate the differences (or indeed the similarities) between them, preferring to leave it to the reader to make sense of the fact that both are labelled 'investigation' in the light of the discussion that follows.

My approach to the question 'What is investigation?' does not expect a single definitive answer but recognizes that the tasks and types of activity labelled as 'investigation' are located within a complex discourse which influences the participants' understanding of the characteristics of the tasks themselves and of students' ideal responses to them. An awareness of this discourse will be essential in order to interpret the significance of features of students' written reports of their investigation and to understand teachers' readings of these texts. It is this discourse that will be considered in this chapter through examination of some of the writing on the subject of 'investigation' that is available in the public domain.

The types of task that are currently labelled as 'investigations' and the activities which are called 'investigating' have been present in some mathematics classrooms in the United Kingdom for many years and are, in particular, to be found described in the pages of publications of the Association of Teachers of Mathematics (ATM) at least as far back as the 1960s.[1] The purpose of this chapter, however, is not to provide a historical review of the presence of these activities within the mathematics curriculum, but to create a picture of the current discourse associated with the term *investigation*, considering the historical development of this discourse to the extent that it throws useful light on the present situation. A personal and historical account of the development of investigation from its early years may be found in Barbara Jaworski's book in this series (Jaworski, 1994), including a review of some of the critical professional literature that identifies tensions within the discourse.

One of my major motivations in undertaking this study was my concern with students' difficulty in presenting their investigative work for examination at GCSE level. As one of the most significant factors in relation to this concern is the institutionalized nature of the investigation as part of the examination system, it seems appropriate to focus primarily on publications relating to the role of investigation within an examination context and thus to take the publication of the Cockcroft report in 1982 as a critical starting point. Prior to the publication of this report, only a small minority of pupils sat examinations at 16+ which included any investigational element[2] and, where they did, this was considered to be experimental or appropriate only for lower attaining pupils (p. 162). Since then, however, 'investigation' has become part of the official mathematics curriculum, incorporated into all 16+ examinations in the form of GCSE coursework and eventually into the National Curriculum in the form of Attainment Target 1 'Using and Applying Mathematics'.

'Investigation' is not, however, a simple or uncontested term. In this chapter, the 'official' discourse found in the Cockcroft report itself and in the publications of the examination boards will be examined. I am taking as 'official' those texts published or endorsed by government departments or agencies and by the examination boards — in other words, texts that may be taken to define policy and examination practice. When considering how 'investigation' is experienced in schools by teachers and by pupils, however, this 'official' discourse is only one influence; there is also a 'practical' discourse, addressed to teachers and to the pupils themselves through the media of text books, teachers' guides, pupils' guides to doing coursework, journal articles describing particular investigations or recommending particular forms of classroom practice, etc. In addition, there is a 'professional' discourse, to be found in professional journals and in books intended for pre-service or in-service education of teachers, which discusses both theoretical and practical issues related to 'investigation'. Although the overt intentions, contents and styles of these three discourses are very different, they all contribute towards the construction of the 'investigation' as a phenomenon in mathematics education. In considering these three types of source, the fundamental questions remain the same:

What are the properties of 'investigation'?

and

What are the desired properties of students' work on investigative tasks (and, in particular, the properties of the writing they produce)?

The distinction between these three public aspects of the discourse of 'investigation' is not as simple as this categorization might suggest; there are overlaps in authorship and in content of the various publications. For example, the same individual author[3] might have contributed to the Non-Statutory Guidance for the National Curriculum (NCC, 1989), published a practical guide to doing and assessing coursework, and written a journal article discussing some of the reasons why teachers find it difficult to use investigative approaches in the classroom. Similarly, statements about, for example, the need for teachers to allow pupils to follow different paths in an investigation may also be found in 'official', 'practical' and 'professional' texts. The distinction between them lies essentially in the authority of each type of text in relation to its subject matter and its constructed readers and in the rhetorical nature of the text itself. In the case of the 'official' discourse, the subject matter of the text is unquestionable and the reader is constructed explicitly or implicitly as an instrument of the text, bringing to it no opinions or possibility of challenging the message; such texts are statements of what is. Of course, the social context of these texts also contributes to their authority and to the ways in which they are read by teachers and others. The examination syllabus, for example, by its very existence defines the content and form of an important part of school mathematics. There is no room for the teacher-reader to contest its message other than by choosing to accept the message of an alternative examination board. The 'practical' discourse, while presenting the nature of 'investigation' as fixed, allows that there may be doubt about the reader's position in relation to it. In particular, it is expected that the reader may experience difficulty in its implementation and possibly uncertainty (arising from ignorance rather than opposition) about its value. The text thus attempts to persuade and advise its readers as well as to instruct them. In the 'professional' discourse, the subject matter itself is contestable and the text tends to be structured as an argument; the reader is constructed as a colleague, or at least as someone who might in the future have that status, whose possibly opposing opinions are to be taken seriously. This discourse includes some texts which are critical of the inclusion of 'investigation' in the mathematics curriculum or of some of the characteristics of its concrete manifestations.

'Official' Discourse

'Investigation' and ideas associated with it may be found in a large number of government sponsored publications as well as numerous publications by the examining boards. I intend, however, to discuss only a small selection of the official texts which have been most influential in the introduction of 'investigations' into secondary school mathematics classrooms and, especially, into the formal system of public examination. Other official publications do not differ significantly in the concepts they contain in relation to 'investigation'.

The Cockcroft Report

The widespread institutionalization of the idea that something called 'investigation' has a legitimate role within mathematics education may be traced back to the report of the Cockcroft Committee and its often- (and possibly over-) quoted paragraph 243. While stating that they had no desire to 'indicate a definitive style for the teaching of mathematics', the authors nevertheless stated that 'mathematics teaching at all levels should include opportunities' for six modes of work:

- exposition by the teacher;
- discussion between teacher and pupils and between pupils themselves;
- appropriate practical work;
- consolidation and practice of fundamental skills and routines;
- problem solving, including the application of mathematics to everyday situations;
- investigational work. (Cockcroft, 1982, p. 71)

The format of this section lends itself to a reading of the list as exhaustive and the six elements as mutually exclusive. Indeed, the term *elements*, which is used in the report itself, further strengthens a reading that sees the six as fundamentally different and separate from one another. Although such an interpretation was not made explicit within the report, most of the response by the teaching profession has treated the list in this way. Indeed, some energy was put into attempts to define the difference between problem solving and investigation (e.g. ATM, 1984) or to attack the distinction between them (Wells, 1993).[4]

In a subsequent section, the report goes on to attempt to define investigational work, in particular to attack the idea of 'the investigation' as a substantial and separate piece of work:

> We suspect that there are many teachers who think of 'mathematical investigations' as being in some way similar to the 'projects' which in recent years have become common as a way of working in many areas of the curriculum; in other words, that a mathematical investigation is an extensive piece of work which will take quite a long time to complete. . . . But although this is one of the forms which

> mathematical investigations can take, it is by no means the only form nor need it be the most common. Investigations need be neither lengthy nor difficult. At the most fundamental level, and perhaps most frequently, they should start in response to pupils' questions, perhaps during exposition by the teacher . . . (pp. 73–4)

Nevertheless, the overwhelming use of the nominalization[5] *investigations* throughout this section (rather than the term *investigational work* found in paragraph 243 itself) further reinforces the interpretation that there is a clearly defined object to be labelled 'an investigation'. The above passage is inherently ambiguous in its construction of its central concept.

This section starts with the statement that

> The idea of investigation is fundamental both to the study of mathematics itself and also to an understanding of the ways in which mathematics can be used to extend knowledge and to solve problems in very many fields. (p. 73)

but does not attempt to justify the statement by any further reference to the nature of mathematical activity. The nature of investigation itself is also defined only implicitly, largely through the use of a small number of examples of types of questions which might be pursued. Two of these questions, 'could we have done the same thing with three other numbers?' and 'what would happen if . . . ?', suggest the notion of *extension*, which has become of importance in the assessment of coursework. The other two examples are problems involving the generation of multiple ways of achieving the same result; such combinatoric questions are very common in collections of 'investigations' for teachers to use in the classroom such as the ATM's *Points of Departure* series. Three further properties of an investigative way of working may be deduced from this text:

- there may be a variety of equally valid results (although the example provided suggests that this multiplicity arises from the use of different makes of calculator rather than from any broader kind of openness in the original task);
- the method which has been used ought to be discussed;
- there is value in following and subsequently discussing 'false trails'.

The Cockcroft report thus establishes the idea that there is a desirable and clearly distinguishable type of activity that may be labelled 'investigation', and hints at some of this activity's properties. The ways in which these properties have been elaborated and transformed into practice will be a theme throughout this chapter.

Significantly, a later section of the report also makes a clear connection between this discussion of teaching styles and the form of examination at 16+. Having castigated timed written examinations for causing a state of affairs in which

> especially as the examination approaches but often also from a much earlier stage, practical and investigational work finds no place in day-by-day work in mathematics (p. 161)

the conclusion is drawn that

> Because, in our view, assessment procedures in public examinations should be
> such as to encourage good classroom practice, **we believe that provision should
> be made for an element of teacher assessment to be included in the examina-
> tion of pupils of all levels of attainment**. (p. 162, original emphasis)

A clear identification is being made between teacher assessment in public
examinations and 'good classroom practice', including investigational work. This
part of the report, in particular the recommendation emphasized by the use of bold
type in the extract above, may be seen as instrumental in the eventual institutionalization of the 'investigation' as part of GCSE coursework.

GCSE: Coursework Tasks and Assessment Criteria

In order to address the two questions stated at the beginning of this chapter —
'What are the properties of 'investigation'?', and 'What are the desired properties
of students' work on tasks within this domain?' — two main examination board
sources will be considered: the coursework tasks set by the London examining
group (LEAG),[6] and the assessment criteria issued for teachers to use in assessing
them. Although the various examination groups vary in their interpretation of what
constitutes coursework, particularly in the level of prescription of the type and
number of tasks to be undertaken by candidates, the assessment criteria developed
by each group have, from the beginning, been fairly similar — varying in the detail
of their formal application and conversion into marks or grades rather than in the
type of criterion included, although there have been differences in the importance
ascribed to various aspects of the criteria. I do not intend to attempt a full analysis
of the similarities and differences between the coursework practices of all the
examination groups, but rather to describe how their publications contribute to the
construction of the discourse of investigation and coursework within which teachers
and pupils operate in schools.

The introduction of coursework into GCSE examinations was not uncon-
troversial. Following initial attempts to exempt mathematics from the general
requirement to include an element of teacher assessment, it was conceded that the
examination groups might continue to offer syllabuses without teacher assessment
until 1991. This concession clearly marked coursework in mathematics as officially
problematic in some sense. Nevertheless, the National Criteria for GCSE Mathematics which eventually emerged (DES, 1985) prescribed that, from 1991, 'all
schemes of assessment must include a coursework element', which 'may take a
variety of forms including practical and investigational work' (p. 5). Such work is
clearly presented as different and separate from other types of work and is only to
be assessed by coursework; thus it is stated that assessment objective 3.17, 'carry
out practical and investigational work, and undertake extended pieces of work' may
only be assessed by 'work carried out by candidates in addition to time-limited

written examinations' (ibid. p. 2). The syllabuses without coursework during the first few years were thus exempted from this objective.[7] The problematic nature of coursework is reflected in the fact that in the first year of the GCSE examination only approximately 10 per cent of candidates were entered for mathematics syllabuses which included a coursework component (SEAC, 1989).

In the assessment objective cited above, an association appears to be being made between 'practical', 'investigational' and 'extended'. It is not clear whether these are aspects of the same phenomenon or are being listed in opposition to one another. In the first two years of the GCSE examination (1988 and 1989), LEAG attempted to distinguish between different types of task, which it labelled 'Investigation', 'Problem', and 'Practical'. The distinction between these categories is very unclear; while the subject matter of those tasks labelled 'investigation' is, on the whole, 'pure' in that little or no attempt is made to relate either the original problem or its solution to any 'real world' context, the same may also be said of most of those tasks labelled 'problem' or 'practical'. These latter designations appear to be associated to some extent either with a degree of 'real world' context or with the possible (but not in all cases necessary) manipulation of concrete objects. The relevance of any 'real world' context is not, however, maintained throughout the task. In all but one of the tasks set during these two years the ultimate aim for the candidate is to form an abstract generalization of some kind. In subsequent years, while setting tasks with starting points within both 'pure' and 'real world' contexts, the board abandoned its labels. Analysis of the coursework tasks set in 1991 reveals the uniform nature of the tasks, all of which require inductive generalization based on patterns 'spotted' in data generated by the candidate early on in the task. It is suggested by Wolf (1990) that the requirement to assess 'processes' has given rise to the predominance of such 'pure' investigations over 'practical' problems. Not only do stereotypical 'pattern spotting' investigations lend themselves to the use and display of a specific set of processes, they also allow the pupil to 'show off one's mathematical prowess' (p. 142) by displaying a variety of content knowledge and skills in ways that would be inappropriate in a 'practical' problem leading to a 'practical' solution. In effect, the problem of distinguishing between practical and investigational work has been resolved by subsuming the 'practical' within a unified type of 'investigational' task.

The idea of 'extension' has from the start been seen as an additional part of any investigational task. LEAG has dealt with the requirement to assess 'extended' work by providing the opportunity for candidates to create an 'extension' to any of the tasks they undertake. In some cases the nature of this extension is specified and through these specifications we may see that the term *extension* has come to signify the undertaking of a repetition of the original problem with some minor variation. Thus, for example, having investigated the number of routes between opposite vertices on various polyhedra, the candidate is invited to extend 'For example, by changing one or more of the rules, or by combining solids' (LEAG, 1991, p. 13). Although, in some other cases, the nature of the extension is not specified to the same extent, a genre has been established in which the idea of extending a task has become routine and algorithmic. Moreover, the contribution that the quality of work undertaken in the extension makes to the evaluation of the student's work as a whole is negligible; its existence appears almost sufficient to fulfil the assessment criterion. Thus, the advice provided for teachers assessing this task suggests that one of the indicators for awarding a grade A is that the candidate should have made 'a reasonable attempt at the extension' (p. 14), without quantifying or elaborating 'reasonable'.

It may thus be seen that the 'practical' and 'extended' aspects of coursework specified by the GCSE criteria have both, in practice, been absorbed into a single type of task which may be labelled 'investigation'. In what follows it may be assumed that 'coursework' refers to an 'investigation' set in the context of the GCSE examination.

As well as providing the tasks and performance indicators related to each of the tasks set, LEAG included general 'grade descriptions' in their GCSE syllabuses to help teachers assign grades to coursework. In spite of the presence of an expression of caution about the possibility of matching all the descriptors to any one task, the grade descriptions must be seen to prescribe the type of task to be undertaken as well as the nature of pupils' work on the tasks. In particular, the following selection of descriptors is easy to recognize in the context of the sort of inductive generalization task set by LEAG but might be less applicable to some other possible types of task:

> Orders the information systematically and controls the variables.
> Recognizes patterns.
> Makes conjectures about patterns, etc. and tests them.
> Devises simple formulae when generalizing.
> Attempts to verify and justify results.
> States results achieved and draws and states valid conclusions.
> extracted from (LEAG, 1989)

The ultimate aim of such a task appears to be to produce an algebraic generalization; this is specified both at grade C ('devises simple formulae when generalizing') and at grade A ('where appropriate, makes use of symbols when generalizing'). While it has long been part of 'common knowledge' that the presence of algebraic symbols is to be used as a necessary, if not sufficient, criterion for awarding a grade C (Wolf, 1990), it was only in 1993 that this was made explicit by the examination board:

> many coursework tasks have generalized results which could be expressed in algebraic form which is in the intermediate and higher level syllabus. It is expected that the use of such algebra (or symbolism) will be seen in work appropriate for the award of a top grade C. (ULEAC, 1993, p. 23)

As 'algebra' is the only item from the GCSE 'content' syllabus to be included in the general assessment criteria, it plays an important role in determining what types of task might be acceptable and in restricting the degree of choice available to pupils in deciding their route through the task.

The same page of ULEAC's guidance on coursework assessment sounds 'A Word of Caution':

> With investigative work it is always possible for a candidate to take an unexpected or unusual direction. We can never legislate for this and to try to do so might interfere with the whole creative spirit of coursework.

but the relatively low status of this general statement, indicated by its heading and by the qualified modality of its expression ('it is always *possible*', 'to try to do so *might* interfere') seems unlikely to encourage teacher-assessors to deviate from the course prescribed by the absolute statement above ('It is expected that . . . algebra . . . will be seen . . .'). The tension between the ideal of creativity and the desire for clear assessment standards is unlikely to be resolved in favour of the 'creative spirit'.

As was seen above, the Cockcroft report contained some ambiguity about whether the 'investigation' was a separate activity or whether 'investigative' ways of working were integral to everyday classroom activity. Although the setting of distinct tasks labelled as 'coursework tasks' and the self-contained nature of the tasks themselves clearly characterizes coursework as something separate from everyday classroom activity, the examination board nevertheless officially endorses the opposite (integrationist) point of view.

1.1   The coursework component is more than merely a method of assessment, it is, perhaps above all else, an instrument to facilitate and encourage curriculum development . . . particularly in relation to the recommendations on Methodology set out in the Cockcroft report and towards developing mathematics at Key Stage 4 of the National Curriculum. . . .

1.2.1 Coursework should encourage good practice. The elements of such, as defined in Cockcroft paragraph 243, should be in evidence whilst students are undertaking coursework tasks.

1.2.2 Coursework should be an integral part of the Mathematics curriculum and not simply a bolt on exercise aimed at satisfying new assessment criteria. (ibid. p. 3)

The tension between rhetoric and practice is a strong indicator of the problematic nature of the Cockcroft paragraph 243 definition of 'good practice' (note that this attempt to encourage curriculum development was published more than ten years after the Cockcroft Report), and in particular of the attempt to develop it through the imposition of new assessment methods.

The National Curriculum

There is a discernible degree of continuity between the characteristics of the official discourse of 'investigation' that have been identified above and the publications which elaborated the introduction of the mathematics National Curriculum: the report of the Mathematics Working Group (DES/WO, 1988) and the Non-Statutory

Guidance (NCC, 1989). I do not, therefore, intend to consider these publications in detail. It is, however, worth remarking that, in spite of the continued insistence that schools:

> must . . . ensure that aspects of using, applying and investigating are integrated and embedded into the ways in which mathematics is taught and learnt (NCC, 1989, p. D6)

the structure of the statutory orders, by including a separate Attainment Target entitled 'Using and Applying Mathematics', strengthens the separation of process from content.

Summary of 'Investigation' in the 'Official' Discourse

Some properties of 'investigation' emerge unambiguously from this analysis of official documents:

- it is essentially mathematical in some way that, by implication, other types of school mathematics are not;
- its content is to do with pattern, relationships, generalization;
- its learning objectives are predominantly related to 'process' rather than 'content';
- it is exploratory and creative and may have multiple valid outcomes;
- it is part of 'good classroom practice', and hence
- it ought to be assessed.

A further property that has developed, particularly since the introduction of GCSE and the National Curriculum, is the identification of 'investigation' with 'pure' mathematics.

There are, however, a number of areas of uncertainty and tension within the discourse. One of the most important of these areas relates to the difference between, on the one hand, using terms such as *investigational work* or *investigating* and, on the other, referring to *an investigation*. Is investigation a general strategy which 'permeates' (NCC, 1989) the curriculum, or is it a particular type of identifiable task? The official discourse slips between these two uses; at the level of general principles and justificatory rhetoric the former interpretation appears to be favoured, but when practical examples are called for, particularly in the context of assessment, separate and usually substantial tasks are identified. Similarly, the initial claim in the Cockcroft report that a mathematical investigation does not have to be 'an extensive piece of work that will take a long time to complete' (Cockcroft, 1982, p. 73) is in tension with the value placed upon undertaking 'extended' work and creating 'extensions' to tasks. Again, assessment requirements favour the lengthy task, particularly as creating an 'extension' is one of the indicators of high pupil attainment.

In considering the desired properties of pupils' work in the domain of 'investigation' there is a further tension between the value placed on multiple methods and outcomes and on creativity when general principles are expressed and the requirement for standardization and comparability within the assessment context of GCSE coursework. In the manifestation of coursework governed by the London examination board this tension appears to have led to high value being placed on inductive algebraic generalizations arising from a stereotypical investigation task.

'Practical' Discourse

It is not my intention here to review the field of publications offering practical advice on 'doing investigations' to teachers and pupils, but to identify the main issues within this discourse which are of relevance to the current study of mathematical writing. As my focus is on the discourse of GCSE coursework, it is relevant to consider publications which concentrate on the preparation, presentation and assessment of investigations for examination purposes. Of particular interest is the advice related specifically to the written form of coursework texts. In this section, I shall analyse the desired properties of pupils' coursework as constructed by a guide for teachers (Pirie, 1988) and a guide for pupils (Bull, 1990). The choice of these two publications is, to some extent, arbitrary; they are not representative in any formal sense. On the other hand, neither may be considered to be 'maverick' as they are each published as part of a series of similar guides in other subject areas by a well established publishing house. Both authors have credentials[8] which contribute to the authority of their texts in relation to their intended audiences of teachers and pupils. These texts may thus be seen to be part of the mainstream of the discourse.

Advice for Teachers

GCSE Coursework Mathematics: A Teachers' Guide to Organisation and Assessment (Pirie, 1988) reiterates many of the themes identified in the discourse of the Cockcroft report and the official GCSE publications. This includes reference to the idea that pupils are to be 'encouraged to create their own mathematics' (p. 7) and repeated stress on the idea of the curriculum development aim of the introduction of coursework being to change the emphasis from content to process, even to the extent of suggesting that teachers should 'Make it overt that you are not interested in "an answer" but in evidence of thinking mathematically' (p. 13). The focus of the guide is on coursework as examination, rather than on investigative ways of working in general (although all the examples of pupils' work provided are of an investigative nature). Nevertheless, it is acknowledged that this way of working is new to many teachers and that both teachers and pupils may have difficulties with it.

In addition to a discussion of the 'process not content' change in classroom practice, the chapter entitled 'Preparing Pupils for Assessed Tasks' concentrates only on communication skills, listed as 'oral exchange, personal recording and formal writing up', suggesting that pupils will need help to develop the skills needed to 'do justice to their mathematical achievements' (p. 14). The distinction between 'personal recording' and 'writing up' and the relation of each to the assessment of coursework is a contested area and Pirie identifies both as problematic because, she claims, 'Neither is normal practice in a traditional classroom'. In particular, there is a need to legitimize 'personal recording' both for pupils and (implied by the degree of effort devoted to the argument) for teachers. An analysis of the following extract highlights some of the key problematic areas:

> When working on an exploratory, practical or extended project, rough notes, side calculations, *aide-memoires* are all useful, if not essential, yet these conflict with the image of mathematics as some symbolic representation which is brief, neat and, above all, right. How many times have you seen pupils, in particular girls, writing on the backs of their hands or desk tops before hazarding an answer in their workbooks? . . . you may meet resistance and a scepticism that, in spite of all, you *will* 'judge' them by their untidiness and their unconventional recording methods. (p. 15; original emphasis)

'Recording' is useful for investigative work but is not used in the normal mathematics classroom. On the other hand, pupils, 'in particular girls', do it secretively (and so presumably already find it useful). In order to persuade pupils to record in a more public way, they must be convinced that such rough work will not be assessed. The question is raised: if the necessary 'rough notes, side calculations, *aide memoires*' are already being written on backs of hands and desk tops and are not to be judged, why do pupils need to be persuaded to make a more permanent or mobile record?

The answer to this question is not provided here but may be inferred from notes accompanying an example of a pupil's work (including both write-up and personal recordings) provided later in the guide. The pupil's write-up contains a table of results (for the 'Painted Cube' task), followed by a series of generalizations expressed in algebraic notation. The author of the guide comments that the teacher needed to look at the pupil's personal recordings in order to clarify what had been done. The personal recordings may thus play a part in the assessment process, although only in order to have a positive influence. At the same time, their private nature is stressed by the suggestion that they may only be so used with the pupil's permission. There is a tension here between the idea of rough jottings as private tools to be used by the pupil without fear that they will be evaluated, and the teacher's need for evidence to support her evaluation of the pupil's work. While Pirie attempts to resolve this tension by emphasizing the pupils' ownership of their rough work, others have resolved it in the opposite direction. In particular, the London examination board denies the private nature of such work, insisting that it should be presented instead of a write-up rather than merely as an optional support.

> Students are encouraged to write up their work as they go along, rather than produce 'nice write-ups' afterwards which have a tendency to omit all the good maths which went into the work. (LEAG, 1991, inside front cover)

In contrast to the detailed justification provided for encouraging pupils to engage in personal recording, difficulties with the write-up are presented as being related to the nature of the writing itself rather than persuading pupils to do it. Thus a classroom activity is suggested to help pupils with developing the necessary skills. In spite of the repeated claim throughout the book that it is process rather than content that is to be assessed, the only suggestions about appropriate forms of writing refer to the presentation of results: teachers and pupils are advised to collect a list of different forms such as tables, graphs, etc. Methods of communication of processes are not explicitly addressed, possibly because the participants in the discourse share no explicit language to describe such aspects.

The desired properties of pupils' write-ups are, however, communicated implicitly in a section of the guide containing annotated examples of pupils' coursework. There are three main issues related to the form in which pupils present their coursework which arise from these examples: the explicit display of processes, the incorporation of algebraic notation, and the interpersonal aspects of the writing.

Explicit display of process

Two contrasting pieces of work on the same problem are presented, each arriving at essentially the same generalized conclusions, although one is expressed in algebraic form while the other is given as a procedure expressed in words. The first piece of work is structured by a narrative of the mental processes gone through by its author: '*I tried one number . . . At this stage I decided to present my answers in a table . . .*' Pirie comments on the clarity of the writing and the fact that it shows the pupils' thinking, claiming that it reveals her 'high mathematical ability' (p. 28). The second piece, in contrast, is structured without narrative as a list of results, starting with specific results and brief observations on those results, and finishing with a list of generalizations. The annotation comments:

> This write-up is an example of a situation where it is not possible to say much, either positively or negatively, about the pupils' ability. This, however, may be the fault of the teacher, if the pupil is unaware of what should be included in a write-up to best display his mathematical talents. (p. 29)

The implicit message to be read by teachers is that achieving a valid conclusion is not sufficient as evidence of mathematical thinking; it is necessary to make the thinking visible through the use of explicit verbal forms. The pupil must not only realize and write down a relationship but must also comment on the fact that she has done so.

Incorporating algebraic notation

In the example described above, the 'good' pupil had introduced algebraic notation as headings in her table and then commented '*When labelling the columns of the table, I realized the obvious relationship*' (p. 28). Again she has provided the reader with a narrative which explains how she obtained her result. This contrasts with the introduction of algebraic notation in the pupil's work on the 'Painted Cube' task mentioned earlier which appears without any such preamble. In this case the annotation reads: 'Sudden algebraic leap. Where did this come from? Was it her own work?' (p. 48).

Although there are several other pieces of work among the eight examples offered that are criticized because the pupil has not shown how she was thinking, this is the only case of a suggestion, based on such an absence of evidence of process, that the pupil's work might have been copied rather than belonging to the pupil herself. It appears that algebraic notation, perhaps because of its particularly high status within school mathematics, must be suspect.

Interpersonal aspects

Most of the examples provided use a personal narrative style, using the first person singular or, where work had been done in groups, using 'we' to refer to the members of the group. The last example, however, uses the passive mood instead, obscuring the pupil's own agency in tackling the problem. For example, she writes:

> *Several boxes were made to find which would hold the most. Before making the boxes a prediction was made* . . . (p. 64)

Pirie comments on this 'curious impersonal style', suggesting that this might lead one to think that the pupil had not done the work herself. Although the impersonal style is not explicitly condemned, the fact that it is seen to be 'curious' strongly suggests that it does not conform to the author's ideas of what is appropriate in the context. The justification for this appears to be that the pupil, by obscuring agency, does not make a claim to ownership of the activity described and the results arising from it. As coursework is to be used to assess the individual pupil, a clear indication of ownership appears to be important for the teacher-reader.

A further issue about which there appears to be some difficulty is that of accuracy of results and the level of sophistication of the mathematical content. At several points in the guide it is stressed that process is more important than content and that pupils need to be persuaded that 'getting it right' is not the main aim of investigative activity. Moreover, a suggested activity for helping pupils to start 'writing-up' recommends that the teacher should avoid marking 'for grammatical or numerical accuracy' (p. 15). Nevertheless, the annotated examples of pupil work are accompanied by several positive comments on the accuracy of results and one example of a pupil said to be 'floundering' as a result of an early error. This tension between valuing error as a necessary part of mathematical investigation and valuing accuracy reflects the impossibility of the tasks of separating process from content and of attempting to define a decontextualized hierarchy of processes. Even if a pupil fulfils process criteria related to, for example, working systematically, forming and testing hypotheses, using a range of mathematical language and forms of representation, a lack of technical accuracy or an 'inappropriate' choice of mathematical tools will lower the value attached to the work. While the discourse of investigation places high value on process, within the practice of assessment there is a tension between this and the simultaneous requirement for pupils to display sophisticated mathematical skills and content knowledge.

Advice for Pupils

Mathematics Coursework: A Students Guide to Success (Bull, 1990) includes advice and examples of pupils' work on both 'investigation' type coursework, involving primarily pure mathematics, and what the author refers to as 'projects', which include both statistical surveys and tasks centred around 'real life' contexts such as 'Holidays' or 'Sport'. Although there is some separate discussion of these two categories, in particular a warning to ensure that a chosen project topic has enough potential for displaying mathematical ability, most of the advice given does not distinguish between the two types.

Addressing pupils, the language used in characterizing investigation and coursework is largely different from that used by publications addressing teachers. The key concepts are, however, very similar. Pupils are advised, for example, not to look for a single correct answer but to 'get involved in the problem' (p. 2). From the examples provided of pupils' work annotated with comments on their degree of 'involvement', it seems that this is closely related to the idea of *extension*; the posing of supplementary problems appears to be particularly desirable.

In distinguishing coursework from answers to examination questions Bull invokes the 'process rather than content' theme, although he simultaneously lays considerable stress on accuracy. The tension between valuing process and valuing mathematical content identified in the guide for teachers is present here as well. In describing the way in which coursework will be assessed, Bull identifies four 'process' areas as the aspects to be considered: understanding, planning, carrying out the task and communicating. In other sections of the book, however, there is considerable stress laid on the importance of using sophisticated mathematical techniques, for example:

> Examine the mathematical content of your work. If the mathematics is merely adding up, then do not expect to gain more than a grade that reflects that you can add up! . . . (p. 120)

In a book that is addressed, at least in theory, to pupils with a wide range of mathematical attainment, the author repeatedly endorses the principle, introduced by Cockcroft and the GCSE, that all pupils should demonstrate what they can do. However, this includes suggesting to some pupils that they ought not to attempt what is beyond them, particularly when it comes to forming generalizations.

Once again, algebra is presented as an important way of discriminating between pupils at different levels. In a sub-section entitled 'Has the Task Been Carried Out Satisfactorily?', satisfactory completion of a task appears to be defined as achieving an algebraic generalization. Although an example of a piece of work which does not achieve this is praised for its 'brilliant' presentation and the effort put in by the pupil, it is simultaneously condemned as 'limited' because it lacks generalization; in particular, it is said to contain only 'a valid (but low level) *generalization in words*' (p. 34; original emphasis). This is contrasted with another piece of work on the same task, assessed as 'worthy of a high grade', which contains '*generalization in symbols*'. The use of italics singles out these expressions as particularly significant. It is stressed, however, that not all pupils will be able to achieve such a high grade. Indeed, they are even advised to avoid the attempt:

> you must not be tempted to generalize if it is beyond your ability. It is very easy to spot someone who has tried to generalize without understanding what is involved. (p. 35)

The message to pupils is thus contradictory: if you use only 'low level' techniques, particularly if you do not use algebra, you will be unable to achieve high grades; on the other hand, if you use algebra you run the risk of being condemned for lacking 'understanding'.

At a number of points throughout the book, pupils are advised to consider their potential readers. The main aspect of this advice identifies the reader as an examiner who has to read a large number of coursework texts and is thus likely to become bored. This is taken to imply that pupils should make their own texts more interesting, both in terms of the mathematical content (although it is suggested that any mathematics teacher or moderator will be interested in any 'good mathematics' (p. 21)) and in terms of presentation:

> So, if your piece of work has that little extra on presentation and interest that makes it easier to read, it may well receive a higher grade. (p. 13)

The reader is also invoked in a plea for 'clarity' because: '*It is not up to the reader to have to work out what you mean*' (p. 37; original emphasis).

A 'common sense' view of communication as potentially transparent reinforces the view of the teacher-reader as an unsympathetic adversary who must be persuaded (forced?) to understand. This contrasts with the picture of the teacher presented by Pirie's advice to teachers, who actively seeks to understand a pupil's methods by calling on oral and personal recording resources as well as the formal 'write-up'.[9] The difference may arise from the different interests of the 'ideal' audiences of the two books. The teachers addressed by Pirie are expected to be concerned with pedagogical aspects of using investigative activities in the mathematics classroom as well as with the technical problems of how to assess the products of that activity; in relation to pupils in their own classes they are likely to take up a position as advocate on the pupils' behalf as well as a position as examiner (the different positions adopted by teachers in relation to the assessment of coursework texts will be returned to in Chapter 9). The pupils addressed by Bull, on the other hand, are constructed as being concerned with 'success' in the coursework examination; this is explicit in the title and is a theme throughout the book. As examination success is determined by the teacher-examiner, it is not surprising that a recurring theme throughout the book is the need to impress and interest a possibly bored and intolerant reader.

Apart from these reader characteristics, a section on improving communication advises the pupil to imagine a reader who 'is intelligent but knows nothing about your assignment and needs to know what you have done and why you have done it' (p. 105). There are obvious difficulties with this act of imagining for pupils who have been working in a class in which all pupils have worked on the same assignment set by the teacher and indeed advised by the very teacher who is then going to read and assess the task. The pupil's imaginary reader is to be constructed to be very different from the person who is known to be the actual reader. Even if it were possible to achieve this feat of imagination, the specification of the imaginary reader's characteristics is ill-defined. The formulation 'intelligent but knows nothing about your assignment' is presumably intended to indicate to the pupil the degree of detail that needs to be included. Unless they already share an understanding of what the implications of being 'intelligent' might be, however, this advice seems unlikely to help them to achieve it.

Similarly, in spite of the stated importance of clarity in communication, little explicit help is provided to illuminate what characteristics it might have. A single example is given of a piece of pupil's work that is said to illustrate poor communication in that 'the reader is unsure of what the student has been doing' (p. 37) but no indication is made of what might have been written to make the reader sure. The most explicit description of the features of good communication is a list of structural components of a piece of coursework including among others, observations and explanations of the task and of the pupils' reasoning. Ways of effectively achieving clarity in each of these components are not discussed. A number of examples of what is labelled 'good communication' are provided but without annotation, so it is not possible for a reader to determine unambiguously what the author intends to indicate is good about them.

One of the listed components of good communication is 'the use of more than one form of presentation' (p. 36) and among the examples of good communication there are extracts of pupils' work containing diagrams, tables, graphs, calculations, as well as paragraphs of verbal text. There is, however, an acknowledgment that this advice is not unproblematic.

> Think about the form of presentation of each item in the assignment. Use a variety
> of forms of presentation. Consider which form will communicate the facts best.
> (p. 105)

The advice is potentially contradictory in that, having considered which form of presentation would communicate the facts best, it might be possible to decide that a single form would be most appropriate and that there is no need for variety. There is a tension between the demands of the particular task being undertaken and the need to display one's mathematical knowledge and skills, including communication skills.

Some stress is laid on the distinction between communication and presentation; it is stated emphatically that 'Communication should not be confused with presentation' (p. 35). Presentation appears to be defined here as elaborate covers and illustrations or the use of a typewriter or wordprocessor. Pupils are repeatedly advised not to waste time on presentation at the expense of their work on the task itself. Nevertheless, many of the examples of pupils' work provided throughout the book include such presentation features and there are many positive comments, for example:

> Here is an example of high-quality presentation. You must not think that you need
> to rush away and start typing everything or use a wordprocessor, but it does look
> good doesn't it? (p. 24)

Taking into account the importance mentioned earlier of 'interesting' the teacher-reader, the book provides an ambivalent message about the visual appearance of coursework. Similarly, it is suggested that poor handwriting, spelling, and grammar and 'unconventional mathematical notation . . . can be tolerated if they are not the result of carelessness or lack of effort' but will not be found in 'high-grade work' (p. 37). As in the case of the use of algebra, discussed above, Bull appears to be attempting to convey different expectations to groups of pupils perceived to be of different abilities: algebra, typing, good spelling, etc. are presented as being beyond the capabilities of many pupils, who will therefore be prevented from attaining high grades however hard they try.

Summary of 'Investigation' in the 'Practical' Discourse

While the differences between the intended audiences are reflected in different emphases in the content of these two guides, on the whole they construct similar pictures of the characteristics of coursework. In particular, both contrast the answer-oriented nature of other school mathematics activities with the importance of 'process' in coursework. At the same time, both texts contain some tension between the value placed on 'process' and a simultaneous valuing of accuracy and other mathematical 'content'. This reflects the inherent difficulty in separating 'process' from 'content'.

Algebra is identified for both teachers and pupils as an area of particular significance in distinguishing the 'best' pupils. However, while the use of algebraic notation is highly valued, it may simultaneously be read as a sign of lack of understanding or even cheating if it is not accompanied by appropriate supporting evidence. The nature of this necessary supporting evidence is not made explicit.

One area of difference between the two guides is in the distinction made between 'personal recording' and 'writing-up'. While the guide for teachers makes much of this, it is absent from the guide for pupils. Bull focuses entirely on the 'write-up' and even suggests that this is all that is necessary. This is clearly a contested area, as may be seen from the fact that the London examination board sees a need to provide their own advice. It is possible that other texts within the 'practical' discourse may take a range of different positions on this question.

The guides also differ in the related area of 'presentation'. While much is made of the importance of good presentation in the advice addressed to pupils, it is apparently not an issue for teachers. This difference is related to the different ways in which the teacher-reader of coursework is portrayed in the two texts. The guide for pupils constructs an adversarial role for the teacher as examiner, against whom the pupil must use all available weapons, including presentation. The idea that they might be influenced by presentation is, however, unlikely to be acceptable to teachers taking on the roles of pedagogue and advocate constructed for them by Pirie.

An issue that arises strongly from these analyses is the difficulty that there appears to be in giving explicit advice about the writing of coursework. Both Pirie and Bull provide examples of pupils' work, annotated with comments which express their evaluation of the presentation and communication aspects. These comments do not, however, identify the features which give rise to the evaluations. Teachers and pupils reading these two books must construct their own interpretations of desirable features from the examples provided. It is likely that teachers, with access over time to a much larger number of such examples and with participation in a community engaging in activities which establish conventions and standards, will come to share enough 'common knowledge' to ensure that their evaluations are largely compatible; pupils do not, on the whole, have such opportunities. There is no explicit language available within the discourse of mathematics coursework to describe the desirable features of the communication of investigative activity. While it is possible to list ways of presenting results (tables, graphs, etc.), these represent only a relatively minor part of the writing that pupils must do. A focus on such easily identifiable features may even disadvantage pupils, as Bull suggests: 'Many candidates . . . are obsessed with producing pages of writing, charts, diagrams, pretty pictures and eye-catching covers' (p. 101). The implicit form in which advice is provided is likely to assist mainly those pupils who already have access to the necessary forms of communication and the means of choosing between them, without providing much help for those who do not.

'Professional' Discourse

The professional journals for mathematics teachers, *Mathematics Teaching* and *Mathematics in School*, contain numerous articles describing examples of what may be labelled as investigations and investigative activities in classrooms. However, it is, on the whole, only since the institutionalization of the investigation following Cockcroft and, in particular, the introduction of GCSE coursework that a more critical literature has emerged both in these journals and in other publications, debating the nature of investigation and its classroom incarnations. It is this literature that I consider in this section, identifying the main issues and areas of contention.

The Nature of Investigation

The assertion by Cockcroft and others, that investigation is inherently mathematical in some way that other school mathematics may not be, is to be found once again in the professional discourse. For example, Fielker, responding to paragraph 243 of the Cockcroft report with a claim that the ATM had been advocating investigative work for many years, quotes in support of his argument:

> We do not believe that a clear distinction can be drawn between the activities of the mathematician inventing new mathematics and the child learning mathematics that is new to him. (Wheeler, cited by Fielker (1982), p. 2)

Although this quotation from an earlier ATM document does not itself use the term *investigation*, and does not, indeed, appear to be making a distinction between this and other types of learning activities, the context in which it is used in 1982 suggests an identity between 'investigating', learning 'new' mathematics and 'the activities of the mathematician'. More explicitly, a 1969 ATM Sixth Form Mathematics Bulletin stated one aim of investigations to be:

> to give students experience of doing mathematics . . . The free investigations (in which there is no constraint towards finding a standard result and the investigation may be taken in any desired direction), seem to me to develop insights into the nature of mathematics which are not developed by other kinds of activity. (cited by Wells (1993), p. 8)

Later publications discussing the classroom implications of investigation, also take this identity between investigation and 'real' mathematical activity as given (e.g. Brown, 1990; McCafferty, 1989; Steward, 1989; Whitworth, 1988), while Ernest (1993a) draws an analogy between the culture of the 'progressive' mathematics classroom (including investigative activity) and that of the research mathematics community. A usually dissenting voice, Wells (1993) agrees that investigating and exploring are activities undertaken by research mathematicians. This does not, however, temper the virulence of his attack on the 'investigation' as a distinct object in the mathematics curriculum. Although recognizing the distinction between convergent (problem solving) and divergent (investigating) activities (ATM, 1984; HMI, 1985) he claims that mathematicians will engage in both during their work on a single problem. He thus denies that there is a distinction between 'problem solving' and 'investigation' as defined by Cockcroft.

The development of *an investigation* as a distinct object was one of the themes identified in the official discourse. As Ernest points out, there has been a metonymic shift in meaning from *investigation* as a 'process of inquiry' to *an investigation* as 'the mathematical question or situation which serves as its starting point' (1991, p. 284). This shift and the associated development of stereotypical starting points and subsequently stereotypical methods of solution are the basis of a substantial amount of criticism in the professional discourse (see, for example, Delaney, 1986; Diffey et al., 1988; Hewitt, 1992; Perks and Prestage, 1992; Wells, 1993; Wiliam, 1993). Much of this criticism is aimed specifically at the type of investigation designated by Wells as 'Data-Pattern-Generalization' (DPG) and by Hewitt as 'train spotting' in which numerical data is generated, a pattern 'spotted' and an inductive generalization formed. There appears to be a degree of consensus within the professional discourse that such stereotypical investigations fall short of the expressed ideal of the sort of mathematics done by mathematicians; even Andrews (1992) in his defence of 'train spotting' admits the validity of this criticism. It is further suggested that they 'may even inhibit mathematical thinking' (MacNamara and Roper, 1992a, p. 27).

In spite of early suggestions that teacher assessment (i.e. coursework) would be effective for assessing 'mathematical knowledge' in general (Love, 1981), apart from the short-lived ATM/SEG experimental GCSE with 100 per cent coursework assessing both content and process, the focus on process has become firmly established both in GCSE and in the assessment of the National Curriculum. There is still, however, some contestation of the relationship between 'investigation' and the process/content distinction. For example, McCafferty (1989) bases his evaluation of 'investigative materials' on the extent to which they allow the use of 'specific strategies' irrespective of the content domain, while Diffey et al. (1988) argue for an investigative approach to teaching a 'topic' in mathematics. Steward takes an alternative position, evaluating an investigation on the grounds that it involves 'those aspects of enquiry that are characteristic of mathematical activity' (1989, p. 13), including symmetry, duality, commutativity and closed algebraic structure as well as 'systematic methods'; such aspects are neither part of the 'content' of GCSE mathematics as traditionally defined by syllabuses nor part of the standard set of 'processes' used by other authors.

Another theme apparent in the official and practical discourse was the idea of lack of constraint, lack of a 'standard result' and variation in direction. The desirability of such 'openness' is stated even more strongly in the professional discourse. Indeed, Fielker (1982) specifically criticizes the examples of investigations suggested by the Cockcroft report because of their lack of openness. Similarly, Ball and Ball (1990) condemn DPG investigations because, contrary to the spirit of investigation, they give rise to 'right answers':

> If you are at a high level mathematically the answer is a formula. If you are at a slightly lower level the answer is a number pattern described in words. If you are at a still lower level the answer is a number pattern which you might not be able to describe, but you might at least be able to make some predictions. (p. 10)

As may be seen in the GCSE coursework tasks discussed above and in later chapters this is an accurate characterization of many officially endorsed 'investigations'. The idea of a right answer or a right way of doing an investigation is taken to be inconsistent with the ideals of openness and lack of constraint. Thus Watson (1986) even suggests that the distinction between right and wrong may be brought into question:

> It is often better to bite your lip and let students charge off in the 'wrong' direction because the more of this work you do the less you will be able to define 'wrong'. (p. 18)

There are, nevertheless, problems with such a completely open approach. For example, Tall (1990) relates the story of a boy who 'succeeded' in finding a method for trisecting an angle. In this case, Tall suggests that the boy should not be penalized because he was working in an unfamiliar context and his work was valid within the framework of his existing experience. In other contexts it might be less easy to justify answers or methods which conflict with 'correct' mathematics. This issue is not explicitly addressed within the professional literature; the ideal of 'openness' is uncritically adopted, the only hesitation being related to the question of whether teachers are competent to cope with it.

Writing Coursework

As was seen in the discussion of the 'practical' discourse, the practical advice offered to both teachers and pupils lays great emphasis on the communication and presentation of coursework, reflecting the significance laid on written work in the assessment process. This significance is simultaneously recognized and criticized in the professional literature, the main theme being the mismatch between pupils' mathematical activity and the written product arising from it. McNamara (1993) describes this mismatch:

> Their written reports . . . displayed a mere shadow of the clarity of their thought . . .
> and of their very powerful ability to generalise the situation. In their reports they
> returned to the particular. (p. 23)

She suggests that, because the written texts 'fix' the investigation, they come to represent the investigation itself. The teacher will thus assess the pupil's 'level of engagement in the written task' rather than in the investigation itself. Recognizing this phenomenon and seeing it as unsatisfactory, a common response is to advocate that teacher assessment should take other aspects of pupils' performance into account rather than relying on written work alone. Thus, Bloomfield (1987) and MacNamara and Roper (1992a; 1992b) describe evaluation of investigative work by oral as well as written means, using interviews and informal 'overhearing' of pupils working. These authors, while recognizing that pupils find writing about their mathematical activity difficult, propose no means of overcoming the difficulty other than to avoid it by raising the status of other forms of communication.

There is not, however, unanimity about this position. Ollerton and Hewitt (1989) recognize the concern that teachers have in wishing their pupils to write things down, particularly as they feel they have to justify their own judgments: 'I want to be able to say that not only do I know, but here is the evidence' (p. 25). Their attitude towards writing is ambivalent, suggesting on the one hand that the requirement to write may hold some pupils back in their mathematical achievement, while simultaneously claiming that this may be useful because it provides an opportunity to take time for reflection. Similarly, Whitworth (1988), in an article advocating the use of investigations at A-level advises teachers to

> Stress that recording and reporting their findings is the only way that they can
> successfully redesign and improve any model they produce. (p. 172)

The suggestion that the act of writing may be helpful to the process of doing mathematics echoes Pirie's advocacy of 'personal recording' discussed above, but makes no distinction between the type of writing that might perform this function and the type of writing that is required in order to provide 'evidence' for assessment purposes. Indeed, the desirable characteristics of the writing produced by pupils are not addressed.

Summary of 'Investigation' in the 'Professional' Discourse

There is general agreement, as there was in the official discourse, that the characteristics of ideal investigative work include its similarity to 'real mathematics' and its property of 'openness'. Issues which are contested include the question of whether process or content should be the focus of investigational work. The development of the 'investigation' as a stereotyped distinct object forms a major focus of discussion. It is accepted that the 'Data–Pattern–Generalization' type of investigation is neither 'real mathematics' nor 'open' and that it does not therefore fulfil the ideal characteristics of 'investigation'.

There is some disagreement about the role and importance of written reports of investigative activity. While it is largely assumed in the practical discourse that the object to be assessed is (at least usually) a written product, the professional discourse disputes this; the object to be assessed is the pupil and the pupil's activity. If this is not adequately represented in the written product then there is a problem, which some suggest may be resolved through use of other means of assessment. There is, in any case, agreement on the observation that pupils find it difficult to communicate the full extent of their investigative activity in writing. Little practical consideration is given to ways of resolving this perceived difficulty.

Coherence and Tensions within the Discourse of 'Investigation'

There is explicit agreement within all three aspects of the discourse of 'investigation' about the 'ideal' characteristics of investigational work:

- it is 'real' mathematics;
- it is open, creative, 'empowering' for pupils;
- is should 'permeate' the curriculum.

The degree to which it is acknowledged that, in general, the practice does not (or cannot) live up to these ideals, however, varies considerably. The official discourse, although contrasting the ideal with other types of (not such 'good') practice, does not admit that there might be any problems in implementing it; the teacher-reader is constructed as an instrument who, once properly informed, will transfer the written description of the ideal directly into the classroom. The practical discourse, on the other hand, allows that such investigational work is likely to be unfamiliar to teachers and that they may lack experience and confidence. This acknowledgment of difficulty, however, does not problematize the ideal itself or the assumption that the guidance provided will ensure its practical implementation. The professional discourse explicitly deals with the mismatch between the rhetoric of the ideal and what it identifies as the dominant practice. While authors such as Ollerton (1992) and Andrews (1992) echo the theme of teachers' lack of experience and confidence to explain this mismatch, the nature of the activity itself is also brought into question, particularly in the context of its institutionalization.

There is also agreement that, as investigational work is part of 'good practice' it ought to be assessed, the basis for this being the principle that 'What You Assess Is What You Get' and hence the idea that curriculum development can be 'led' by changes in assessment (Burkhardt, 1988). The official and practical discourse does not represent this as problematic, except in so far as teachers and pupils (being unfamiliar or lacking confidence with such ways of working and assessing) are likely to need extra support to do it effectively. There is no acknowledgment of any mismatch between the ideal and its operationalization through GCSE coursework. The professional discourse, on the other hand, is concerned with a number of problems, ranging from the essentially practical problem of the inadequacy of using a pupil's written work as the sole measure of their mathematical activity, to more fundamental criticisms of the effects of institutionalization on the nature of investigational activity itself. Thus, the professional discourse makes explicit some of the tensions and contradictions implicit within the official and practical discourse. In particular, the ideals of openness and creativity, once operationalized through the provision of examples, advice and assessment schemes, become predictable and even develop into prescribed ways of posing questions or 'extending' problems and rigid algorithms for 'doing investigations'. The development and ubiquity of the stereotypical data–pattern–generalization investigation may be seen as a natural (necessary?) consequence of the traditional positivist assessment paradigm (Galbraith, 1993) within which the national assessment programmes operate. While the essential contradiction between this and the ideal characteristics of investigational work is denied within the official and practical discourse, its existence is explicitly agreed within the professional arena, with extensive discussion and debate revolving around its consequences and possible remedies (e.g. Hewitt, 1992; Lerman, 1989).

Another implicit tension within the official and practical discourse concerns the focus of investigation on content or on process. This tension is again explicitly acknowledged and debated in the professional discourse. While the practical discourse in particular insists that the focus ought to be on process, there is, however, a problem in separating process from content when it comes to the assessment of investigational work: how does the 'difficulty' of the mathematical content affect the value placed upon the mathematical processes used? Given that one of the purposes of public assessment at 16+ is to distinguish between 'successes' and 'failures', it may appear important that there should be at least some level of consistency between the distinctions made by coursework and those made by examination results. (At one point at least one of the examination boards resolved large differences between grades achieved in coursework and grades achieved in examinations by simply favouring the examination result.)[10] Such a desire for consistency would help explain the emphasis in the practical discourse on the need to include appropriate levels of content and the development of the use of an algebraic generalization as an indicator of success.

A further issue of particular interest is the construction of the ideal characteristics of pupils' written reports of investigations. While there is implicit definition of the desired characteristics of pupils' texts through the use of examples, there appears to be no linguistic means available within the discourse to describe these characteristics explicitly. Again there is agreement that this is an area in which there is particular difficulty for pupils. The only advice available, however, is related to the presentation of results and the overall appearance of the text — neither of which (at least officially) has high status (although this is an area in which there are some contradictory messages, at least for pupils). No support is provided for the communication of processes, which are supposedly the main objective of investigative work and assessment by coursework.

The properties of 'investigation' and the desired characteristics of students' work on investigative tasks that have been identified in this chapter will inform the analysis and discussion in subsequent chapters of students' reports of their investigative work and teachers' readings of these reports. This understanding of the discourse of 'investigation' is essential in order to be able to interpret the significance of what students write with reference to the context in which their texts are produced and read.

Notes

1   A keyword search of the *Mathematics Teaching* Index reveals articles in the ATM's journal about 'investigation' or its cognates dating from 1959, including six separate articles in 1968 (compared to seven in 1982 and six in 1990). This does not mean that teachers and pupils in 1959 or 1968 thought of themselves as 'doing investigations'; rather, the compilers of the index saw similarities between the activities described and their own contemporary concept of investigation.

2   There were a number of Mode 3 CSE examinations including coursework components, prepared by individual schools or small groups. There was also a GCE syllabus initiated by the ATM.

3   This is not pointing to a particular individual but is a purely hypothetical example, although it is certainly the case that individuals can be identified who have made contributions to at least two of the types of discourse. There is some question as to whether such an individual should be considered to be 'the same author' in that their authority relationship to their text and to their readers in each case is significantly different.

4   The first edition of this polemic pamphlet was published in 1986; it has been supplemented in two further editions.

5 A nominalization is a noun (in this case *investigation*) formed from a verb (in this case *investigate*). Two of the effects of nominalization are to transform a process into an object and to obscure the agency of the subject who performs the action. This and other linguistic tools for analysing texts will be discussed further in Chapter 6.

6 The London and East Anglian Group. LEAG has subsequently been superseded by the University of London Examinations and Assessment Council (ULEAC) and, most recently, Edexcel as the body responsible for the examinations discussed here.

7 From 1995, examination boards may once again set syllabuses which include no teacher-assessed coursework, but these syllabuses must still assess the investigative processes specified in Attainment Target 1 of the National Curriculum, using instead an invest igation undertaken in timed examination conditions or an examination consisting of short questions intended to assess specific isolated processes. There are already some indications that this change in the form of assessment is further affecting the nature of the object being assessed.

8 Pirie as an established academic in Mathematics Education and Bull as Assistant Senior Moderator with one of the examination groups.

9 It is also interesting to note that, just as the guide for teachers suggests that communication failure in a coursework text may be blamed on the teacher, the guide for pupils lays the blame squarely on the pupil.

10 It is interesting to note a similar issue in relation to the relative status of National Curriculum Teacher Assessment and Key Stage tests. Although they are officially stated to assess different aspects of pupil attainment and to be of equal value, when there are discrepancies between them this is generally seen to be a problem and to suggest that the Teacher Assessment is 'inaccurate' in some way.

Chapter 6

A Critical Linguistic Approach
to Mathematical Text

Before looking in later chapters at the mathematical writing produced by students, it is necessary to develop a means of describing the forms of language they may choose to use. The forms that mathematical language take are of interest, not merely for their own sake, but for the relationships between the various forms and functions of mathematical texts.[1] What difference does it make for the professional mathematician whether her paper is written using the passive voice or with a personal presence, using complex or simple syntax? What difference does it make for the school student whether she chooses to use words or algebraic symbols to express a generalization, to label her answers or leave them to speak for themselves, to use t or x to represent the independent variable in time–distance problems? Possible answers to these questions include: the mathematician's paper may not be published because it is judged not to report serious, important research (cf. Anderson, 1988); the student's work may be awarded a low grade because she is judged to lack certain understanding, knowledge or skills (cf. Flener and Reedy, 1990; Kress, 1990). Written communication is not a simple matter of transmitting what is in the writer's mind onto paper and thence into the reader's mind. Both writer and reader have their own perceptions of and relations to the subject matter and to each other, all of which influence the construction and interpretation of the text. How the reader interprets the text will depend on the resources they bring to bear upon it, including their expectations about the forms of language considered 'appropriate' within the particular situation.

Texts such as research papers and students' examined coursework reports play a significant role in the discourses within which they and their writers and readers are situated. The ways in which they are interpreted by their readers may have far-reaching consequences for their authors. It is, therefore, of importance to writers to know what forms of language are likely to perform the functions they want and what forms are likely to be highly valued within the particular discourse. As a mathematics teacher and teacher educator, it is important to me to find a means of communicating with students about mathematical language, helping them to take control over their writing in order to achieve their intended ends and to be assessed positively by those who are in a position to judge them. The method of text analysis described in this chapter seeks to provide such a means of communicating about mathematical language as well as a way of investigating, describing and critiquing mathematical discourses. My aim in analysing mathematical texts is not so much to create descriptions of the nature of mathematical writing as to provide a means of identifying and interpreting features of mathematical texts that are likely to be of significance to the mathematical and social meanings that may be constructed from them by their readers.

The way in which language reflects and maintains power relationships (like those between academic author and journal editor, student and teacher) has formed a focus of study for Critical Linguistics and Critical Discourse Analysis (see, for example, Fairclough, 1989; 1995; Fowler and Kress, 1979; Hodge and Kress, 1988; 1993). Analyses, which are concerned with the ideological and social aspects of language use, have generally focused on texts arising in social contexts that highlight the strength of power relationships within society, including, for example, advertising, newspaper articles and job interviews. The way in which language is used by the various participants within such contexts is critical to the exercise of power. The recognition that power relationships are also at play within educational and academic settings makes Critical Discourse Analysis a useful and appropriate means of interrogating and interpreting mathematical texts.

The main linguistic tools that will be used to describe the verbal components of mathematical texts are based on Halliday's (1985) functional grammar. These tools may be used to provide a description of any verbal text (in English). Mathematical texts, however, usually contain significant non-verbal components, including algebraic symbols, diagrams, tables and graphs. The analysis of non-verbal parts of texts is less fully developed in the literature; analyses of the syntax of mathematical symbols (Ervinck, 1992; Roe, 1977) have paid little attention to the functions that might be fulfilled by choices between alternative symbolizations or between verbal and symbolic forms, while discussion of graphical elements in mathematics texts (e.g. Shuard and Rothery, 1984) has tended to consider only the difficulties that these may cause for student-readers, taking their form as an unproblematic given. More general work on the analysis and interpretation of visual text is difficult to apply to mathematical texts as the theories underlying the analyses and the examples to which they are applied are far removed from mathematical practices. My main source in attempting to describe graphical elements have been the work of Kress and van Leeuwen (Kress and van Leeuwen, 1990; 1996) who, although not dealing with mathematical texts themselves, provide some general 'grammatical' concepts that have proved useful. Nevertheless, the set of tools for the analysis of visual text that I describe towards the end of this chapter is limited and further work will be required to make it more generally applicable to a wide range of mathematical texts.

It is not sufficient, however, merely to describe the features of the text being analysed. What is of interest is to interpret the functions that these features fulfil for writers and readers. Halliday's functional linguistics is based on the premise that every text contributes to three 'metafunctions': ideational, interpersonal and textual. There is no one-to-one correspondence between a piece of text and a particular function. Rather, Halliday argues that every text fulfils each of these functions and his systemic-functional grammar indicates the ways in which grammatical features of language serve to fulfil them.

The *ideational* or *experiential* function refers to the way in which language expresses 'the categories of one's experience of the world' (Halliday, 1973, p. 38) and one's interpretation of the experience. The aspect of mathematical language that has been most frequently addressed — the naming of mathematical objects — contributes to the ideational function by influencing the types of objects that may be participants in mathematical activity. Consideration of this function allows us to address questions such as:

> *What does this mathematical text suggest mathematics is about? How is new mathematics brought about? What role do human mathematicians play in this?*

The *interpersonal* function expresses social and personal relations between the author and others, 'including all forms of the speaker's intrusion into the speech situation and the speech act' (ibid., p. 41). Pimm's (1984) discussion of the use of *We* is a rare example of concern with the interpersonal in mathematical texts. Given the recent growth of attention to the social in mathematics education generally, it would seem that further attention to the social as it is constructed in mathematical texts would be appropriate. This function is particularly significant in situations (such as assessment) where the relative power of the participants is an important defining factor.

> *Who are the author and the reader of this mathematical text? What is their relationship to each other and to the knowledge constructed in the text?*

The *textual* function is what makes language 'operationally relevant' in its context and 'distinguishes a living message from a mere entry in a grammar or a dictionary' (Halliday, 1973, p. 42). The formation of argument is one obvious way in which the textual function is fulfilled in mathematical texts but other types of 'messages' may also be communicated, including, for example, reports that define, describe or classify and narratives relating the progress of mathematical activity.

> *What is this mathematical text attempting to do? Tell a story? Explain a procedure? Describe? Prove?*

The separation of the three metafunctions, while providing a useful analytical tool, does not take account of interrelations among the three. For example, if a section of text has textual features which identify it as an argument, the fact that it has been included in a supposedly mathematical text suggests that mathematics itself is, at least in part, 'about' making arguments (ideational/experiential) and that the reader is expected or expecting to be persuaded by the writer's argument or at least impressed by its presence (interpersonal). Nevertheless, analysis of these three aspects allows us to gain insight into what a particular text may be achieving and how different choices of language might achieve different things. Indeed, they correspond to three important ways in which mathematical texts may differ: in their subject matter, in the relationships between author and readers and in the formation of argument.

A key concept in this view of language that I have found very useful in considering the interpretation of mathematical texts is that of *choice*. Whenever an utterance is made, the speaker or writer makes choices (not necessarily consciously) between alternative structures and contents. Each choice affects the ways the functions are fulfilled and the meanings that listeners or readers may construct from the utterance. As Kress (1993) argues, these choices are not arbitrary but are motivated by the writer's 'interests' and reflect her 'place in the world, physically, cognitively, socially, culturally, conceptually' (p. 172). The writer has a set of resources which constrain the possibilities available, arising from her individual social and cultural history but also from her current positioning within the discourses in which the text is produced. Similarly, the meanings constructed from a text by its readers will vary with the resources of individual readers and with the discourse(s) within which the text is read. The text itself may provide a reading position from which the text is unproblematic and 'natural', but readers do not necessarily take up this 'ideal' position and may resist the text by interpreting it in a different discourse (Kress, 1989). The features identified by use of linguistic tools must, therefore, be interpreted in the light of an understanding of the particular context in which the text occurs, taking account of the social situation of texts within their contexts of production and interpretation. The 'reading' of the context (Potter and Wetherell, 1987) in this case involves making use of knowledge about mathematics, the explicit conventions of formal mathematical writing, the academic community, the school mathematics curriculum, social practices within the mathematics classroom, assessment practices etc. A particular emphasis in this process is laid on considering the ways in which teachers may interpret features of texts produced by students. This will be followed up in later chapters where I report an investigation of mathematics teachers' reading and assessment practices.

Throughout this chapter, possible interpretations of linguistic features are illustrated using extracts from two types of text: an academic mathematics research paper (Dye, 1991) and secondary school students' reports of investigative work.[2] Clearly there are substantial differences between the two genres. It is, however, interesting to be able to compare them and to examine the extent to which the characteristics of mature mathematical writing are found (and considered to be appropriate) in students' writing in the light of the claim that one of the purposes of investigative work is to enable children to engage in activity that is like that of 'real' mathematicians. I would contend that the method of analysis described in this chapter is more widely applicable, requiring, however, knowledge of the particular context in order to make interpretation possible. It must be remembered that, where interpretations of extracts of text are offered, these do not attempt to discover the intentions of the author but the possible meanings that may be constructed by a reader within the given discourse.

Linguistic Analysis of Mathematical Texts

The grammatical features related to each of the three metafunctions of language and their interpretation will be discussed separately although, as mentioned earlier, the functions themselves are not so easily separated.

The Ideational Function: Presenting a Picture of the Nature of Mathematics

The central question to be addressed by using the analytical tools discussed in this section is 'What is mathematics (as it appears in the text being analysed)?'. This general question, which makes the assumption that the text under consideration is in some sense about mathematics, includes the following more specific issues:

- What sort of events, activities and objects are considered to be mathematical?
- How is 'new' mathematics brought about (or created or discovered)?
- What is the role of human beings in mathematics?

The significance of answers to each of these questions must be considered in the light of existing differences and debates within mathematics and mathematics education, for example, the absolutist/social constructivist divide in the philosophical basis of mathematics (Ernest, 1991) and educational questions about the relative importance of mathematical processes or content matter.

In analysing the picture of mathematics and mathematical activity presented in a text, a significant role is played by examining the transitivity system, that is, the types of processes and the types of participants that are active in them. Halliday identifies six main types of processes: material, mental, relational, behavioural, existential and verbal, of which the first three types are the most common. At the coarsest level of analysis, the relative weightings of the different types of process are indicative of the nature of mathematical activity presented in the text. A high proportion of material processes may be interpreted as suggesting a mathematics that is constructed by doing; mental processes may suggest that mathematics is a pre-existing entity that is sensed (discovered) by mathematicians; relational processes present a picture of mathematics as a system of relationships between objects. Given the importance of the formation of generalizations in mathematics and the way in which this is used as a marker of a successful GCSE candidate, it is of particular interest in the case of students' texts to note whether a generalization is expressed as a relation:

$$(TOP\ LENGTH + BOTTOM\ LENGTH) \times SLANT\ LENGTH = No.\ OF\ TRIANGLES$$

or as a material procedure:

> *If you add the top length and the bottom length, then multiply by the slant length, you get the number of unit triangles.*

The procedural formulation is likely to be less highly valued than the relational one as it may be seen as representing an earlier stage of development of algebraic thinking.[3]

Halliday (1985) claims that in much scientific writing 'relational processes tend to be the most frequent and perhaps the most informative of the primary clause types' (p. 124). They may be further categorized as either attributive (i.e. stating a property or attribute of an object) or identifying (i.e. stating an identity between two objects). Huddleston et al. (cited in Halliday, 1966) found a high proportion (32/200) of all clauses in scientific English texts to involve identifying. Stating identities is clearly of importance in mathematics and is frequently expressed by the use of an equals sign. The use of the equals sign is of interest in its own right in examining students' texts. While it frequently does play such an identifying role, there is also evidence that it is frequently used to play other roles. In particular, Kieran (1981) reports persistent use of an 'operator' concept of the equals sign by students at all levels which suggests that it is fulfilling a material rather than a relational role. Another common role is as a logical connective between statements, for example:

$$5x + 3 = 2x - 15$$
$$= 5x = 2x - 18$$

Such usages are likely to be considered to be mathematically incorrect by a secondary school teacher-assessor; a recent handbook for mathematics teachers (Backhouse et al., 1992) picks out use of the equals sign as a connective as its single 'example of bad practice' (p. 126) to illustrate writing that does not 'make sense when read aloud'.

In examining the picture of the nature of mathematics presented in a text, it is clearly significant to ask not only what types of process take place but also what kinds of objects are participants in the text and hence what sorts of objects are the actors in mathematical processes or are affected by these processes. In most discussions of mathematical language, consideration of the representation of mathematical objects in text has concentrated on the naming of these objects and, in particular, on the ways in which the vocabulary of naming in mathematics is related to the vocabularies of other areas of language use, including metaphorical uses, (e.g. Pimm, 1987) or on the nature of the symbolic system of written representation (e.g. Ervinck, 1992). The use of various kinds of 'specialist' vocabulary is relevant to the interpersonal aspects of a text discussed below. In this section, however, my concern is with the types of objects themselves.

Mathematics characteristically treats relations and other processes as objects in their own right which may in turn act and be acted upon. For example, a function may be defined initially as a relation between two quantities but may also be seen as an object that can itself be transformed, combined with others of the same type, operated upon, and so on. Similarly, a process such as rotating through a given angle may be treated as an object that may then, for example, be used as an element of a group. Grammatically, this transformation is represented by the nominalization of processes: the creation of process-objects such as *rotation*, *permutation* and *relation*. Such nominalization has a number of effects on what it is possible to say with and about such process-objects. Firstly, it brings the process into immediate relation with another verb and hence, where this verb is relational, with other nominals; it allows the process to act as the theme of a clause (performing a *textual* function — see below); it also allows the process to be presented as a cause or effect (Halliday, 1966). The power of the use of nominalized process-objects may be illustrated by this example taken from a piece of GCSE coursework.[4] The author starts by describing a number pattern:

> *As you can see the unit no. increases by two every time the top length increases by one.*

He then is able to extend his generalization to a wider range of situations:

> *This can be done by using any slant no. but if you change this you may find that **the unit increases** may be different.*

By expressing the process of increasing as a nominal, he shifts the focus from the particular property of the original pattern to a more general relationship between a range of patterns:

> *This time the **unit increase** is by 4 instead of 2.*

And this newly created object may now have properties of its own and be seen to change:

> *On the next one when you increase the slant **it** increases to 6.*

A further consequence of the use of nominalizations that is seen to be important in Critical Linguistics is the obscuring of agency; the transformation of process into object removes the grammatical need to specify the actor in the process. In the context of mathematics, the use of, for example, *rotation* or *permutation* without any indication that these processes are actually performed by anyone fits in with an absolutist image of mathematics as a system that exists independently of human action. As Halliday and Martin (1993) point out, there is a difference between objectification and objectivity but, in the rationalizations for their practices provided by scientists and other academic writers, the two are often confused.

Another powerful feature of many mathematical texts is the symbolization of mathematical objects which allows them not only to act and to be acted upon but also to be combined and manipulated to form new objects. As was discussed in Chapter 2, it appears that, for many people, the use of symbols is what characterizes mathematical language and even mathematics itself; this has implications similar to those of the use of specialist vocabulary. While I am not concerned here with the grammar of mathematical symbolism, its presence or absence is relevant to the image of mathematics that is presented in a text and, for some readers, the extent to which the text itself is considered to be 'mathematical'. The role of symbolism is discussed further in a later section of this chapter.

While mathematical symbols and the grammatical category of nominalization are significant in affecting the type of mathematics and mathematical activity portrayed in a text, further significant types of participant may also be identified by reference to their role and importance in mathematics, although not necessarily by their grammatical form. These include:

- *human beings*, who may be further categorized as *specific* individuals (e.g. the author, the individual addressee, a named third party) or as *general* human participants (usually addressed as 'you' or referred to as 'one' during the explanation of a general process, or exhorted to action by the use of imperatives);
- *basic* objects such as numbers or shapes and objects *derived* from these[5] such as factors, products, lengths or areas;
- *relational* objects such as patterns or formulae;
- *representational* objects such as tables, diagrams or graphs.

Of particular interest is the place of human beings in the text and in the doing of mathematics: the extent of their presence and the sorts of processes in which they act. Is the main role of human beings to 'see' or 'discover' (perhaps suggesting a Platonist view of mathematics), or do they manipulate shapes and symbols (the main activity of pupils in the mathematics classroom)? The interpretations offered here, being out of context, can only be illustrative of the possible significance of different roles. As mentioned earlier, the presence of human beings as agents in mathematical activity is obscured by the use of nominalizations. A similar function is performed by the use of representational objects as actors in verbal processes, i.e. *the table shows that* . . . rather than *I have shown in the table that* . . . , which obscures the writer's presence as author as well as mathematician. The use of passive rather than active forms of verbs is a further way of obscuring agency that is much used in academic writing.

In considering the portrayal of mathematical activity, it is also important to determine how causal relationships are represented in the text: that is, what types of objects cause or are caused. Here again the presence or absence of humans as causal agents is significant in the extent to which mathematics is seen as an autonomous system. For example, in an academic mathematical paper previously established facts (labelled by numbers and hence further distanced from the activity which originally established them) are presented as causes of other facts without any intervening activity:

By (4), (6) the other Brianchon point of the former edge is (1, −1, 1).

In contrast, a Year 9 pupil's rough work shows mathematical facts and relationships to be dependent upon human action:

whenever there is one dot inside and you count up the perimeter and the area will be exactly half it

The importance of explanation and proof in mathematics is also to be seen in the frequency with which expressions of causality occur in a text. The ways in which such explanations, proofs and arguments may be constructed textually will be discussed later.

The Interpersonal Function: The Roles and Relationships of the Author and Reader

The interpersonal function concerns not only the relationship between the author and her reader(s) but also the ways in which the author and the reader are constructed as individuals, distinguished by Fairclough (1992c) as the 'identity' function. In asking 'Who is the author of this text?', the areas of interest include her attitude and degree of authority towards mathematics in general and towards the particular mathematical task being undertaken. The analysis should also consider how the reader's relationships to mathematics and to the task are constructed within the text. This includes asking the question: 'Why is the constructed reader reading this text?' which may itself involve considering the relationship between author and reader. An important aspect of this relationship is its symmetry or asymmetry: to what extent are the participants 'equal' members of a community of mathematicians or is there greater authority ascribed to one or to the other? How intimate is their apparent relationship?

One of the most obvious ways in which interpersonal relationships are expressed in a text is through the use of personal pronouns. This has been remarked upon by authors concerned with ideological aspects of language use in general (Fairclough, 1989; Fowler and Kress, 1979) and by those specifically concerned with the nature of academic scientific writing (Bazerman, 1981; Tarone et al., 1981) and the language of mathematics education (Pimm, 1984; 1987). The use of first person pronouns (I and we) may indicate the author's personal involvement with the activity portrayed in the text; Tarone et al. (1981) suggest that the academic science authors they studied used the first person when claiming personal responsibility for procedural decisions rather than when following standard procedures. It may also indicate an expectation that the reader will be interested in this personal aspect as, for example, a teacher might be concerned to know to what extent the mathematics presented was the product of work done by an individual student. In one piece of coursework, a student[6] introduced the original problem thus:

> *The problem that we were given was . . .*

and used the plural pronoun to refer to the group as a whole throughout the first part of his text. When he started his 'extension', however, he claimed individual ownership of both problem and solution:

> *For my extension I am going to . . .*

In the assessment context in which this text was situated it was important that the author should make this personal claim because of the weight given not only to understanding and performing adequately (which could be achieved and evaluated in a group setting) but also to posing an appropriate, original extension question (which can only be done as an individual). In contrast, the academic mathematics paper used to illustrate this chapter uses the first person plural throughout in spite of the fact that it was written by a single author, claiming that:

We shall show that . . .

and thus suggesting that the author is not speaking alone but with the authority of a community of mathematicians that 'guarantees the generalized transmissability of that discourse' (Greimas, 1990).

While such uses of the first person may draw attention to the activity and authority of the author, *we* may also be used in an inclusive way to imply that the reader is also actively involved in the doing of mathematics. For example, from the same academic paper:

We saw in section 2.2 that . . .

and

By Theorem 1 we may assume that H is H*.

gives the reader a share in the responsibility for constructing the argument. Not all readers, however, may be happy with accepting this responsibility; Pimm (1987) comments on similar uses of the first person plural in a mathematics text book:

> The effect on me of reading this book was to emphasize that choices had been made, ostensibly on my behalf, without me being involved. The least that is re-quired is my passive acquiescence in what follows. In accepting the provided goals and methods, I am persuaded to agree to the author's attempts to absorb me into the action. Am I therefore responsible in part, for what happens? (pp. 72–3)

The ways in which the second person pronoun is used are also of interest. Addressing the reader as *you* may indicate a claim to a relatively close relationship between author and reader or between reader and subject matter. For example, one boy wrote in his coursework:

On this grid you will notice that it has coloured boxes around the numbers.

By including the words *you will notice* it appears that the author is addressing an individual reader personally and directing her attention with a degree of authority; it also suggests that the reader ought to be interested in the details of the mathematics presented in the text. On the other hand, some uses of *you* appear to be attempts to provide expressions of general processes rather than being addressed to individual readers. This seems to be the case particularly where children are struggling both to formulate generalizations and to communicate them. For example, the generalization by Year 9 students:

the area would be half of the perimeter if you add one to the area

contains a mixture of relational and procedural forms as well as a combination of a general relationship between two properties of a shape and an action by a human agent. Martin (1989) points out that 'mature' writers will use one form consistently; such lack of consistency of expression is thus likely to be interpreted negatively by a teacher/assessor as a lack of maturity or a mathematical deficiency.

While considering the significance of different ways of using personal pronouns it is also relevant to mention their absence. As mentioned in the previous section, constructions such as use of the passive voice obscure the presence of human beings in the text. This not only affects the picture of the nature of mathematical activity but also distances the author from the reader, setting up a formal relationship between them rather than an intimate one.

One characteristic of academic mathematics texts (and some school texts) is the conventional use of imperatives such as *consider, suppose, define, let x be . . .* Like the use of *we*, these implicate the reader, who is addressed implicitly by the imperative form, in the responsibility for the construction of the mathematical argument. Rotman (1988) draws a distinction between the use of inclusive ('Let's go' although the 'Let's' may be only implicit) and exclusive ('Go') imperatives in mathematical writing. Inclusive imperatives, which Rotman identifies as mental processes like those above, are addressed to a 'thinker' and 'demand that speaker and hearer institute and inhabit a common world or that they share some specific argued conviction about an item in such a world' (p. 9). Exclusive imperatives are addressed to the reader as a 'scribbler' who must perform some material action (*integrate, multiply, drop a perpendicular . . .*). Such use of imperatives and of other conventional and specialist vocabulary and constructions characteristic of academic mathematics marks an author's claim to be a member of the mathematical community which uses such specialist language and, hence, enables her to speak with an authoritative voice about mathematical subject matter. At the same time, it constructs a reader who is also a member of the same community and is thus in some sense a colleague (although the nature of this relationship may vary according to the type of action demanded). In academic writing this assumption of mutual membership of the mathematics community is to be expected. In the school context, however, there are tensions between the need for the pupil to display her familiarity and facility with conventional mathematical language and the demand sometimes made by assessment criteria to explain the processes she has gone through so explicitly that 'someone who knows no mathematics' can understand it. A pupil who addresses the teacher-assessor with authority as a colleague may even be perceived as arrogant. When some students' coursework texts were read by teachers and researchers at a meeting of the British Society for Research into Learning Mathematics, several expressed negative reactions to the text of a student who had adopted an authoritative position in his writing.

> An interpersonal feature of one child's work was commented upon negatively. He wrote:
>
> > *'When I had finished writing out this table I had seen another pattern. Can you see it?'*
>
> This way of addressing the reader was seen as inappropriate. It is, however, typical of the way that children are themselves addressed either by the writers of mathematics

text books and work cards or (usually orally) by their teachers. This boy seems to have identified and copied one of the features of the mathematical texts provided for him without realising that it might be considered inappropriate in his own writing. (Morgan, 1992a, p. 12)

Relations between author, reader and subject matter may also be seen in the modality of a text: 'indications of the degree of likelihood, probability, weight or authority the speaker attaches to the utterance' (Hodge and Kress, 1993, p. 9). This may be expressed through use of modal auxiliary verbs (*must, will, could*, etc.), adverbs (*certainly, possibly*), or adjectives (e.g. *I am sure that . . .*). Expressions of certainty are particularly sensitive in the relationship between pupil and teacher-assessor where they may be interpreted as inappropriate claims to knowledge or authority.[7]

The Textual Function: The Creation of a Mathematical Text

In this section, the way in which the text is constructed as a coherent, meaningful unity is considered: what sort of text is it? This will be addressed by examining internal features which contribute to the way in which the text is constructed as well as the overall structure of the text as a whole. Answers to this question, as mentioned above, also contribute to the ideational and interpersonal functions of the text. By constructing a particular kind of text as a part of mathematics the nature of the discourse of mathematics is implicated, as are the expectations of the participants about what constitutes appropriate writing within the given context.

By examining the types of theme that a writer has chosen to use, a picture can emerge of what sort of things the text as a whole is about. The *theme* of a clause is an indication of the main subject matter of the clause; in English it is not only the starting-point of the message but is also realized by being positioned at the start of the clause (Halliday, 1985, p. 39). Vande Kopple (1991) citing Fries, for example, contrasts two descriptions of houses, one of which presents a picture of movement through the house with a progression of clauses whose themes refer to location (e.g. *To the right . . . , Through the door . . . , Upstairs . . .* , etc.), while the other orients the reader's attention on the house as a set of components by thematizing the contents rather than their locations (e.g. *There is a table . . . , The dining room . . . ,* etc.). Where textual themes occur, these focus a reader's attention on the progression of the argument or story. Given the high status of deductive reasoning in the mathematics community, we might expect to find expressions of logical reasoning thematized. For example, the presence in a report of mathematical activity of a large number of themes expressing reasoning (e.g. *Hence, Therefore, By Theorem 1*, etc.) would serve to construct the text as a deductive argument, while a predominance of temporal themes (e.g. *First, Next, Then*, etc.) would construct a story or report recounting what happened or, if used with imperatives, would construct an algorithm.

It is also worth examining the way in which reasoning is constructed in the text. Martin (1989) points out that reasoning can be expressed through the use of conjunctions (*because, so*), nouns (*the reason is . . .*), verbs (*X causes Y*) or prepositions (*by, because of*). It may also be expressed less explicitly through the juxtaposition of causally related statements. Conjunctions and juxtaposition are characteristic of spoken rather than written text — what Altenberg describes as 'the unpremeditated, rambling progression of conversational discourse' (1987, p. 61) — while Martin (1989) claims that 'mature' writing tends to express causal relation-ships through nouns, verbs and prepositions. Inexperienced writers may well use the less explicit juxtaposition of statements. A problem with such lack of explicit-ness is raised by Swatton (1992) in the context of assessment of processes in school science; he points out the difficulty in determining whether a hypothesis has been formulated (and hence assessing a specified criterion) unless explicit causal language is used. In any assessment context this could also be significant because writing that uses forms of language characteristic of speech may be judged to be expressing less 'mature' forms of thought as well. This distinction between forms of reasoning in speech and in writing is, however, a general one which may not necessarily apply to mathematical discourse. In his discussion of a study examining the ordering of cause and result in conversation and in 'public informative prose' Altenberg (1987) suggests that the order cause–result, because it is chronological, is more common in conversation while formal writing often reformulates this into the order result–cause. While it seems that, for example, scientific explanation might favour the result–cause order, the status of deductive thinking in mathematics might lead one to expect a greater emphasis on reasoning from cause to result. Interpretation of the expression of reasoning in mathematical texts, therefore, requires further exam-ination of the writing and reading of such texts; it cannot be assumed that this spoken–written distinction is generally valid in all areas of discourse.

As well as looking at internal characteristics of the text it is important to consider the overall structure of the text as a whole. Do various parts of the text fulfil different functions and how clearly are these defined? Such sections may be signalled by explicit labelling, by paragraphing or other lay-out devices, or only by changes in content matter or style. In interpreting an element of a text, readers are influenced by its position and by what they expect to see at that point in the text. If the structure is unclear or unconventional this is likely to affect the meanings that the reader ascribes to the text, her evaluation of it and of its author. Hon (1992), for example, in a report addressed to classroom teachers, describes the conventional structure of science investigation reports written by adults and suggests that where children omit some of the 'more-or-less obligatory elements' (p. 4) this is 'the result of a misunderstanding of the exact nature of the writing task' (p. 11).

Non-verbal Features of Mathematical Texts

Non-verbal features play an important part in most mathematical texts. In particu-lar, the system of mathematical symbolism plays a crucial role in the activity of doing mathematics as well as being 'one of the subject's most apparent and distinct-ive features' (Pimm, 1987, p. 138). Algebraic symbolism is rather different from other non-verbal features, not only because it can be translated into words and read in a linear way similar to verbal text but because of the significance of its role within mathematics. In addition to symbols, mathematical texts may contain what Shuard and Rothery call 'graphic language', including tables, graphs, diagrams, plans and maps, pictorial illustrations (1984, p. 45). These features share the characteristic of non-linearity and cannot be unambiguously translated into words. As well as these discrete features of the texts, 'presentation' (i.e. graphological aspects such as the spacing of the text and the use of colour and underlining) may influence the ways in which a text is read.

The Role of Algebraic Symbolism

By representing an object, quantity, action or relationship by a symbol in a mathematical text, it is declared to be 'mathematical' and thus of significance. At the same time symbolizing is an act of abstraction allowing the writer and the reader to focus only on the formal properties of the symbol itself and allowing 'manipulation to move faster and more seamlessly by blurring the distinction between symbol and object' (Pimm, 1987, p. 139). Mathematics itself thus appears as a domain in which the main activity is manipulation of symbols rather than of concepts or 'real world' objects. Symbols are not, however, always manipulated within the text. In students' texts a symbolically expressed generalization may stand alone as the 'answer', suggesting that the purpose of the task undertaken was to produce this expression. In such cases the symbols are the product of the mathematical activity rather than a tool to be used during the process and mathematical activity is directed towards forming an algebraic expression. While I have suggested that extensive manipulation of symbols and the presentation of symbolic expressions as products present a picture of mathematics as a primarily symbolic activity, it is important to consider to what extent the symbols are explicitly linked to their referents. The algebraic product may be 'translated' back into 'real world' terms thus maintaining a picture of mathematics as modelling a concrete reality.

Halmos points out one of the interpersonal effects of the use of symbols in mathematical text:

> if it looks like computational hash, with a page full of symbols, it will have a frightening, complicated aspect. (Steenrod, Halmos, Schiffer, and Dieudonné, 1973, p. 45)

Since he was advising writers of academic papers, this would suggest that it is not only non-mathematicians who have a negative emotional reaction to excessive use of symbols. The extent of their presence in a text is, however, one way in which the author claims authority as an 'expert' member of the community of mathematicians — one who is not frightened and does not consider the symbolism complicated. The claim to expert status is particularly strong where new notation is coined within the text to signify 'new' mathematics created by the author (although there is also the possibility that the type of new symbol chosen may be seen by a reader as inappropriate — a 'category mistake' (Pimm, 1987, p. 145)). As with the use of specialist vocabulary and conventional language discussed above, there is also an assumption that the reader will be a member of the same community, sharing the ability to interpret the symbolic language. The claim to expert status is, of course, dependent to some extent on the type of symbols used and on the context within which the writing is situated. The use of numerals by themselves would not be considered of particularly high status in most areas of mathematics. In GCSE coursework, in particular, it appears that use of algebraic symbolism is an unwritten criterion for attaining a grade of C or above at GCSE (Wolf, 1990) and is thus seen to mark off those students who are capable of progressing to higher mathematics from the rest.

Diagrams, Tables and Graphs

The tools for analysis of 'visual' forms of text are less fully developed in the literature than those for verbal text. The main source that has informed this section is the work of Kress and van Leeuwen (1990; 1996) who, working in a Hallidayan tradition, have attempted to construct a 'grammar' for visual forms of communication, identifying features of pictures and diagrams that serve ideational, interpersonal and textual functions. While Kress and van Leeuwen's grammar provides some useful tools and concepts, its empirical basis does not on the whole include mathematical texts and its application and adequacy in the case of mathematics has yet to be fully developed. Unlike the linguistic tools described above, therefore, the tools for analysing graphic components considered in this section have had, to a large extent, to be derived through an empirical examination of actual texts.[8] The texts I have used are students' investigation reports; the tools developed, therefore, are certainly not comprehensive and may have limited application to other types of text. Interpretations of the features identified are also made only within the school mathematics assessment context. The development of a fully comprehensive means of describing and interpreting graphic forms in mathematical texts in general has not been attempted.

Although there are structural and functional differences between diagrams, tables and graphs, these elements all share the characteristic that their components are not readily translatable into a linear verbal form. The ways in which they are read and integrated into a whole text may thus be distinguished from verbal text and from algebraic symbolism. Much of this section refers to diagrams; many of the features of diagrams that are identified as significant to the analysis are, however, equally relevant to the consideration of graphs and of tables. Where graphs or tables have features that are not found in diagrams these are dealt with specifically.

'Neatness'

Diagrams which are drawn with a ruler, with largely correct proportions or exact measurements, possibly with great detail and apparent care, positioned between the margins and parallel to the edges of the paper may be categorized as 'neat'. The prime function of 'neatness' is interpersonal; it indicates that the text is formal and that there is some distance in the relationship between author and reader. This distance may be physical, in that detail and clarity are necessary if there is no possibility of oral communication to supplement the diagram — diagrams drawn on the back of an envelope in the course of a personal conversation are unlikely to have many 'neat' qualities. The distance may also be a social one, the neatness being a mark of respect for the reader, or it may be an 'intellectual' distance, indicating the degree to which the reader is constructed as sharing the resources needed to understand the diagram. In the case of coursework texts, where the reader is a teacher-examiner, neatness may serve as an indicator of the amount of care and effort that the student-author has expended on the task as a whole.

A neat diagram is thus clearly addressed to a possibly distant audience. A rough diagram (one which lacks most of the qualities of neatness listed above), on the other hand, either is addressed to an audience that is constructed as intimate (socially and intellectually) or appears as a 'private' diagram, drawn for the personal use of the author rather than as part of the communication with a reader. Of course, if such a 'private' diagram has been included in a text that is intended to be read by others this means that it does have a public communicative function. In the coursework context, this function would be likely to be to demonstrate that the student/author has done the required 'investigation', trying out specific examples for herself before recording the results more formally elsewhere. The roughness of such diagrams may also be taken as an indicator that they are the original work of the author herself as copying would be likely to have been done with greater care.

The degree of neatness may also serve a textual function, indicating to the reader how she should make sense of the diagram's role within the structure of the whole text. As suggested above, rough diagrams, being private, may be read as background material which provides evidence of process but which does not contribute to the thread of argument. Just as they were drawn without much care or attention to detail, it is not necessary for the reader to pay much attention to their detailed properties. A diagram that is neat, on the other hand, may form an important part of the argument, serving as explanation or justification. The textual function of a diagram can also be inferred from the way in which it is integrated into the text (see below). Where there is a mismatch between the degree of neatness and the reader's perception of the textual function it is likely that a negative judgment will be formed by the reader. Thus, a very neat diagram or set of diagrams which is read as background 'working out' may be judged to be a 'waste of time', while a very rough diagram which is read as forming part of an explanation may lead the reader to judge the author to be lazy or careless.

Labelling

One of the ways in which the functions of a diagram are indicated is through the form of labelling attached to it. Three forms of labelling are of particular significance in the context of mathematics coursework: question numbers, specific quantities or measurements and variable names.[9] A question number used as a label for a diagram, or indeed for any other segment of text, indicates that it is the answer or part of the answer to a question specified by the set task. It is thus a sign that the student-author's activity in doing the mathematics is directed by an external authority rather than being autonomous or creative. Specific quantities or measurements marked on a diagram suggest that the diagram is a specific example, either drawn in the process of experimenting before forming a generalization or given as a demonstration of the truth of a generalization (obviously depending on the position of the example within the text as a whole). In both cases the drawing implies that the physical object portrayed in the diagram is real, at least in the sense that it can be counted or measured, and that it is the subject matter of the mathematical problem. In the case of those diagrams apparently drawn during an experimental phase, such labels play a role similar to that of 'neatness', indicating that they are being presented for the reader's attention as part of the main flow of the argument rather than as background 'rough' work.

In contrast, a diagram labelled with variable names focuses on the general, i.e. the features that the object represented has in common with other similar objects, rather than the particular quantities or measurements that identify the unique object represented. The subject matter of the mathematical text is thus more abstract; the relationships between the properties of the physical objects represented are more important than the properties themselves.

Naturalism

The presence of diagrams in a mathematical text implies that the mathematics involved is, at least to some extent, about the concrete objects portrayed. Even abstract and general geometric objects are given a concrete and particular form by being represented in a diagram.[10] However, it is also relevant to consider the extent to which the representation is abstract and schematic or naturalistic.[11] For example, a student writing about the investigation 'Frogs' might draw her diagrams with naturalistic pictures of frogs (as they appear in the SMILE computer programme and in most published introductions to the investigation) or she might choose to use abstract iconic representations such as circles or squares. The latter, more abstract approach is likely to be judged by the teacher/assessor to demonstrate a higher level of mathematical thinking. Kress and van Leeuwen (1996) distinguish the 'abstract coding orientations, which are used by sociocultural elites' to inform the way in which texts in academic and scientific contexts are read:

> The ability to produce and/or read texts grounded in this coding orientation is a mark of social distinction, of being an 'educated person' (p. 170)

Equally, a failure to produce such abstraction may serve as a mark of a lack of this social or intellectual distinction.

The point of view from which three dimensional objects are represented is one of the features of a diagram that contributes to its naturalism or abstractness. Where perspective is provided, the concrete reality of the object is emphasized. This

Figure 6.1: A naturalistic diagram of a pile of rods

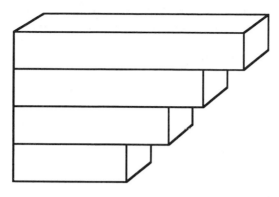

Figure 6.2: An abstract diagram of a pile of rods

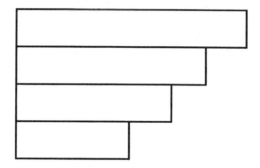

highlights the practical nature of the activity involving the object. For example, a pile of rods for the 'Topples' task (LEAG, 1991) that is drawn showing perspective (Figure 6.1) suggests through its naturalism that physical features of the rods such as the material they are made of may be significant to the problem, while the drawing without perspective (Figure 6.2) focuses more unambiguously on the length of the rods as the only important variable. In the case of mathematics GCSE coursework it seems unlikely that teacher/examiners would expect variables such as friction to be effectively taken into account by children. It is likely, therefore, that the less naturalistic frontal view would be considered more appropriate.

Dynamic signs of activity

While some diagrams have what Kress and van Leeuwen (1996) call an *analytical structure* which displays an object and its attributes (Figure 6.3), others have an *action structure* which suggests that a process is taking place or has taken place (Figure 6.4).

Kress and van Leeuwen (1990) identify directional vectors within a diagram as the main indication of such processes as they connect the actor to the goal of

Figure 6.3: A diagram with analytic structure (corresponding to a relational verbal statement: This trapezium contains 21 inner triangles*)*

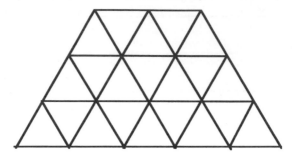

Figure 6.4: A diagram with action structure (corresponding to a material verbal statement: To find the perimeter, count the dots around the outside*)*

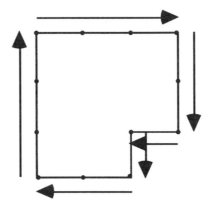

the action. A mathematical diagram with such an action structure not only identifies the process as part of the subject matter of mathematics but also suggests that the process is independent of human activity as it involves only the objects represented in the diagram. This analysis, however, assumes that the participants and process are entirely contained within the diagram itself and does not take account of the possible role of the author or reader as actor upon the objects portrayed. While Kress and van Leeuwen do discuss the case of, for example, traffic signs, in which the reader is the elided actor addressed in the imperative, e.g. 'Go this way', the action represented in such signs is expected to take place in the 'real world' outside the diagram. In the context of a mathematical text it may be the diagram itself that is to be acted upon.

Diagrams, like symbolism, can act as tools in the activity of doing mathematics as well as acting as representations of the objects or products of mathematical activity. This role may be indicated within the diagram in the shape of marks which suggest the author's processes and guide the way in which the reader should actively make sense of the diagram. For example, arrows may not only indicate the route which the reader's gaze should take but may also show how the diagram might be moved or transformed in the reader's imagination. Dots or other tally marks suggest that counting has taken place or should be done by the reader. Within a table, arrows or other indicators may also be used to identify values that are to be combined or compared in some way; a conventional example of such a dynamic table is a table of differences used as a tool for analysing the structure of a number sequence. Such uses suggest both concrete objects and material action (manipulating the diagram itself either physically or in imagination or performing an operation such as counting, measuring or subtracting) to be the subject matter of mathematics. They also suggest that the reader's role is an active one, reconstructing the processes described by the author rather than merely receiving an account of their outcomes.

Different ways of representing data can also present different views of the nature of the subject matter. The use of a line graph rather than a list or table of values or a bar chart 'creates something like a dynamic process (transcodable as "change", "grow", "decrease" etc.)' (Kress and van Leeuwen, 1996, p. 105). The participants are themselves dynamic variables rather than discrete and static objects. A graph may thus be interpreted to make a general active statement that could be verbalized as *The area increases steadily*, while a table presenting the 'same' information makes a series of relational statements about specific instances: *The area when b = 1 is 6; the area when b = 2 is 8; the area when b = 3 is 10.*

Integration into the text

In interpreting the roles of diagrams, graphs and tables it is necessary to look at how they are integrated into the body of the text. What sort of verbal references (if any) are made to them and how are they positioned on the page? For example, integrating a table with the words *I put the results in a table* suggests a focus on the author's processes; *here is a table* suggests that the table is seen as a product in its own right or as a sign of the author's mathematical expertise; *in the table you can see* suggests an expectation that the reader will be actively involved in making sense of the mathematics. Where no verbal reference is made to the table this may suggest that its role in the text should be taken for granted as a standard component of the genre.

The layout of the page may also indicate the textual functions of different parts of the text. Kress and van Leeuwen (1996) relate left–right ordering on the page to the given–new structure of the information contained in it (corresponding to the direction in which we read verbal text). Where, for example, a page is arranged with diagrams on the left hand side and a table of results on the right, this gives priority to the diagrams as representations of what is given and unquestionable while the table is presented as an interpretation of these 'facts' and a creation of the author. An ordering from top to bottom of the page may be taken to suggest a development either temporally in the narrative (i.e. what happened first, second, etc.) or logically in the argument. For example, a hypothesis stated in words or symbolic form at the top of the page, followed below by a specific diagram labelled with measurements and a calculation suggests that the diagram plays the role of confirmation of the hypothesis while the opposite ordering suggests that the hypothesis has been formed on the basis of the evidence provided by the example represented in the diagram.

'Presentation'

In contrasting spoken and written language, Halliday (1989) argues that writing does not have paralinguistic features such as intonation and gestures which form an important part of the context of speaking. I would suggest, however, that there are features of written language which play similar roles. In particular, the use of devices such as underlining, italics, colour, different sizes of letters, etc. 'may have clear linguistic implications, perhaps related to the semantic structure of the utterance (as in advertising or newspaper articles) or even to its grammatical structure' (Crystal and Davy, 1969, p. 17) and thus can provide guidance to the reader about the status and relative importance of the various parts of the text. In formal academic writing, such devices are generally used sparingly and with limited conventional meanings. They are to be found, however, in published texts intended for children and are extensively used in mathematics text books (Shuard and Rothery, 1984, p. 20)).

The use of colour, for example, may thus mark a text as being produced by or for a child, the colour being included either to entertain by creating visual interest or to help guide the reader by highlighting important parts of the text. By way of contrast, a piece of coursework that is typed or word-processed appears to be claiming to be a formal 'adult' text, setting itself apart as different from the hand-written work of the everyday mathematics classroom. The presence of features such as title pages, lists of contents, etc. similarly suggest a claim to be a 'publication'. Such devices may, however, be interpreted by a teacher/assessor to be a 'waste of time', distracting from the more important mathematical content matter.

Applying the Analytical Tools

In this chapter, linguistic and non-linguistic features of mathematical texts have been identified as contributing to the construction of ideational, interpersonal and textual meanings in the texts; this is summarized in Table 6.1. The functions that have been considered are those related to mathematics and mathematical activity in the discourses of the community of academic mathematicians and of the secondary school mathematics classroom and assessment system; there are likely to be other areas of meaning that have not been considered. While I have attempted to suggest possible interpretations for the various choice of these features, it is only within the context of a complete text that the interpretation can be made, particularly as apparently contradictory features may coexist within a single text. Indeed, similar features may function differently in different contexts; for example, Dowling (1992) remarks on the different functions served by cartoons in mathematics text books

Table 6.1: Summary of tools for analysing mathematical text

	verbal	non-verbal
ideational	The types of processes, in particular the uses made of the equals sign and the types of processes used in the expression of generalizations; The types of participants in these processes; The portrayal or suppression of agency through nominalizations, non-human actors, and non-active forms of verbs; The nature and extent of the expression of causal relationships.	The presentation of symbolism as 'tool' or as 'answer'; The extent to which the symbols are explicitly linked to their referents; The role of graphic entities as 'tool' or 'product'; Labelling by variable names or specific quantities; Abstract or naturalistic nature of representational diagrams; Analytic or action structure of diagrams.
interpersonal	The use of personal pronouns; The extent of specialist mathematical vocabulary and conventional forms of language such as imperatives; The expression of certainty and authority in the modality of clauses.	The extent of symbol use; The use of newly coined or unconventional symbols; 'Neatness' as an indication of the 'distance' between writer and reader; Diagrams indicating action on the part of author or reader; Colour, typing, question numbers etc.
textual	Thematic progression; The ways in which reasoning is expressed; The overall structure of the text.	'Neatness' as an indicator of 'public' or 'private'; How symbolic and graphic elements are integrated into the text as a whole through the use of verbal language; The layout of the page; Title page, list of contents etc.

intended for 'high ability' and 'low ability' students. The features that have been identified should be seen as things to examine in the texts being analysed and interpreted in the light of the suggestions made here, taking into account the complete text and the contexts of production and interpretation. This does not mean that there may not be further, unanticipated features that prove to be significant during the analysis.

It should be noted that there is no suggestion that the author of a text has made conscious decisions to choose to use particular features in order to express the types of meaning considered in this analysis. Rather, the individual's positioning within a particular social structure and consequent understanding of the nature of the genre within which she is writing makes it 'natural' for her to make these choices because they appear 'appropriate' to the task she is undertaking. They may or may not appear similarly appropriate to a reader, depending on the discourse within which that reader is positioned. The analyst, however, must stand apart from making such judgments as the concept of 'appropriateness' is itself socially constructed and is indeed one of the ideological concepts that is to be 'demystified' by the analysis. While she must share in the 'member's resources' (Fairclough, 1989) used by the participants to produce and interpret the text, the analyst must use these with self-consciousness in the light of 'rational understanding of, and theories of, society' (p. 167).

Notes

1   While the main focus of this book is on written texts, almost everything that is said here is equally applicable to spoken texts. Where I use the terms *writer* and *reader*, therefore, I could in most cases equally have used *speaker* and *listener*.

2   The reports of investigative work were written by students with varying degrees of experience, ranging from Year 9 students (aged 13–14) who had never written such reports before, to Year 11 students (aged 15–16) producing their final reports for submission as coursework for examination at GCSE.

3   Van Dormolen (1986) draws parallels between this distinction between procedural and relational thinking and Freudenthal's (1978) distinction of levels of language. However, whereas Freudenthal is clear that it is the *language* that is at a lower level in the procedural example, van Dormolen slips between referring to levels of language and levels of knowledge.

4   This example is taken from one of the case study texts discussed in later chapters.

5   It is not always possible to make a clear distinction between basic objects and objects derived from them as what is taken as 'basic' depends on the particular problem that forms the context.

6   This example is taken from one of the case study texts discussed in later chapters.

7   This phenomenon of mismatch between forms of language that may legitimately be used by different participants in an asymmetric discourse and the effects of the use of the language of the 'other' group has been observed in a number of social settings by ethnographers (see e.g. Cazden, 1988).

8   The tools were derived in order to make it possible to describe identifiable differences within and between children's texts. The fact that the differences were identifiable and appeared significant to me during this process suggests that they have some relevance to the issues that concern me in relation to the discourses of investigation and assessment. An analyst with different interests and resources may well be able to see other differences and derive other tools to describe them. It is, of course, possible that such further tools would enable additional insights into the investigational texts themselves.

9   I am using the term 'variable names' to refer both to symbolic labels, such as a conventional *n* or a more contextually meaningful *T.L.* (for 'Top Length'), and to verbal labels such as *difference* or *top length*. In each case the label is identifying a generally significant feature of the object represented in the diagram without quantifying it within the particular diagram.

10   It is interesting to note that, in spite of the geometric nature of the subject matter of the academic article referred to earlier (Dye, 1991) and an explicit appeal to physical imagery contained in its introductory section, the article contains no diagrams. The

generality and abstract nature of the argument are thus emphasized. Within academic mathematics there is dispute about the status of graphic representations with a general historic trend away from the visual towards symbolic, deductive modes of argument. This trend has been justified by a demand for greater rigour, based at least in part on the suggestion that the eye is fallible. Davis (1993), however, argues for higher status for the visual, claiming that there are 'graphical displays . . . from which certain pure or applied mathematical conclusions can be derived almost by inspection' (p. 336). While admitting that pictures can deceive (he uses a proof that all triangles are isosceles as an example), Davis is arguing within a paradigm that assumes that pictures are 'transparent'; the reader would not be deceived if the diagram were drawn 'properly'.

11   The distinction between abstract and naturalistic images is identified by Kress and van Leeuwen (1996) as part of the *modality* of the text — the degree of 'reality' claimed for the image is part of the interpersonal function. In the particular context of mathematical texts, however, the contribution made by abstraction or naturalism to the picture of the nature of mathematics as an abstract system or as applicable to (or derived from) the real world seems more significant — hence I am considering this as performing a primarily ideational function.

Chapter 7

Reading Investigative Mathematical Texts

In the previous chapter I outlined a set of tools for describing mathematical texts and interpreting the functions that features of such texts might perform within mathematical and educational discourses. In this chapter I offer some examples of the application of these tools in order to characterize written texts produced within the practice of GCSE investigative coursework. My intention is not only to illustrate how the analytic tools may be applied but also to provide some further insight into the discourse of mathematical investigation itself.[1] This will be done through analyses of coursework tasks set for GCSE candidates and of students' written reports of their work on these tasks.[2]

The Tasks

In order to make sense of students' reports of their investigations, some knowledge of the tasks they were responding to is needed. The two tasks involved here were set by the London examining board (LEAG) for candidates who were entered for the GCSE examination in the summer of 1991. 'Topples' was undertaken while the students were in the first year of the two year course leading up to the GCSE, and 'Inner Triangles' was undertaken in the second year. There are strong similarities between the two tasks: both are structured[3] with specific questions to which students are expected to respond; both expect students to collect and organize data, form and 'explain' a generalization, and 'extend' their work. There is also a fundamental difference in that 'Inner Triangles' deals with 'pure' mathematical structures while 'Topples' is considered a 'practical' task in that the data must be gathered from physical experimentation. The descriptions that follow are based on the text of the tasks presented to students and the 'performance indicators' issued by the examination board to guide teachers' assessment of the tasks (LEAG, 1991).

'Inner Triangles'

The 'Inner Triangles' task asks students to determine a relationship between the dimensions of a trapezium drawn on isometric paper (see Figure 7.1) and the number of small 'unit' triangles it contains.

Figure 7.1:   A trapezium containing 'inner triangles'

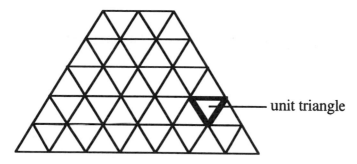

unit triangle

The first part of this task is presented in a formal way that might be characterized as similar to a school text book with the structure: definitions, example, exercise. Students are informed of the subject matter and terminology of the task and are then asked to find the number of unit triangles given the dimensions for two specified examples and to find the dimensions given the number of unit triangles for a further two examples. This traditional formality is also expressed through the impersonal nature of the language, for example:

> *The diagram below shows a trapezium drawn on triangular lattice or isometric paper.*

There is no human agency here; it is the diagram which 'shows' while the creator of the diagram is hidden by the use of the passive *drawn*. The lexicon throughout the task is tightly restricted; the mathematical objects and the attributes of these objects which are to be considered in the question (trapezium, unit triangle, dimensions, top length, bottom length, slant length) are named unambiguously and these names are used repeatedly and precisely throughout the task. One of the effects of this formality is to suggest that the subject matter of this investigation is not negotiable by any individual student but may even be a part of the conventional body of school mathematics.

In spite of the 'text book' formality, even in this early part of the task there are features that (although perhaps hidden from many students) do not conform to the conventions of that genre. The student is instructed to:

> *Give the dimensions of a trapezium containing (a) 8 unit triangles, (b) 32 unit triangles.*

In spite of the appearance of simplicity and the use of the 'school maths' format (imperative instruction, single stem with multiple questions), there is not in fact a unique answer for either part of this question. While this may be signalled by the use of the indefinite article, there is no indication given in the task that more than one answer for each part should be sought. The performance indicators (provided by the examination board to guide teacher-assessors), however, suggest that finding more than one answer could be used to differentiate between students at grades F and E. It seems that the 'better' student is expected to read through the simple directed nature of the given question to answer a more complex question that lies behind it. This is, after all, an 'investigation' and multiple answers are to be expected from anyone who knows the rules of the game.

Following this initial exercise, the student is instructed to

> *Investigate the relationship between the dimensions of a trapezium and the number of unit triangles it contains.*

In spite of the use of the word *investigate* (which might suggest some degree of choice for the student), both the goal and the method of the investigation are tightly defined. The student is to investigate 'the relationship', the definite article and the singular noun suggesting that there is only one correct answer to this investigation. This is echoed by the performance indicators which specify the formula which students are expected to obtain in order to achieve a grade C or B (although in practice, of course, there are a number of alternative ways of expressing the relationship). Moreover, the student is then advised how to report on her investigation:

> *show all your working,*
> *explain your strategies,*
> *make use of specific cases,*
> *generalize your results,*
> *prove or explain any generalizations.*

This list prescribes an inductive approach to the problem through using specific examples and generalizing from them. Its ordering also suggests a hierarchy within the list of processes (given the convention of school mathematics that questions will progress from easier to more difficult). This hierarchy is confirmed to some extent by the performance indicators. For example, 'explanation of methodology' is expected for a grade D while there is no expectation of proof or explanation of the mathematics until grade A where:

> *The quality of explanation of **why** the generalized result is as it is, defines the level of Grade A.* (original emphasis)

Finally, an 'Optional Extension' suggests that the student may extend the task. Although the student appears to be being allowed unlimited freedom to extend 'in any way', this freedom is immediately curtailed by placing constraints on the types of extensions that are allowed — the student must look only at figures within figures drawn on isometric paper.

To summarize: this task is located within 'school maths' although the specific subject matter is new and thus requires initial definitions and examples. The student's activity at the beginning of the task is closely determined and it is not expected that the lowest attaining students will progress beyond answering specific closed questions. Those who progress further, however, are allowed some limited autonomy in deciding both the goal of their investigation and its methods. The type of reasoning expected is inductive although 'explanation' is expected at the highest grade levels.

Figure 7.2:   A pile of rods

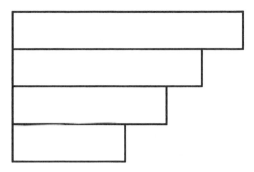

'Topples'

Like 'Inner Triangles', the 'Topples' task is highly structured and the nature of the student's activity is highly specified. It differs, however, in the practical, physical nature of the subject matter and in the degree of formality in the text. The students are instructed to build piles of rods in such a way that each rod in the pile is one 'unit of length' greater than the one beneath it (Figure 7.2). As in 'Inner Triangles', students are asked to investigate a relationship between variables in the situation — in this case between the length of the rod at the bottom of the pile and the length of the rod which first makes the pile 'topple'. Although this task might be described as a 'practical' task and although the collection of the data is performed practically and necessarily with a degree of experimental uncertainty, it is clear that practical activity is not what is valued most highly. What is required is the discovery of an abstract relationship between numbers. This is made explicit in the performance indicators for the task which start by stating:

> *The generalization for this task is well within the syllabus at intermediate and higher level; it is a simple linear function. We would therefore expect to see an algebraic (symbolic) representation of this generalization from candidates at grade C and above.*

It is interesting to note that the practical, empirical nature of the task is mentioned just twice in the performance indicators: once for the highest attainers who are expected to offer 'some explanation of why the pile topples' (which must surely lie within the domain of physics or mechanics rather than GCSE mathematics), and once for the lowest attainers whose results 'are likely to be . . . not very accurate' — a clear distinction between mental and manual activity for these two groups of students.

The student is frequently addressed directly, both through use of the personal pronoun *you* and through imperative instructions. This less conventionally formal style is also seen in 'asides' such as:

> *Make sure that the rods increase by one unit of length at a time.*

and in the tentative modality of the instruction:

> *Make any observations that you can.*

The image of the reader conjured up by the use of this less formal address is of a student who is perhaps less mature than that addressed by the 'Inner Triangles' task and less able to cope with a more conventional mathematical style. The 'Topples' task was set for students during the first year of their two year GCSE course and was intended for all groups of students, whereas 'Inner Triangles' was restricted to those entered at the Intermediate or Higher levels[4] of the examination. It is interesting to speculate whether the authors of the tasks made these linguistic distinctions deliberately, based on their beliefs about the capabilities of the students.

At the beginning of the task, after the procedure for building piles of rods has been described, students are instructed to 'investigate'. They are not given guidance as to which examples they should look at but are advised to record and tabulate their results, to make observations, generalize and explain. Finally, they are asked to respond to questions about piles of a size presumably beyond that which may be constructed practically. No suggestions are provided to the students of what methods they might use to answer these final questions but they are asked to 'explain your working', suggesting that the method chosen is likely to be important. In spite of the lengthy description of practical activity given at the beginning, it is clear from the specific tasks required of the student that carrying out the practical activity is less important than performing the standard 'investigation' algorithm and answering hypothetical questions in a non-practical way. The performance indicators even suggest that, for the highest attaining students, the task is really about algebraic notation and manipulation rather than about piles of rods:

> *From the candidates at grades B and A we would expect to see use of this algebraic form in the two specific cases given.*

To summarize: this task starts with practical activity, involving experimentation with physical apparatus; its subject matter rapidly moves, however, towards abstract patterns of numbers and, for the highest attaining candidates, algebraic manipulation. Although the student's activity appears initially to be relatively open exploration, this is directed towards gaining specific answers. The model of reasoning is essentially inductive. The image of the student reader is less mature and less mathematically sophisticated than that suggested by the 'Inner Triangles' task.

Much of the official and professional discourse surrounding coursework and investigations suggests that value is laid on students' freedom to determine their own questions and methods. This freedom is signalled in both these tasks by the instruction to the student to 'investigate'. The signal is, however, ambiguous as in each case the subject matter of the investigation is tightly defined. The methods to be used are also largely determined by the use of imperatives and the explicit listing of processes to be undertaken.[5] Moreover, it is clear that, whatever variation between students might be permissible in the course of doing the tasks, they are all supposed to be aiming at the same uniquely correct 'answer' in the form of an algebraic generalization (although this uniqueness may only be signalled to the teacher by being stated in the performance indicators). Thus, in 'Inner Triangles', the student is instructed to 'generalize your results', suggesting (by the possessive pronoun) student ownership of the results and possible variation between different students, while the performance indicators state that 'The results are . . .', claiming absolute authority and no room for variation. There is a tension between, on the one hand, the principle of student exploration and autonomy expressed in the official and professional rhetoric of investigations and reflected in the use of the word *investigate* and, on the other hand, the absolutist nature of mathematics expressed in these texts. This tension may be a consequence of the assessment context in which the texts are located. Although a note inside the front cover of the collection of tasks and performance indicators (LEAG, 1991) states that the performance indicators

> are provided as a *guide* to assessing the level of performance demonstrated by the student. They are *not* hurdles and must be treated flexibly. Alternative approaches to solving the problem or tackling the task must be assessed using different measures of performance (original emphasis)

the forms of language used within the tasks and within the performance indicators associated with individual tasks do not reflect such flexibility.

The Students' Texts

I now turn to look at the characteristics of writing produced by students in response to these two tasks. It is clear that no one text can adequately characterize a genre. This is, perhaps, particularly so in an educational setting where texts produced by students are likely often to be considered imperfect and inappropriate. It may be more useful, therefore, to look at a range of texts and to ask in what ways they are similar and how they differ. The student texts that will be examined here are those produced by five pupils. Richard and Clive investigated 'Inner Triangles', Ellen and Sandra investigated 'Topples', while Steven responded to both tasks. This set of texts was chosen to represent a range of different characteristics, though all achieved similar grades from their teacher-examiner.[6]

Ideational Aspects

As the two tasks differ in their subject matter, 'Inner Triangles' being 'pure' while 'Topples' is 'practical', it might be expected that the picture of the nature of mathematics and mathematical activity portrayed in the students' texts would differ accordingly. As we shall see, however, the situation is not quite as simple as that. Examination of the participants and processes and the role of human mathematicians in the texts reveal differences both between tasks and between individual student texts.

One of the most striking features of Clive's (IT)[7] text is the large number of statements declaring the existence of relational and representational objects:

> *Here is another quick conversion table.*

> *Below is a formula . . . here it is.*

> *. . . I found a formula . . . here it is.*

> *. . . there were a lot of patterns and formulas . . .*

These tables, formulae and patterns clearly play a significant part in Clive's text. Not only are they present in the text but their presence is declared, drawn to the reader's attention by the use of existential statements. The subject matter is presented as being about patterns and formulae. Although the task is about geometric objects and Clive includes a number of diagrams of these objects in his text, the form and integration of the diagrams also reinforce the idea that the problem is primarily about patterns. For example, two diagrams, although in the form of trapezia, appear not to represent individual trapezia but rather whole sets of trapezia used to generate a number pattern (one of these is shown in Figure 7.3). The commentary on the diagrams focuses the reader's attention on the numbers rather than on the geometrical figures:

> *The numbers can be added together to get the next row of numbers.*
> *It can also tell you the answer . . .*

The referent of the word *it* in the extract above is not explicit but appears, perhaps because of a lack of appropriate technical vocabulary, to be 'pointing' (Rowland, 1992) to the pattern of numbers.

The origin of the tables in Clive's (IT) text is obscured. They are merely declared to exist and on only one occasion (in the final part of the extension) is there any suggestion of human agency in the production of a table when the author claims ownership, declaring *Here is my conversion table*. The general lack of explicit human agency may indicate obliquely that most of the tables were constructed by other group members or by the group as a whole rather than by the author himself (and are, therefore, not to be claimed personally by the author). However, the image of *table* presented in the text is of a pre-existing basic object, rather than a deliberately constructed organizing mechanism or problem solving tool. Unlike tables, the formulae are *worked out* or *found* and ownership by the group or by the author himself is claimed each time a formula is introduced. The

Figure 7.3: Clive's diagram

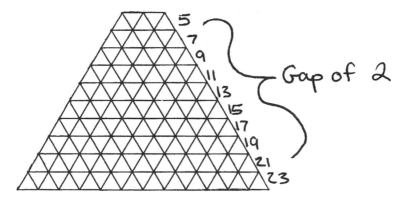

formulae are thus presented as the product of human activity. Since the overall purpose of the piece of coursework is to allow the teacher to assess the author, what the author has achieved must be made clear to the reader. Whereas the tables appear as autonomously existing entities, the formulae represent personal achievements.

In contrast, Richard's (IT) text, which consists almost entirely of diagrams, tables and symbols with a few verbal labels but no longer passages of verbal text, appears to lay more stress on the basic objects of the problem (triangles and hexagons), on the measurements derived from them, and on the answers to the specific questions posed by the task. The only processes indicated are relational ones, using the equals sign to assign values to dimensions and to express relationships between variables. There is no explicit presence of any human activity; the author's agency in producing the mathematics is obscured by the use of nominalized headings such as *Working out, Results* and *Extension*. The focus of Richard's (IT) text is clearly on the product of any mathematical activity rather than on the activity itself. While Clive's (IT) focus on pattern and on the human processes involved in observing patterns and deriving formulae conforms to the value laid on process and personal activity within 'investigation' discourse, Richard's (IT) focus on measurements and results seems located more within a traditional 'school maths' genre.

Two of the 'Topples' texts, by Sandra and Ellen, place material objects and their behaviour as their central subject matter. This may be seen in Ellen's (T) capitalization of *Rods* and overlexicalization (using variously and often interchangeably: *rod, number of units, number n unit, unit number of rod(s), unit of rod, n unit rod, unit, length of rod*) and in Sandra's (T) prominent display of naturalistic diagrams of piles of rods (Figure 7.4), drawn in perspective and in colour, showing in some cases two rods joined together to form the required length, thus focusing on a wide range of physical properties of the rods rather than solely on their length.

Even here, however, there are differences. An examination of the actors and processes in Ellen's (T) text presents a picture of a mathematical world in which material objects behave in ways which are independent of human activity. For example, when asked to explain her results, Ellen responds with an answer which makes no mention of the process of building piles:

Figure 7.4: Sandra's pile of rods

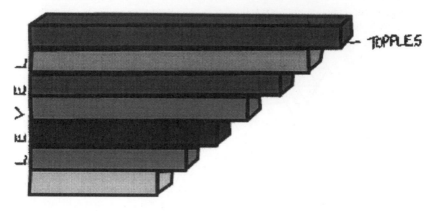

The smaller the unit at the bottom the more likely the load will fall quicker, i.e. a one unit rod can't even balance a 2 unit rod, yet a 3 unit rod can balance 8 units.

Even in her statement of the original problem, it may be seen in comparing her introduction with that provided by the examination board that she has obscured all human involvement in the practical activity of building the piles of rods. For example, the warning about the importance of the way in which the rods are placed on top of one another is changed from a description of 'careful' human behaviour to a statement that 'The Rods have to be verticle (sic)'. A property of the pile of rods substitutes for the human act of building the pile. Even the author's own task is changed from 'to investigate the relationship . . .' to 'to see when the blocks topple'; she has the role of a passive observer of the physical world rather than an active participant. The role of humans in Ellen's text is to observe and to engage in problem solving processes at the level of decision making (performing mental processes) rather than carrying out tasks (material processes). Thus, at the beginning of the section with the formulae, she states:

I thought I had a formular (sic)

and she introduces one part of the extension work, explaining the problem in terms of her own thought processes:

This time I decided to have the units go up in 2's.

The role of human beings is thus presented as one of observing and deciding what to observe, calculating and thinking rather than engaging directly with the material world.

In Sandra's (T) text, a relatively large number of both mental and material processes are ascribed to human actors. While the author herself is shown only to be carrying out the tasks prescribed by the set questions (working out answers, thinking of an extension), she makes extensive use of the general *you* and *we* as actors in more specific activities, including calculations, building piles of rods, observing, comparing results and thinking. Mathematics is thus shown to be a human activity and, at the same time, this activity is generalized. Thus the description of the first extension:

> *You can try and build a pile by joining them together and see when they topple, in the same way as the original experiment and compare them together.*

It provides a procedure that could be followed by any mathematician rather than a specific account of what Sandra herself did. Unlike Ellen, however, Sandra makes it clear that actually manipulating the physical apparatus is an important part of the mathematical activity involved in the task. The author's own activity is signalled in inconsistent ways. In labelling the various sections of question 1, for example, she first copies the imperative instructions from the question paper:

> *b) Tabulate Results*

then indicates her own personal involvement in the activity:

> *c) How I worked them out*

and finally uses a nominalization:

> *d) Predictions*

which obscures her own role as the agent making the predictions. Such inconsistencies in the style of the text suggest a lack of control over linguistic resources that may be interpreted by a reader as a sign of immaturity in the writer.

Steven's responses to both tasks show representational and relational objects (tables, patterns, formulae) playing an important role. They are stressed by the use of headings and colour and announced to the reader by declarations such as 'I have found a formula'. The practical activity of drawing and counting triangles (IT) or building piles of rods (T) is in the background, indicated by a small number of examples (IT) or a paraphrase of the introductory practical instructions given by the task (T). These signs of physical activity are restricted to the early parts of both texts and are soon superseded by a focus on numbers, patterns and relationships between patterns. In this passage from Steven's (IT) text, the author's own activity is obscured, while lengths and numbers are presented as changing largely autonomously, with little human intervention.

> *As you can see the unit No. increases by two every time the top length increases by one. This can be done by using any slant No. but if you change this you may find that the unit increases may be different. e.g. [table 2] This time the unit increase is by 4 instead of 2. On the next one when you increase the slant to three it increases to 6. [table 3] As you can see the difference is six. Another interesting pattern is*

> the way in which the unit No's increase when the top length stays the same and just the slant increases. [table 4] The first increase is by 5, from 3 to 8 and then from 8 to 15 is 7, and finally 15 to 24 is increased by 9. This shows that it increases by the same amount as before but increases by 2. So it would go: 5, 7, 9, 11, . . . This pattern works whatever the top number is.

The process of varying the values in the problem is not shown as something done by the author himself; rather, it shifts from being a process that may be carried out by any mathematician (*if you change this* or *when you increase the slant*), to a process performed by mathematical objects themselves (*the unit No. increases by two every time the top length increases by one*) or by some unspecified agent (*15 to 24 is increased by 9*), and finally to an object which may itself have properties and variations (*The first increase is by 5 . . . This shows that it increases by the same amount as before*). This nominalization opens up the possibility of a higher complexity of generalization, taking account of relationships between three variables rather than just two at a time and considering rates of change as well as individual changes. Similarly, in Steven's (T) text, the 'topple pile' is treated as an abstract quantity which 'goes up' autonomously:

> There is one definite pattern that I can pick up. The topple pile goes up in three and then two and then three and so on.

While the author is present in the text, his role is to 'pick up' an existing pattern rather than to perform material actions or to create anything new. The major human involvement in both Steven's texts involves finding patterns and formulae or reading information from tables.

Interpersonal Aspects

The student texts differ substantially in their formality and in the roles that they construct for their reader. While some of the texts are consistent throughout, others suggest a changing relationship between author, reader and subject matter, often shifting from a formal to a less formal, more personal approach as the task progresses from fulfilling specified instructions to more open investigation.

Richard's (IT) and Sandra's (T) texts are both highly formal and impersonal, containing virtually no references to the authors' own activity or attitudes. In both cases, the vocabulary used is restricted, repetitious and consistent, suggesting a concern with 'correct' and precise use of language and hence a formal relationship with the reader. This may, however, also give the impression of a lack of fluency with the language. For example, Sandra uses the phrase *Length of rod that first makes the pile topple* (a phrase which was used in the question paper) not only when writing in full sentences but also as a label for a variable and as a heading for a column of a table where it would perhaps be more usual to find a more abbreviated phrase. In contrast, Clive (IT) both uses his own words to describe his extension task and demonstrates his personal involvement by using the first person:

> *For my extension I am going to see how many triangles in a triangle and also how many hexagons are in a hexagon.*

The informal, speech-like quality of this problem statement contrasts vividly with the formal statement of the original problem:

> *Investigate the relationship between the dimensions of a trapezium and the number of unit triangles it contains.*

Clive's own language is not only less formal in its lexis (e.g. *see* rather than *investigate*) but is also less precise in its mathematical formulation. Unlike the precise technical expression of *the relationship between the dimensions of a trapezium and the number of unit triangles it contains*, the phrase *how many triangles in a triangle*, while quite clear within this particular context because of the work that has gone before, could be interpreted in different ways within the context of different tasks (e.g. if posed following solution of the 'How many squares on a chess board' problem). The informal language suggests an informal and sympathetic relationship between author and reader; the reader is assumed to share a common understanding of the problem and to be willing to interpret potentially ambiguous expressions in the way that was intended by the author. At the same time, the paraphrasing of the instructions given in the task statement may be taken as a sign that the author has understood the task and made it his own. On the other hand, a less sympathetic reader (one who resists the 'ideal' reading position (Kress, 1989) offered by the text) might interpret the lack of specialist language (in particular, the lack of mathematical symbolism throughout Clive's text) as a sign of poor ability in mathematics.

Another aspect of the formality of Sandra's (T) text is its presentation, which is both meticulous and decorative, making extensive use of colour. Again, there are repetitive aspects of this; there is great consistency in the size, lettering and colour of the page headings, for example, and the tables are all constructed to be the same size and with their columns aligned at the same oblique angle. The colour, although it also makes the text attractive to look at, is used in a way that suggests that its intention is more functional. Keys to the colours used in the diagrams are included, implying that the colour should help the reader to make sense of the diagrams. All these features serve to construct this as a formal and public text, addressed to an audience which has a very distant relationship with the author — possibly distant both in space and in status.

As well as differences in the degree of formality in the relationship between the student authors and their readers there are differences in the roles constructed for the readers by the text: their reasons for reading the text and the ways in which they might interact with the mathematical material. As might be anticipated given the context in which the texts were produced, all the texts, to some extent, portray their reader as an assessor, demonstrating that the requirements of the tasks have been fulfilled by numbering sections in accord with the question paper or by labelling answers, results and formulae. While assessment appears to be the full extent of the reader's role in some texts, others suggest that the reader might also be interested in the mathematics. For example, Steven (IT) addresses his reader as a colleague who is expected to take an active part in making sense of the mathematics. She is addressed directly in order to bring her attention to the significant features of the tables:

> ***As you can see*** *the unit no. increases by two every time the top length increases by one.*

At another point, the reader's attention is drawn to *another interesting pattern*, suggesting that she is expected to share the author's enthusiastic attitude towards his findings. The relationship between author and reader is thus constructed as one in which a general competence and interest in mathematics is shared but in which the author himself has expert knowledge about the particular problem considered in this text. Similarly, Ellen (T) advises her reader on how to read a table:

> *If you take a look at the differences on the table it shows it goes up in 3's but when the number of units is 8 and topples at 20 it changes to 1. The pattern stops then to my surprise starts up again.*
> *Unfortunately I was unable to find a way of telling when the rods were going to topple on top of what length of rod.*

This reader too is expected to be interested and involved in trying to make sense of the data. As well as making a claim to ownership of this part of the task, however, Ellen is laying herself open to criticism because of her inability to find a formula to fit her data. The comments on the lack of consistency in her results and her failure to find a formula suggest that she sees her reader as a trusted colleague who will share and appreciate her surprise rather than condemning her.

Textual Aspects

All the texts have features which make them appear, at least to some extent, to be 'school maths'. In all cases the questions posed in the given task provide at least some of the structure for the students' texts through the use of question numbers or copied headings. The strength of this aspect, however, varies between the texts. In the case of Sandra (T), in spite of her decorative presentation, it is reinforced by her extensive use of the wording from the question paper and by the 'question–answer' structure of much of her text. Ellen (T), on the other hand, also uses headings such as *Introduction*, *Formula* and *Extension* which serve to structure the text around the components of 'investigation'.

Apart from Richard's (IT) text, which is consistent in its bare 'school maths' structure, the students' texts each contain some sort of mixture of question-and-answer, narrative, descriptive report and, to a lesser extent, explanation. Several of the texts include short sections of narrative, reporting their own actions, for example: *I found a formula for hexagons quite quickly* (Clive (IT)) and *This time*

I decided to have the units go up in 2's. Eg. I started with a 1 unit rod and straight away put a 3 unit rod on it (Ellen (T)). Extended passages of cohesive writing, however, are relatively rare; Steven's two texts containing more than the others. An examination of such extended passages makes it possible to see how their thematic structure helps to construct various kinds of text. For example, the sequence of existential and topical themes in the following extract (T) appear to construct it as a descriptive report:

> **There is one definite pattern** *that I can pick up.* **The topple pile** *goes up in three and then two and then three and so on.* **This** *is just in the results I have.* **It** *may not be continuous all the way through.*

In the first sentence the existential declaration in the thematic position focuses the reader's attention on the existence of the pattern rather than on the fact that it was 'picked up'. The topical themes in the subsequent sentences maintain the focus on the properties of the pattern rather than on the author's actions. The last section of Steven's (T) text appears to contain an attempt to present an argument, using themes which suggest a train of reasoning:

> **I have taken a look** *at my early results and seen that a 2 unit starter has a topple rod length of 5 units* **so** *if I multiply* *them by 10 I get a starting rod of 20 and a topple rod of 50.*
> **Or alternately I have found** *another formula . . .* **First I tried** *it on an answer I knew . . .* **So now I will try** *this with the result in hand . . .*

The reasoning, however, presents a justification for the chain of actions carried out by the author rather than a logical explanation of the results achieved.

One of the sentences from the extract of Steven's (IT) text whose ideational aspects were discussed earlier presents an interesting example of the way in which a transformation can shift the focus of a statement:

> *Another interesting pattern is the way in which the unit Nos increase when the top length stays the same and just the slant increases.*

By presenting the sentence in this form rather than the unmarked alternative

> *The way in which the unit Nos increase when the top length stays the same and just the slant increases is another interesting pattern.*

the reader's attention is drawn primarily not to the topic of the next section of the text (in which top lengths are kept the same while the slant length is varied) but to the fact that it is another interesting pattern. The focus of the text is thus seen to be the system of patterns described rather than the details of the individual patterns.

The analyses of student texts that I have presented in this chapter are only partial; I have chosen extracts to illustrate the application of the tools described in Chapter 6 and to show some of the similarities and differences between different students' texts that such a linguistic approach can identify and describe. In a few places, I have speculated how some of the features of the writing might be interpreted by teachers and how their assessment of a student might be influenced by the form of his or her text. The next section of this book now turns to a more thorough investigation of the question of how teachers respond to student writing, including an empirical study of teachers reading and assessing the student texts that have been discussed here. The linguistic tools that have been developed will be used both to inform the analysis of teachers' discourse and to shed further light on the aspects of student writing that appear to be significant to the assessment process.

Notes

1   The relationship between the analysis of such texts and knowledge of the discourse in which they are located is dialectical. Some knowledge of the discourse of investigation (as described in Chapter 5 through analysis of published texts *about* investigation) is essential in order to make sense of the texts; analysis of the texts provides further insight into the discourse, which informs the analysis . . .
2   The analyses presented here are illustrative and hence incomplete. Fuller analyses may be found in Morgan (1995).
3   The relatively high level of structure in these tasks is in tension with the value laid on 'openness' and 'student empowerment' in the discourse of investigation. It is, nevertheless, typical of a significant proportion of published investigations and conforms in each case to the Data–Pattern–Generalization stereotypical form (see Chapter 5).
4   The GCSE examination is set at three levels: Foundation, Intermediate and Higher. The grades available at the lower levels are restricted. Decisions about which level a student is to attempt are often not made until the final year of the course. The students whose work is considered here were all entered at Intermediate level (maximum available grade C).
5   Since 1991 some changes have taken place in the setting of coursework tasks by the London examination board. In particular, there seems to be rather less explicit guidance provided in the text of the tasks about the methods to be used. This does not, however, mean that students have more freedom to choose their own methods. Rather, the authority that in 1991 was invested in the text is, by 1994, delegated to the individual teacher who is instructed that he or she

> should suggest to candidates, at the appropriate tiers of entry, that they:
> * make and record any observations and comments;
> * record any results or data;
> * try to work in an ordered, systematic manner
> * . . .   (ULEAC, 1994)

and so on.
6   The rationale for selecting these particular texts and fuller analyses of each of them are given in Morgan (1995).
7   For convenience and clarity, the texts responding to the 'Inner Triangles' task are labelled (IT) and those responding to 'Topples' are labelled (T).

Chapter 8

The Assessment of Investigations and Teacher Assessment

The fact that reports of investigative work written by students are used as assessment instruments in an external examination is one of the most important aspects of the social context within which they are embedded. As well as affecting the types of tasks that may be tackled and the types of responses that may be valued, the formal assessment context must also affect the relationship between the student-authors and their teacher-readers. The choices made (consciously or unconsciously) by student-authors are shaped by this, as are the ways in which teachers read the texts produced; the nature of the assessment must, therefore, play an important part in any attempt to analyse and understand the texts produced by students and the discourse within which they are embedded.

In this chapter, methods of assessing investigative work are discussed in the context of similar new developments in assessment internationally which aim to reflect, if not lead, curriculum development in mathematics education. The relationship between the values of the discourse of investigative work and its assessment is discussed. In particular, the assessment of divergent and creative work and the assessment of the use of mathematical forms of communication are considered.

One of the crucial features of coursework that distinguishes it from other forms of public examination in the UK is the fact that it is assessed by teachers themselves rather than by external examiners. As assessors of a coursework text, teachers assign value to the whole text and to particular features of the text. These values not only serve to assign a grade to an individual student's text and hence to the student herself but also influence the teacher's behaviour in the classroom and, to the extent that they are communicated to students, the writing of the texts themselves. In this chapter, therefore, issues related to teacher assessment are considered, including the question of its consistency and the small amount of research into teachers' assessment practices. As my major focus is the role of the form of the student's written text, I shall also look at the relationship between this and teachers' evaluations of writing.

New Developments in Assessment

Although the particular form of the introduction of investigative tasks and their assessment in the UK has some unique features, there has recently been a considerable amount of international concern with the development of new modes of assessment in mathematics, including assessment of extended projects and of problem solving skills (e.g. Charles and Silver, 1989; Houston, 1993; Lesh and Lamon, 1992; Niss, 1993). In particular, 'performance' or 'authentic' assessment is being discussed: that is, assessment which supposedly either reflects 'good classroom practice' or actually assesses the learning that takes place during everyday classroom activity, often involving teachers directly in the assessment process. While the general interest in assessment across the curriculum may have arisen from political concern with 'standards' and 'accountability' (Eisner, 1993), the concern of many mathematics educators with 'authentic' assessment has been related to the belief, stated very clearly by Burkhardt (1988) and by Ridgway and Schoenfeld (1994), that the success of curriculum development depends on the use of assessment that reflects and supports the aims of the curriculum. This belief has been an explicitly stated motivation in the development of mathematics coursework assessment in the UK at Advanced-level (Sulke, 1990) and undergraduate level (Haines, 1991) as well as at GCSE (Cockcroft, 1982; ULEAC, 1993). In considering assessment led curriculum innovation, such as GCSE coursework, it is necessary to consider the extent to which the assessment-led nature of the innovation may distort its curriculum focused aims.

The development of such new methods of assessment in mathematics has been largely 'intuitive' (Collis, 1992), and, Ruthven argues, once the new methods become established, they become 'cocooned in a seductive technical apparatus based on implausibly rational models of knowledge and learning' (Ruthven, 1994, p. 449).[1] Inadequately theorized assessment methods and practices thus come to define the curriculum. There are a number of tensions and contradictions between the espoused aims of curriculum developments and the consequences of assessment practices. For example, Galbraith (1993) argues that the constructivist views of the nature of learning and problem solving that have driven curriculum reform are incompatible with the view that the assessment of open-ended problems can provide a measure of problem solving ability. Moreover, he rejects the generally accepted idea that external assessment requirements should be used to influence the curriculum on the grounds that, viewed from a critical perspective, it is

> ultimately disempowering to teachers in impeding the growth of full professional responsibility, and to students in making their choices and interests irrelevant. (p. 82)

This contention calls into question the extent to which investigations, institutionalized through the GCSE examination, can fulfil the ideal of student empowerment current in the investigation discourse described in Chapter 5.

Methods of Assessing Investigative Work

As teacher assessment of coursework at GCSE was about to be introduced, Foxman et al. (1986) reported on a debate comparing different approaches to the assessment of investigative work. They identified three approaches which they label: 'Mathematical process criteria', 'Judgment on autonomous merit' and 'Simple focusing categories'. These parallel the 'analytic', 'general impression' and 'focused holistic' approaches to assessing problem solving identified by Lester and Kroll (1990). Most of the GCSE examination boards initially developed generic 'mathematical process criteria' reflecting heuristic models of problem solving and making no distinction between the criteria to be applied to different tasks. In the case of the London examination board, the set of criteria was formulated into 'grade descriptions' of work at three different levels; for example, a student gaining a grade A would be expected to demonstrate, among other things, that she 'chooses efficient strategies' and 'orders the information systematically and controls the variables' (ULEAC, 1993, p. 62). Wiliam (1994) identifies two major problems with such assessment schemes. Firstly, they take no account of the difficulty of the mathematics involved in a given problem; for example, the criterion 'formulates general rules' makes no distinction between the formulation of a simple linear rule and one involving much more complex relationships. Secondly, the heuristic model behind the criteria defines a progression through the task; where a student's work diverges from the defined progression it becomes difficult to assess. In consequence, the tasks offered to students have become stereotyped because:

> it appears that teachers have 'played safe', and used only coursework tasks that conform to the model of progression and the particular calibration implicit in the generic descriptors. (p. 53)

In response to the difficulties that teachers experienced in applying such generic criteria, the London examination board also issue task specific 'performance indicators' exemplifying the typical outcomes of a given task for students at each grade level. For example, for a student to gain a grade B for the investigation 'Inner Triangles' the teacher-assessor is advised to 'Look specifically for . . . recognition that top length − bottom length = slant height' (LEAG, 1991, p. 80). In spite of statements from the examination board that alternative outcomes may be equally valid and should be assessed as such, Wiliam, drawing on his experience of work with teachers during the development of the Graded Achievement in Mathematics (GAIM) scheme, claims that:

> by delineating particular 'canonical' responses, the task-specific schemes appear to lead teachers to direct students towards approaches that yield more easily 'assessable' responses. (1994, p. 54)

The characteristics of the assessment scheme are thus in conflict with some of the stated aims of the curriculum development they are supposed to support, in particular the aim of valuing students' individual, alternative and creative responses.

Assessing Creativity

As was seen in Chapter 5, the discourse of investigations values diversity and creativity. These are not, however, traditionally valued by assessment practices in mathematics (Galbraith, 1993) and there are problems for teachers in attempting to come to terms with them. For example, concern is expressed by Tall (1990) as he relates an anecdote about a boy whose coursework reporting his 'discovery' of a method of trisecting an angle was rejected by his teacher-assessor; the impossibility of the conclusion apparently overshadowed the value of the mathematical thinking that had gone into the project. Before the introduction of GCSE coursework, Haylock suggested that mathematics teachers' attempts to promote systematic approaches had produced the 'dull, predictable and narrow' responses that children provided to his questions seeking to measure divergent production (1985, p. 550) while the tension between the values placed on accuracy and on creativity gave rise to conflict for the assessor. As Lester and Kroll point out, having reviewed a number of alternative schemes for assessing students' problem solving behaviour, none adequately measure a student's 'willingness to take risks' (Lester and Kroll, 1990, p. 69).

Indeed, valuing and encouraging risk taking seem antithetical to the desire for reliability in teacher assessments. Even where this tension has been recognized, there seems to have been little attempt at a reconciliation. For example, Ahmed and Bufton addressing teachers beginning to use investigative work, comment:

> Whilst we like and strive to be different, we like and strive for our pupils to be 'the same' in their mathematical development and thinking. Once we recognise this conflict we can accept that some pupils will indeed respond differently and surprisingly to our open ended starters. (Ahmed and Bufton, undated, p. 6)

They do not suggest how such acceptance should be achieved and valued. In reporting their project on the development of mathematical modelling skills, Tanner and Jones (1994) also deny that variety of outcomes is a serious problem for assessors, claiming that:

> Good solutions are 'reliably recognizable' (Scriven, 1980). Mathematicians work to a set of assumptions, often unstated, related to generality, economy and elegance. Teaching students mathematics must include acculturation into these assumptions. (p. 422)

Although the authors recognize that there are differences between the traditional culture of the mathematics classroom and the mathematical culture they describe, they again do not address the question of the acculturation of the teachers themselves, perhaps assuming that this is merely a question of will on their part. What teachers 'reliably recognize' as good solutions must be constrained by their knowledge and experience of the examination system and of school mathematics as well as by their own beliefs about mathematics (which do not necessarily coincide with the assumptions listed by Tanner and Jones).

While the valuing of creativity is a relatively new development in school mathematics, it has a longer tradition in some other subject areas. Here too, however, its assessment is not unproblematic, as may be seen in considering a report by

Dixon and Brown (1985) on teachers' and examiners' ratings and comments on the 'response to literature' aspect of 'A' level English students' coursework and examination scripts. The value placed on originality (here labelled 'personal involvement' and 'imagination') is made explicit:

> when received ideas are substituted for personal involvement, and uninspired and routine writing sets aside the imaginative experience, there are solid grounds for refusing a B grade mark — or possibly even a pass — to such work. (p. 18)

Yet an examination of the implicit assessment criteria revealed in the assessors' comments shows that, while students were condemned for following their teacher's opinions (although the assessors had been provided with no evidence about the teaching that may have occurred), they were praised for showing understanding of the 'intention' of the author whose work they were discussing. This suggests that only those 'personal' responses which coincided with the interpretations of the assessor would be valued. Clearly, as Haylock (1987) points out, 'appropriateness' is also required in order to validate creative production.

In the context of GCSE as a nationally recognized and externally moderated examination, it is not surprising that teachers should be concerned that their assessments should be seen to be consistent with those of others. This concern has given rise to the deliberate construction of consensus through the publication of performance indicators and assessment schemes, through in-service training and school level collaboration, and through the process of official moderation by external examiners. This process may, however, serve more to ensure that teachers advise students towards standard responses than to help teachers to know how to value creative ones; as Pike and Murray (1991) are pleased to report: 'problems with rogue strands, off beat ideas etc . . . soon disappear' (p. 33) when teachers have been involved in such in-service activities. While there is evidence that supports the view that mathematics teachers are remarkably consistent in their assessments of coursework, there does not appear to have been any investigation either of the extent of 'original' content in students' coursework texts or of teachers' assessment practices when faced with work that they perceive as unusual. In Chapter 11 I will describe the results of my own attempt to investigate teachers' responses to unanticipated features of students' work.

The Assessment of 'Mathematical Communication'

Although the procedures and sets of criteria for the assessment of investigative work vary between the various GCSE examination boards, all of them include some assessment of 'communication'. The actual nature of the forms of communication is specified to varying extents by the different boards. Figure 8.1 shows the parts of the London board's grade descriptions that refer to the forms of communication expected to be used by students; this is not untypical of the examination boards.

Figure 8.1: Forms of mathematical communication expected of students by the London examination board (extracts from ULEAC, 1993, p. 16)

At grade F:	Produces some sketches and graphs and, where appropriate, computer output. Able to make limited use of mathematical terms.
At grade C:	Uses an adequate range of mathematical language and symbols, including appropriate visual forms and, where appropriate, computer output. Uses some mathematical words relevant to the task and is generally familiar with the vocabulary of Level 1.
At grade A:	Where appropriate, makes use of symbols when generalizing. Selects the most appropriate methods for communicating results. Makes effective use of a range of mathematical language and notation, diagrams, charts and, where appropriate, computer output.

The picture of the nature of mathematical communication constructed by such assessment criteria is a collection of discrete components: vocabulary, algebraic symbolism, forms of visual representation such as tables, graphs, etc. While it is clear from other criteria that extended writing is expected, for example, the student awarded a grade A: 'Communicates clearly the work undertaken giving reasons for the strategies used and explaining some assumptions made', the characteristics of writing that provides reasons and explains assumptions are not specified. As was seen in Chapter 2, this does not provide an adequate description; in particular, it fails to take account of higher level characteristics of a mathematical text, for example, the ways in which arguments are formed. This omission is consistent with Spencer et al.'s (1983) finding that teachers in curriculum areas other than English tend to associate the language of their subject only with its specialist vocabulary rather than with its stylistic aspects. Similarly, Langer and Applebee (1987) report that:

> While teachers can easily recognize (and reward) correct information, they have more trouble articulating the rhetoric or the rules of evidence that govern effective argument within their particular discipline. (p. 149)

Such a lack of explicit knowledge of the range of features that characterize mathematical forms of communication within the investigation report genre does not necessarily mean that teachers are unable to recognize examples and judge them to be 'appropriate'. In the context of assessment of students' journal writing, Waywood (1994) claimed that teachers reading students' mathematical journals were able to 'intuitively' distinguish between different types of writing (recount, summary, dialogue) and to value them differently 'even though they couldn't articulate what stimulated the recognition' (p. 332). Appeal to teacher intuition, however, while contributing to the likelihood that teacher assessment of communication in mathematics will be consistent, does not provide any help for the student who does not share such intuition and needs help to acquire the language skills necessary to produce the more highly valued forms of text.

Teacher Assessment

In spite of the recent increased international interest in 'authentic' or 'performance' assessment, including assessment carried out by teachers, there has been very little research into its practical implications. Since the introduction of the UK National Curriculum, there has been some increase, particularly at the primary level. This appears to have been motivated largely by the novelty of the introduction of 'high stakes' assessment at this level and by a perception that such assessment is likely to be problematic for primary teachers, perhaps because of perceived tensions between the values inherent in such assessment and the 'child centred' culture of many primary teachers (Gipps et al., 1995). As Torrance (1995) points out in discussing the introduction of GCSE, secondary teachers:

> drew on their previous experience and understanding of what assessment 'is' — their structure of belief about what constitutes assessment and what its purpose is — in order to make sense of the changes and make decisions about how they should implement them. (p. 50)

Because secondary teachers were already involved in some aspects of examination practice, the extension of their involvement to include a greater degree of teacher assessment may have been accommodated more easily. The process of assessment itself appears generally not to be seen as problematic at the secondary level, although concern has been expressed about the integration (or lack of integration) of assessment tasks into the classroom.

The Creation of Consensus in Assessment of Investigative Work

There has been some concern expressed about the validity of current methods of assessing investigative work in mathematics, particularly about the extent to which assessment of the written product alone provides a true and full record of the student's mathematical achievement (Bloomfield, 1987; MacNamara and Roper, 1992a; 1992b; Tanner and Jones, 1994). In practice, however, more attention has been paid to the question of reliability. The measure of the success of a scheme for teacher assessment appears to be taken to be the extent to which teachers arrive at the same judgment and the achievement of consensus among assessors is taken as a sign that the judgments themselves are in some sense 'objective' (as for example in Hoge and Colardarci's (1989) review of research into the 'accuracy' of teacher assessment) or that the assessment scheme 'reflects those values of the intellectual community from which the tasks were derived' (Haines and Izard, 1994, p. 379). Such reliability does not, however, guarantee that an objective statement of those values is possible.

The training in the assessment of mathematics coursework provided for teachers at the time of the introduction of GCSE consisted largely of meetings at which groups of teachers attempted to achieve agreement in their assessments of pieces of students' work. Evidence of the success of this process in achieving consistent marking is largely anecdotal (e.g. Banwell, 1987; Pike and Murray, 1991; Wiliam, 1993), though Gill (1993) provides an account of work with student teachers which suggests that, through working in groups, even inexperienced assessors can very rapidly come to close agreement about the level of investigative and practical work. Apart from the consensus achieved through the communal development of 'standards', the official process of moderation by the external authority of the examination boards must also have contributed to the development of teachers' assessment practices. Teacher assessment in English has a much longer tradition, using similar methods to induct teachers into the formation of holistic judgments of students' work, and here there is considerable evidence of consistency (e.g. Britton, Martin and Rosen, 1966; Cooper, 1977).

In spite of the 'objective' appearance of the use of an assessment scheme based on either generic criteria or task-specific performance indicators, the practical application of the scheme relies on the existence of a consensus among the assessors about their meaning; such a consensus is constructed socially. Gill (1993) and Ruthven (1987; 1995) suggest that it is based on the application of a general construct of 'level' or 'ability' rather than on the use of detailed criteria; indeed, the consensus arrived at by Gill's student teachers was achieved without access to any stated criteria. Roper and MacNamara (1993) found that groups of secondary teachers and of primary teachers assessing the mathematical processes in the same pieces of work, using the same set of criteria (National Curriculum Attainment Target 1), achieved largely consistent assessments within each phase but differed considerably across phases. This suggests that the constructs of 'level' of secondary and of primary teachers have been developed independently and are determined more by group membership than by any 'objective' meaning that might be attached to the criteria.

An examination of the wording of the generic criteria issued by the London examination board (ULEAC, 1993) reveals one significant feature to be the frequent use of subjective qualifiers. In the description of a grade A candidate, 'clear' and 'appropriate' each occur four times with 'relevant' occurring twice; for grade C again 'appropriate' is used several times together with 'clear' and 'adequate', while for grade F the candidate's work is described as 'fairly clear' and 'not always relevant'. The application of such terms can only be understood in a relative way — dependent on the social context and the particular audience reading the student's work. Their undefined character supports the contention that the criteria describe a general construct of what constitutes a good piece of work or a poor piece of work rather than defining its separate properties. The use of such 'transcendental signifiers', by reserving any determination of their meaning to those in authority (teachers and examiners), excludes some students from access to the means of fulfilling the criteria (Cherryholmes, 1988).[2] One of my aims in subsequent chapters of this book is to develop a more explicit understanding of what such terms might mean in practice.

Research on Teachers' Assessment Practices

While the concern with reliability addressed in the previous section focuses largely on the outcomes of teachers' assessment activity, my concern is more with the nature of the activity itself — the ways in which teachers make sense of students' texts rather than the grades they allocate to them. Very little detailed consideration has been paid to teachers' assessment practices. Indeed, this was one of the issues raised by Gipps (1992) and Torrance (1992) in their call for research to provide foundations for the implementation of the National Curriculum assessment procedures. Radnor and Shaw (1995) note that publications related to the moderation of GCSE coursework have not drawn upon 'detailed fieldwork with teachers and schools' (p. 127) and thus have provided little insight into the processes.

The development of the assessment of GCSE coursework and of the National Curriculum Attainment Target 1 in mathematics appears to have been based on the premise that the assessment of mathematical processes, while not necessarily easy, is not problematic. An ethnographic study of teacher assessment of a comparable component of the English curriculum (Filer, 1993) suggests, however, that there are problems related to teacher assessment of students' processes. Although this study was located in the primary school, the issues raised are nevertheless relevant to teacher assessment of processes at all levels. Filer presents a case study of an infant teacher assessing children's writing processes (including such aspects as 'organization' and 'imaginativeness of expression'). Her analysis suggests that this assessment was strongly influenced by the 'knowledge content' of the writing although this influence was not acknowledged by the teacher or the assessment scheme. The teacher displayed strong expectations about the content of the writing and, in practice, only accepted deviations from the stereotyped content from those children who were capable of writing clearly and independently. It was thus impossible for her to assess criteria such as 'imaginativeness of expression' for those children whose technical skills were less, in spite of the fact that such skills were supposedly assessed separately. When considering this analysis in relation to the assessment of mathematics coursework, it suggests that both 'content' and the technical aspects of the writing may affect teachers' assessments of a student's level of achievement in the 'processes' that are the official subject of the assessment. In particular, deviations from the expected response may be less likely to be valued when the student has poor language skills or is perceived to be of 'low ability'.

A Belgian study of teacher behaviour, while set in a classroom context very different from that involved in investigative work, raises some issues that are of interest in considering teachers' assessment practices in general. Rapaille's (1986) analysis of high school mathematics teachers' assessment processes in 'natural' conditions (through recording 'thinking aloud') makes use of a model of teacher assessment behaviour that involves the use of a 'norm product' and a set of 'possible products' that might arise from the work of a given group of pupils on a given task. While the unique nature of Rapaille's 'norm product' appears inappropriate in a context in which alternative products may be equally valid and creativity is valued, Miller suggests a similar, more relevant, concept in considering teachers' reading of student writing in English:

> Typically, a teacher anticipates seeing 'what they did' with the assignment . . . At the same time that the teacher has imagined intentions for the text, the teacher also

> has realistic doubts that these intentions will be fulfilled ... The teacher who is reading begins, then, with a semi-Platonic model: Each text to be read is conceived of as only a shadow of the Ideal text, but any embodiment of the Ideal in practice would be a surprise to the teacher. (Miller, 1982, cited in Gilbert, 1989)

The characteristics of any such 'Ideal text' in mathematics teachers' practice in respect to investigations are explored in later chapters of this book.

Having determined the norm product for a question in a mathematics test and broken it down into its various components, Rapaille analyses a teacher's treatment of those components of students' answers which differed from the norm. Some differences were observed between the same teacher's treatment of similar divergent components of answers by different pupils and Rapaille's analysis of the teacher's commentary suggests that such differences are the result of 'external' factors, including the influence of the student's answers to previous questions.

The influence of 'external' factors on the teacher's treatment of student deviations from the norm is also remarked by Broadfoot (1995) in her study of primary teachers' administration of the National Curriculum Standard Attainment Tasks (SATs). As well as expressing concern about the lack of standardization in the context in which the tasks were carried out and in the amount of help provided, Broadfoot provides examples of teachers who interpreted the level criteria differently according to their expectations of particular pupils, effectively making the supposedly 'standard' test results match their own previous assessment of the pupil. It appears again that the teachers were making use of a general construct of ability (see also Abbott et al., 1994), though the question of how their previous assessments were arrived at is not considered. One explanation for this practice of reinterpreting the criteria to fit the child's perceived level is teachers' 'perfectly understandable' wish 'to do the best for their own candidates' (Radnor and Shaw, 1995, p. 141). Several authors comment on the tensions that this wish creates for teachers involved in 'high stakes' assessment procedures, both in the administration and in the assessment of the work. Scott (1991) and Paechter (1995) report variations in practice between teachers and between schools in the amount of support provided to secondary school pupils while carrying out school-based assessment tasks. Paechter, in a study of the first Standard Assessment Tasks (SATs) for Technology, remarks on the conflicts that teachers experienced between their roles as teacher and as examiner, in particular, the divergence between the concept of being 'fair' to the pupils and that of administering a 'fair' test. These conflicting roles and divergent concepts of 'fairness' are likely also to play a role in teachers' terminal assessment practices.

In studying teachers' assessment practice, however 'reliable' the results it cannot be assumed that teachers will all use the same methods or share the same attitudes towards the assessment process. In a study of primary teachers' assessment of their pupils' National Curriculum levels, Gipps et al. (1995) analysed teachers' self-reports of their practice to categorize three different types of teacher: 'intuitives', 'evidence gatherers' and 'systematic planners'. There is no evidence suggesting that such different practices might result in different summative assessments of individual students' performance and, as more direct methods of gaining access to the teachers' actual practice were not used, these categories may perhaps only be taken as indicating different sets of attitudes towards assessment. The very different procedures involved in the administration of coursework assessment at GCSE and the more general cultural differences between primary and secondary schools and teachers mean that the specific categories defined by Gipps et al. are unlikely to be applicable in the context of the present study. Nevertheless, their analysis does point to the importance of recognizing the complexity of teachers' assessment practices and the possibility of substantial differences both between individuals and between groups of teachers.

The Relationship between Form and Content in Teacher Assessment

While the ability to use 'appropriate' forms of mathematical communication is one of the criteria applied in the assessment of coursework, it is generally assumed that it is both possible and desirable to apply the other criteria (related to, for example, problem solving strategies or the choice and accurate use of mathematical techniques) independently of the quality of the writing. This separation of 'form' from 'content' is based on an assumption that writing is transparent in conveying the writer's meanings to the reader and that the meanings that are so conveyed are concerned only with the explicit subject matter of the assessment task. Such an assumption, however, is challenged by theories of communication which take into account the social context of the interaction between writer, reader and text and by research into teachers' assessment of student writing.

The relationship between the forms of language used and the meanings that are read from a text is discussed by Hodge and Kress (1993), who stress that language conveys messages about the social situation and, drawing on Bernstein, that different social classes have differentiated access to certain forms of language. Readers (and listeners) make judgments about writers (and speakers), mediated through expectations of class, which become judgments about intelligence, character, grasp of subject matter etc. Kress (1990) exemplifies the effect of this in an educational context through his analysis of two economics essays awarded very different marks by the teacher. While both cover the same areas of 'content' without error, the language of one shows less control over conventional forms of academic argument and was thus assessed to show less control of the subject matter. Conversely, because of the asymmetrical relationship between student and teacher-assessor, forms of language that might in other social settings convey authority on the part of the writer may not be interpreted as such in the assessment situation.

Sociological and sociolinguistic studies of the discourse of classrooms (e.g. Cazden, 1988; Edwards and Mercer, 1987; Mehan, 1979) have indicated the influence of the form of children's language on the teacher's acceptance of the correctness, value and appropriateness of the utterance. These studies have been primarily concerned with oral discourse but the conclusion that, in order to be judged positively, students' responses need to be both 'academically correct and interactionally appropriate' (Mehan, 1979, p. 133) is equally applicable to written discourse.

Teachers also have expectations for writing that students must fulfil in order to be judged to be successful both in their control of language and in their grasp of the subject matter. Such 'ground rules' (Sheeran and Barnes, 1991) for school writing vary both between curriculum areas and between different contexts and tasks within a given subject area, and, as Sheeran and Barnes point out, are not always made explicitly available to students.

Much of the research into the ways in which teachers assess written work has focused on teachers of English. While the interests of English teachers in relation to the assessment of student writing are clearly different from those of teachers of other subjects, the findings do point to the difficulty of separating judgments of content from those related to form, even for those teachers who might be expected to have more sophisticated knowledge about language. When forming a holistic judgment of students' essays, Harris (1977) found that, although the teachers studied stated that their most important and frequently used assessment criteria were related to the quality of the content and organization of the essays, they were in practice strongly influenced by mechanics (i.e. spelling, punctuation) and word usage. When an essay that had been rated above average in all areas except organization was changed in order to make the diction, sentence structure and mechanics below average, Harris reports that the teacher-assessors 'could see no value in the theme at all, and the content was also rated below average' (p. 18). The research findings in general are not, however, consistent in discerning the relative weights given by teachers to the various aspects of the texts. For example, Stewart et al. (Stewart and Grobe, 1979; Stewart and Leaman, 1983) found teachers to be more influenced by mechanical accuracy than by 'syntactic maturity', and Cavallero (1991) found mechanics and organization to be more influential than content or vocabulary, while Freedman (1979) found mechanics and sentence structure to be less important than content and organization. Similarly apparently contradictory and inconclusive results have been reported in relation to the influence of handwriting on the marking of English examination papers and essays (Briggs, 1980; Massey, 1983; Soloff, 1973). One of the problems with interpreting such research lies in the fact that the aspects of the form of the student texts considered are at a level of generality which does not allow any consideration of the relationships between form and meaning. A simple rating of either the whole text or of its components thus provides little indication of the sorts of meanings that the teacher-reader may be constructing from the text.

An experimental study with English teachers at high school and college level by Hake and Williams (1981), however, by focusing on a single aspect of style, makes it possible to speculate about the reasons for teachers' preferences. Essays were constructed to vary only in their use of a nominal or a verbal expression of the 'same' propositions. Hake and Williams report that:

> the syntactic complexity of a nominal paper seemed sufficient to trigger judgments of a paper's profundity and of the superiority of its logic and organisation . . . graders preferred the nominal style so strongly that it appears to have influenced their discursive judgments about other, more general components of the essay (p. 437)

although, interestingly, the teachers of the most senior students appeared to be negatively influenced by a nominal style when it was used in an otherwise generally lower quality paper, suggesting that weaker students 'will be punished for acquiring a visible surface characteristic of the prose that is often most highly rewarded' (p. 440).

While Hake and Williams suggest that it is the 'syntactic complexity' of the nominal style that influences judgments about content and organization, more general indicators of complexity (Stewart and Grobe, 1979; Stewart and Leaman, 1983) do not appear to have had similar effects. An alternative explanation might take into account the conventions of academic writing which generally expect the impersonal style that is achieved through the use of nominalizations. Those students who comply with the conventions may be considered to have grasped not only the genre but also the content, particularly by those teacher-readers labelled by Hake and Williams as 'less sophisticated'. Anderson's (1988) studies of the reading of academic scientific articles also found that papers which had been rewritten in 'simpler' language were judged to be reporting less valuable research. Anderson concludes that:

> Although we assume that the complexity of a text is related to the complexity of the subject matter, that is to do with the ideational function, we may find that the over-elaborate style is really to do with the interpersonal function. (p. 156)

In a school setting, in contrast, Gilbert (1989) citing a study by Freedman in which teachers had been asked to assess essays written by 'professional writers' believing them to have been written by students, notes that the teachers 'reacted badly' to aspects of the professionals' essays, such as the use of nominalizations, which served to distance the author from the text or to express authority and confidence (p. 51). Each of these studies is based within a particular social context with its accompanying conventions and relationships between writers and readers. While their findings may be taken as an indication that the use of a nominal style or other complex syntactic forms is likely to be influential in the ways in which teachers assess a student's text, the precise nature of that influence (both the value and the meanings associated with the various forms) is likely to vary between contexts.

The importance of considering the context in which the text is read and judged is clear in a study by Hayes et al. (1992) which found that groups of teachers and of students formed different opinions about the 'personality' of the writers of essays. Some texts which were condemned by teachers for displaying negative character traits such as 'pretentious' were praised by students as 'creative'. While there was consistency within each of the two groups, the finding that they differed in their judgments suggests that, although both were aware of the audience and purposes for which the essays had been written (college admission), the resources for judging the appropriateness of the text were not shared. While Hayes et al. do not provide any analysis of the particular features of the texts that were associated with the various character traits, their study points to the potential significance to the assessment process of interpersonal aspects of texts as well as to a possible mismatch between teacher and student expectations and perceptions of those interpersonal aspects.

The studies discussed above have all been concerned with 'general purpose' writing in which a holistic judgment of the quality of the essay has been made. The specific 'content' of the writing in such a context, while clearly contributing to the teachers' judgments, is probably not as great a concern for the teachers as it would be in writing based within other curriculum areas. Studies of the assessment of written work in science, however, suggest that features of the form of students' writing also contribute to teachers evaluation of the writers' level of scientific understanding. Wade and Wood (1979) look in some detail at the writing on the same two science tasks by two 12–13-year-old boys, one judged by his teacher to be 'high ability' and the other 'low ability', the judgments being made largely on the basis of written work. The authors identify substantial differences between the language used by the two students. The 'high ability' boy's writing is neat and technically accurate; it also makes use of cohesive devices ('this is because', 'then you . . .') to create a coherent text. The 'low ability' boy's work, on the other hand, is scruffy with many errors in spelling, punctuation and the use of capital letters. When considering the content of the two texts, however, Wade and Wood point out that the 'high ability' boy:

> is not thinking clearly: 'When a candle is burning in air it keeps lit until the candle goes out' is hardly an explanation of anything. 'This is because the heat given from the candle goes to the water out and pushed in the jar' is confused and does not make the link with using up part of the air. (p. 136)

They claim that there is evidence that the 'lower ability' boy's scientific understanding is actually better in some respects:

> 'Chlorophyll comse out of the leeF and turns the alcohol turns green' is more perceptive than 'The alcohol went dark greenish colour'. (p. 137)

They suggest that the student with poor language skills is 'doubly penalized'. Not only is he not given credit for scientific understanding, but the feedback provided by his teacher, 'Use sentences', refers only to his language use without giving him the specific help he needs to use punctuation more effectively. It would appear that the teacher is strongly influenced by the linguistic features of the text in forming an impression of its scientific value.

Studies by Spear (1984, 1989) of the influence of the gender of student writers on science teachers' judgments suggest not only that teachers claim to be able to recognize a writer's gender from qualities of their writing but also that the value placed on the content matter of a text may vary according to whether it is attributed to a boy or to a girl. While science teachers ascribe a number of apparently positive qualities to girls' written work (e.g. neatness, care, quality of language) these were often interpreted negatively in relation to their grasp of the subject matter.

The written work of girls is principally described as being 'neat', 'well presented' and 'thorough'. Girls obviously 'try hard' and 'are conscientious'. Although all these valuations are positive, they refer to behavioural traits rather than to mental ones. By focusing upon the conscientiousness of girls, teachers seem to overlook or devalue the actual content of girls' work. The reverse tends to happen when boys' work is considered. Teachers prefer to focus upon boys' innate cognitive abilities and to excuse their inferior behavioural traits. (Spear, 1989, p. 276)

Taking into account Spear's earlier (1984) finding that teachers generally valued the same text more highly if it was attributed to a boy than if it was attributed to a girl, this suggests that features such as neatness, presentation and length of the text may be interpreted differently when they occur in boys' or in girls' texts. Spear suggests that the reported differences are associated with gender differences in participation and achievement in science and in perceptions of aptitude and interest in the subject. In different subject areas the effects may vary, although patterns of participation and perception of interest in mathematics may be similar to those in science. These findings again indicate the complexity of the contextual factors that must be taken into account when interpreting teachers' readings of student texts.

Very little attention has been paid to mathematics teachers' assessment of students' written work, perhaps because of the extent of the dominant paradigm of assessment which assumes that answers in mathematics are unambiguously right or wrong. One exception, looking at students' work in a traditional style of 'problem solving' in the US, is a study by Flener and Reedy (1990) which found that some teachers were unwilling to accept answers that were expressed in unconventional forms, even rejecting an answer because it used x rather than t as a variable name in a time–distance problem. New developments in assessment which involve more open problems have not, on the whole, addressed the issue of the more diverse responses from students. This neglect is questioned by Collis (1992), who, in critiquing new approaches to assessment in the US, provides examples of students' writing in response to an open question in the innovative California Assessment Program. Students were asked to give exact descriptions of figures that would allow them to be drawn accurately by an imaginary audience ('talking to a student in your class on the telephone'). While many students responded with answers in a 'non-mathematical' genre that nevertheless fulfilled the requirement for exactness, the assessment criteria only allowed credit to be given to those students who had given answers which used technical mathematical terminology to describe the figures. Collis identifies a mismatch between the student expectations (arising from the wording of the problem) and the expectations of the examiners, and suggests that the type of response expected by the examiners should be indicated more clearly to the students. This critique, however, while recognizing that different styles of writing may be produced by students and may be equally effective or acceptable in some contexts, nevertheless still assumes that a more precise statement of the problem or a different set of assessment criteria would ensure that valid assessments of students' mathematical understanding would be achieved.

It seems that teachers' judgments are largely formed in an 'intuitive' way. The 'intuition' is formed within a social context in which teachers come to share certain expectations of students' work. These expectations are, however, shared through practice rather than through explicit statements; even where criteria are applied, the use of 'appropriateness' as an assessment criterion reserves knowledge of the meaning of the criterion to those who already know, without providing guidance for the student who does not already share the teacher's expectations — this is likely to disadvantage some groups of students. This notion of 'appropriateness' in relation to the assessment of investigative work needs to be explored. In particular, what is the nature of 'appropriate' forms of mathematical communication? The model of the nature of mathematical language explicitly acknowledged by the examination boards and by teachers is largely restricted to a set of specialist vocabulary and visual forms which does not provide an adequate description.

The 'common sense' view of assessment assumes that it is possible to identify unambiguously and hence evaluate objectively the object of the assessment. There are, however, difficulties in disentangling the content of a text from its form or, where (as in mathematics coursework) the object of assessment is the student's processes, the processes used from the content knowledge and skills. These difficulties are not solely practical, although there is substantial evidence that teachers' assessments are influenced by features of student's work that are not the explicitly stated object of assessment; there are also logical problems in attempting to separate the form of a text from its meaning. While some features of students' writing have been identified that appear to influence teachers' judgments, the context dependent nature of the reading of such features must, however, be recognized; what is valued in one context may be deemed inappropriate in another. The next section of this book explores in more detail the ways in which teachers form their judgments.

Notes

1   A possible exception to this is the development of some aspects of the assessment related to the 'Realistic Mathematics Education' curriculum development in the Netherlands (van den Heuvel-Panhuizen, 1996). The more systematic approach adopted here may have arisen because of the principled opposition of some of those involved in the curriculum development (including, in particular, Freudenthal) to any kind of formal assessment.

2   As Bourdieu (1974) contends:

> the more vaguely what [examinations] ask for is defined, whether it be by a question of knowledge or of presentation, and the less specific the criteria adopted by the examiners, the more they favour the privileged. (p. 40)

There is indeed some evidence that the introduction of coursework across the curriculum has widened the gap between groups of students with high and low achievement (Abrams, 1991). As Linn et al. (1991) point out, the evaluation of assessment methods needs to (but usually does not) include consideration of the intended and unintended consequences for the curriculum and for individuals and groups.

Chapter 9

Investigating Teachers Reading Coursework

The written texts produced by students do not stand alone as independent phenomena. They are situated within the wider context of the activities of students, teachers, external moderators, and other interested parties. The interactions between these participants and their interactions with oral and written texts as producers (speakers/writers) and as consumers (hearers/readers) all play a role in constituting the discourse of GCSE investigative mathematics. One of the most significant aspects of this discourse is the fact that coursework forms part of a summative, externally validated examination. The results of this examination can have significant consequences for teachers' professional standing as well as for individual students' future educational and employment opportunities and the relationships between the participants in the discourse are strongly influenced by this examination context. Recognition of these factors must be central to any attempt to understand the texts produced by students. In particular, the teacher, who reads the students' texts and has the primary responsibility for assessing them, plays a crucial role in this context. In order to gain insight into the context in which students' investigation reports are situated, I have therefore sought to explore, through interviews with teachers experienced in working with students undertaking GCSE coursework, the discourse of the assessment of coursework in general as well as teachers' specific practices in reading selected coursework texts. Those features of students' written texts which were identified as significant in this assessment process will be considered in Chapter 10. In this chapter I discuss the ways in which these interviews illuminated the teachers' roles as reader and assessor.

The Sample of Teachers

In all, eleven teachers from six schools were interviewed. It is clear that this small group of teachers may in no sense be considered a representative sample. They were, as a group, relatively highly experienced both in terms of their years of teaching and in terms of their levels of responsibility within both school and department. They were more than usually experienced with the examination of coursework, all but two having been involved with this before it became compulsory. Their willingness to be interviewed also suggests a degree of interest and commitment to coursework, although several also expressed doubts about their own expertise.

Having said this, the study of experienced teachers is likely to identify more stable practices and their professional status may be influential in shaping the practices of their less experienced colleagues. I do not claim to make any universal generalizations on the basis of the data collected from these interviews. Rather, my intention is to describe a range of practices and to point to areas of tension and conflict within the discourse of coursework, both between different teachers and within individuals engaged in reading and assessing coursework texts.

Design of the Teacher Interviews

In order to investigate the ways in which teachers read students' written work and respond to its various features I could not rely solely on the teachers' self-reporting of their practices. Not only were such reports unlikely to reflect practice fully or accurately but it also seemed unlikely that they would address the specific issues I was interested in. In particular, my early exploratory discussions with teachers suggested to me that most of them did not appear to have access to ways of describing features of students' texts, even when these might have a concrete effect upon their reading practices. For example, both a narrative of mental processes and a narrative of material actions were likely to be described merely as 'telling what was done'. Teachers' responses to the question 'What is "good" communication in coursework?' tended to list structural features, such as 'introduction', 'findings', 'explanation' and 'conclusion', and highly visible non-verbal features, such as tables, graphs and diagrams. In general, however, teachers seemed able to give little indication of the form that features such as 'explanation' or 'findings' might take, other than that they should be 'well presented' or 'clear'. The teachers' responses (however inadequate) are, of course, significant in that they form part of what appears to be 'common sense' teacher talk and are likely to reflect the sort of advice and feedback that is provided to students, but descriptors such as 'clear' do not help a novice or an outsider to understand what is actually expected; they are unanalysed 'transcendental signifieds' which, by assuming (without necessary justification) that all participants share a common understanding of their meaning, serve to maintain teachers' authority within the discourse (Cherryholmes, 1988). In order to attempt to analyse such 'common sense' terms I decided that it was necessary to examine teachers' responses to concrete examples of students' writing as well as their self-reports of their assessment practices.

Each teacher's interview was based on one of the two coursework tasks: 'Inner Triangles' or 'Topples' described in Chapter 7. The first of these may be considered to be a 'pure' investigation, while the second involves use of practical equipment and was designated a 'practical task' by the examination board. The use of these contrasting tasks provides the opportunity to identify which aspects of the teachers' reading practices vary between the two tasks, building up a picture of a complex genre, and which are common to both and may thus be part of a general coursework practice. The three student texts for each of the tasks discussed in Chapter 7 were read and assessed during the interviews. Using these complete authentic student texts meant that there were inevitably many complex textual features that could not be 'controlled'. Some previous research using 'discourse based' interviews (Herrington, 1985; Odell and Goswami, 1982) has sought to control the features that might be considered by constructing rather than using authentic texts. I felt, however, that the length and complexity of coursework texts would make it impossible to isolate the influence of specific features without oversimplification and without overdetermination of the teachers' possible responses through my own preconceptions. I therefore decided to use authentic texts to allow a fuller exploration of teachers' reading and assessment practices. Six of the teachers from three schools read the selection of three complete 'Inner Triangles' texts, while five teachers from another three schools read the selection of three 'Topples' texts. All of the teachers also read short extracts from three further 'Inner Triangles' texts, focusing on the way in which generalizations had been expressed.

The design for the interviews sought to provide a setting in which teachers' responses to features of students' texts that I had identified through consideration of the literature and during my analysis of the texts themselves might be investigated, while simultaneously maintaining the possibility of exploring other aspects of the teachers' reading that arose during the interviews. This would allow me to make sense of how the students' texts were situated within school mathematics practices. The setting in which the teachers were operating was not, however, 'natural'; this must be taken into account when interpreting the results.

Several days in advance, each teacher was given the statement of the task so that they could familiarize themselves with it and consider what they would look for in students' responses. At the beginning of the interview, I asked them in general terms to tell me about what they would look for when assessing responses to the task. The primary objective of this was to elicit the teacher's 'common sense' notions of the nature of coursework writing and assessment and to identify those features of students' work that the teacher herself claimed to consider significant.

During the second part of the interview, the teachers were asked to read and assess each of the three student texts, talking aloud as they did so to explain their judgments, then, after all three texts had been read, to rank them in order of merit.[1] This part of the interview was intended to gain insight into the ways in which the teacher makes sense of her reading of the student texts and into the nature of her assessment practice. By providing student texts with specific contrasting features, I hoped to be able to see the influence of these features on the teacher's reading and assessment. However, by constructing the purpose of the reading as assessment rather than as discussion of textual features, the identification of other, unanticipated features would not be inhibited. Moreover, there was more likelihood that the teacher would adopt a position within the discourse of coursework assessment rather than being clearly situated within the interview discourse. The question of teachers' positioning within the coursework assessment discourse or within the interview discourse is discussed below.

In the final part of the interview, the teacher was presented with three extracts from further students' texts, representing the students' presentation of a generalized solution to the 'Inner Triangles' task. Again, these extracts were chosen to display a number of contrasting features. This time, the teachers were encouraged to focus on the form of the text rather than attempting to assess its author. They were asked to say which of the extracts was expressed the best and what advice they would offer to each of the students to help them to improve their work. Through this I hoped to encourage teachers to identify specific textual features rather than just general overall impressions. Although the brevity of the extracts meant that the features that might be discussed were strictly limited, the fact that they were related to the formation of a generalized solution means that they are of particular significance within the mathematics coursework discourse.

The Teacher as Interviewee

In interpreting responses to questions concerning the reading and assessment of texts, it must be remembered that the questioning, the reading of the text and the judgments made by the reader are always situated within a context which affects, among other things, the understanding by the participants of the nature of the text being read and of their reasons for reading it. What sort of text is it? What might be the circumstances of its production and consumption? What are the generic criteria by which it ought to be judged? Is the aim of the task seen to be to assess the student's work or to evaluate the teacher's assessment? However carefully the interview may be designed to create conditions in which 'authentic' readings may be made by the interviewee, it is impossible to control the positionings that s/he may adopt. This raises questions about the interpretation of discourse-based interview data in general. For example, Odell and Goswami (1982) and Herrington (1985), while paying attention to the design of the interview itself in order to maximize the likelihood of an 'authentic' response, do not examine the responses achieved in a critical manner that questions the position from which the response is given or the social context, both immediate and wider, within which the response has been constructed. Their analyses, by reducing their data to mere counts of types of reasons given for judgments, assume that each interview provides a static picture of the homogeneous practice of an individual. This type of analysis is in a positivist tradition of the type criticized by, among others, Mishler (1986) and Jensen (1989) as inappropriate for data produced through social interaction.

The idea of 'positioning' as a factor in the analysis of interview data is discussed by Evans (1994). He suggests that subjects are positioned by the practices at play in the setting of the interview (in the case of his own study of adult students' numeracy he identifies these as Academic Mathematics and Research Interviewing). Then, depending on this positioning of the individual, further practices may be called up which 'provide the context for that subject's thinking and affect in that setting' (p. 323). Evans' study suggests that the positioning of interviewees, by making certain practices more or less likely to be called up, affected not only expressions of beliefs or feelings but also performance on the mathematical tasks which formed the focus of the interviews. In interpreting the data from the interviews, it is thus relevant to consider the positioning of the teacher-interviewees and its possible influence on their judgments about students' texts.

As well as the teachers' positioning as interviewees, the practice of GCSE coursework assessment involves a number of different, and sometimes contradictory positions that teachers may at various times adopt. As teachers of individual students, they are clearly in a pedagogic relationship: concerned to further the students' mathematical learning. They are also concerned to ensure that each student achieves as highly as possible on external examinations, not only because of personal loyalty to individual students but also in order to secure the teacher's own professional standing in the eyes of the school management and others who might have influence on their promotion or employment prospects. At the same time, however, the teacher assessing coursework is acting as an agent of the external examination board and as such is guided by the rules of that body. Failure to abide by those rules, causing major changes in students' grades following the moderation process, would be likely to result in loss of standing in relation to students, parents and the school. The external assessment context also ensures that concepts such as standardization, rigour and evidence play a part in the teachers' discourse.

In analysing interviews with the eleven teachers, the following distinct (and in some cases potentially contradictory) positions were identified:

- examiner, using externally determined criteria;
- examiner, setting and using her own criteria;
- teacher/advocate, looking for opportunities to give credit to a student;
- teacher/adviser, suggesting ways of meeting the criteria;
- teacher/pedagogue, suggesting ways in which a student might improve her perceived level of mathematical competence;
- imaginary naive reader;
- interested mathematician;
- interviewee.

Each of the teachers adopted more than one of these positions, sometimes shifting rapidly between several of them. Later in this chapter, a comparison of two teachers, Fiona and Joan will illustrate the ways in which these positions were manifested in the interviews, the significance of shifts between different positions, and the usefulness of the notion of position as an explanatory tool.

The tension between taking on an examiner role and acting as teacher/advocate or adviser is a familiar one for teachers involved in any summative assessment as they seek both to uphold the integrity of the examination and to 'do their best' on behalf of their own students. It is to be expected that one way in which this tension may be resolved is by appeal to the anonymous authority of the examination board, although some of the teachers appeared to be able to adopt a more authoritative position themselves as examiners entitled to determine their own interpretation of the official criteria. The suggestion that students should attempt to address an audience who 'knows nothing' about the problem was mentioned by several teachers as being advice that they offered to their students; some also appeared at times to attempt to imagine themselves into such a position of ignorance in order to judge the effectiveness of a student text. Positioning as a reader interested in the mathematical content of the text being read occurred infrequently, probably because of the routine nature of much of the coursework produced. Where it did occur, however, there was a tension between this position and that of examiner. For example, Dan expressed interest in Richard's investigation of the area of stars:

> *Perimeter times slant height . . . mm! . . . Blimey, I would definitely have liked a bit more explanation of that, cos that's quite interesting isn't it. The perimeter multiplied by the slant height gives you the area inside, that's quite an interesting find which I doubt if many other people did so it's quite innovative and something a bit different but given us absolutely no . . . not even 'oh gosh look at this' would have been . . .[2]*

On the one hand, Dan would like more explanation of this result because he finds it interesting and possibly wishes to understand the mathematics of it himself. The modality of the exclamations, the repetition of 'interesting', and the statements that it is 'innovative' and 'different' suggest a personal involvement with the subject matter. At the same time, he is evaluating Richard's work as an examiner, comparing it to other students' work and then criticizing it because no evidence or comment has been given to 'us'. The change from using 'I' to using the first person plural here marks Dan's shift from reading as an interested individual to reading as an examiner acting as part of a group with common expectations. The suggestion that 'oh gosh look at this' would be an appropriate comment is an evaluative suggestion also from a position as examiner; such a comment would not help an interested reader to understand the mathematics. While, as an individual, Dan is curious about the mathematics, as an examiner, his concern seems to be more with the way in which the work is presented.

Although the format of the interviews was designed to construct the teachers as expert informants demonstrating their normal practice, there were occasions when it appeared that this role was not fully adopted. Joan, for example, expressed insecurity about her assessment of Clive's work:

> *. . . so probably a level 7 again. But you're going to tell me now that somebody else has done this and come up with something completely different — but don't tell me that.*

She appears to be seeing herself in the interview situation as an examinee trying to come up with the 'right' answer. Similarly, Charles, on finding that the author of the third Topples text he read had arrived at a different result from that given in the first two texts, reacted to this difficulty not by treating it as a problem that might arise during the assessment of a set of coursework scripts but by accusing the interviewer of giving him a trick question: '*You horror! Could I have looked at these in any order?*' It appears that, at least at these points in the interviews, Joan and Charles were positioned as interviewees rather than within the practice of coursework assessment. Such explicit examples are rare but their existence suggests that there may have been other points at which the teachers were attempting to justify themselves and their judgments to the interviewer rather than merely 'thinking aloud' while undertaking their normal assessment practice. This may, in particular, be indicated where general descriptions of practice were given to back up comments on specific texts. This possibility, however, does not invalidate the interview data in general. The justifications used by the teachers must be drawn from their repertoire of 'members' resources' related to coursework and its assessment. As such, they form a part of this discourse and need to be reconciled with the rest of their practice.

In their analysis of the discourse of scientists, Gilbert and Mulkay (1984) explained apparent contradictions (in the ways in which errors were accounted for) as arising from the scientists' simultaneous participation in two practices with different sets of beliefs about the nature of scientific knowledge and activity. Similarly, the teachers discussed here were participants in the practices both of teaching and of examination as well as that of the interview. As Galbraith (1993) points out, the 'constructivist' paradigm associated with the current discourse of teaching is not compatible with the 'conventional' paradigm of external examinations. Contradictions within the teachers' discourse should not, therefore, be interpreted as indications of irrationality or incompetence but as signs of movement between the various practices in which they are situated in the process of making sense of the text being read and of their own relationship to the text and to its author.

Analysing the Interviews

It is important to recognize that answers provided by teachers in an interview situation cannot be taken as an absolute, objective indication of the 'truth' about the way they read and assess their students' texts. Not only may the teacher, in being removed from her normal setting, be deprived of 'resources — shared knowledge with which to approach the task, shared values, familiar procedures for analysing data, widely agreed on criteria — which may be essential for succeeding with a given task' (Doheny-Farina and Odell, 1985, p. 507), but in asking a teacher to verbalize her practice and to explain or justify it she may be prompted to reflect on it in new ways. The interaction between interviewer and interviewee constructs a new text (Mellin-Olsen, 1993; Mishler, 1986; Paget, 1983) which must be interpreted within its own context. My analysis of the texts produced during the interviews was, therefore, informed by consideration of the whole context within which the interviews took place and the way in which the participants are positioned within that context.

Given the theoretical standpoint on the motivated nature, lack of transparency and contextuality of language use taken in my analysis of students' written texts, it would have been contradictory for me to adopt a more naive representational view of the data arising from interviews, which are also essentially linguistic events. As the language of interviews was not itself the object of study, it was not appropriate to undertake full textual analysis of entire interviews. However, many of the tools of textual analysis described in Chapter 6 for use in the analysis of written mathematics have also proved useful to help answer Jensen's (1989) criticism of much interview-based research:

> It is the exception rather than the rule that qualitative researchers *analyze* the language of their materials. Even if the importance of language is acknowledged in an abstract sense, very often the interviews only appear as quotations illuminating the researcher's own narrative, so that the reader is left wondering how the discourse of the interview was transformed into the discourse of the report. (p. 100; original emphasis)

These tools assisted the 'transformation' from the discourse of the interview at two points in the analysis: firstly at the stage of identifying parts of the interview text which might be particularly significant and subsequently in a more detailed analysis of the nature of this significance.

The first approach to an interview transcript involved the identification of passages which were of interest either because they addressed certain themes which had been identified *a priori*:

- the linguistic or other symbolic forms used in students' writing (e.g. diagrams, tables, 'algebra');
- a student's use of personal narrative and logical argument;
- the explicit statement and use of criteria either provided by the examination board or particular to the school or individual teacher;
- creativity, originality or error;

or because they contained what Jensen (1989) refers to as 'linguistic danger signals'. Such signals[3] include:

- the hiding of agency (through passives or nominalizations);
- changes in personal pronoun use or tense, which may indicate distancing, differing degrees of generalization, or a change between different practices;[4]
- positive or negative modality;
- emphasis through repetition of related semantic terms — a sign of the ideational significance and possibly contested nature of the theme.

Having thus selected passages of interest, further themes were identified within these passages which appeared significant either to an individual teacher or to groups of teachers. The process was recursive as the identification of additional themes through the use of linguistic signals necessitated a return to the original data to discover other occurrences of these themes.

Teachers' explanations and justifications of their judgments were also identified at this stage. Describing the ways in which teachers explain their own actions and those of others is an important aspect of building up a picture of what events

and ideas are significant within the discourse. The expression of causal relationships was therefore of interest to the analysis of the interview texts. However, as
Polkinghorne (1988) points out, 'logico-mathematical reasoning' is not the only
form of explanation used:

> People ordinarily explain their own actions and the actions of others by means of
> a plot. In the narrative schema for organizing information, an event is understood
> to have been explained when its role and significance in relation to a human
> project is identified. (p. 21)

The narratives[5] that teachers relate may also reveal the interpretive resources they
are using to make sense of the practice of assessment or to justify their judgments.
They 'can be thought of as impression-management, as the presentation of their
professional selves' (Cortazzi, 1993, p. 42) and can provide insight into the objects,
events and causal relationships that are significant for the teachers.

Having identified themes and passages of the interviews related to them, the
analysis proceeded to consider the nature of the teachers' reading practices and
interpretive resources used in relation to each theme, including their orientation
towards the students and the texts and their positioning as pedagogue, examiner and
interviewee. This was achieved through close attention to the interview texts, again
making use of the tools of critical text analysis described above and in Chapter 6.
Linguistic features of particular significance in this analysis include the modality of
the text and uses of personal pronouns as these affect the expression of relationships between the teacher, the student text, the student-author and other participants
in the assessment context.

Variation and Validity in Teacher Assessment

One of the important issues that arose immediately from the interviews was the
amount of variability that appeared between the teachers, both in the approaches
they took to the assessment process and, to a rather lesser extent, in the rankings
they made of the texts. In the development and evaluation of any form of assessment, the issues of validity (the extent to which the assessment scheme assesses
that which it claims to assess) and reliability (the extent to which the same result
will be achieved on different occasions or by different assessors) must be considered. As was seen in Chapter 8, there has been some concern about the validity
of the coursework assessment process, expressed mainly in teachers' professional
journals. Official and public concern, expressed by examination boards, government and the media, has centred on the issue of reliability. It seems that there
has been some measure of success in achieving the desired consistency in teacher
assessment of coursework. Reliability in the results achieved does not, however,
necessarily mean that teachers are using the same criteria or that the results can
genuinely communicate a valid assessment of the student's mathematical achievement. As Wiliam (1994) states, 'To put it crudely, it is not necessary for the

raters (or anybody else) to know what they are doing, only that they do it right' (p. 60) — where 'right' means 'in agreement with other raters'.

While the concern with reliability focuses largely on the outcomes of teachers' assessment activity, my concern is rather with the nature of the activity itself — the ways in which teachers make sense of students' texts rather than the grades they eventually allocate to them. It cannot be assumed that teachers will all use the same methods or share the same attitudes towards the assessment process. Indeed, although there has been little detailed research into teachers' assessment practices, what there is (e.g. Flener and Reedy, 1990; Gipps et al., 1995) points to the importance of recognizing the complexity of teachers' assessment practices and the possibility of substantial differences in practices both between individuals and between groups of teachers.

In the remainder of this chapter, these issues of validity and reliability of the assessment of investigative coursework will be explored through looking in some detail at the practices of two teachers, Fiona and Joan, reading and assessing the same student's text (Richard's 'Inner Triangles' text). Throughout my interviews with teachers assessing students' investigative coursework, I frequently encountered occasions when the teachers appeared to be experiencing tensions between their various roles in reading and evaluating students' coursework texts. Often this meant that they expressed difficulty in arriving at an evaluation of a section of text or discomfort about the judgments they made. Because of the demands of the examination system, teachers have to find some way of resolving these tensions in order to arrive at a single final assessment of each piece of work. Different individual teachers do not necessarily do this in the same way and, I shall argue, this has consequences for both the reliability and the validity of the resulting assessment.

A Comparison of Two Teachers Reading Richard's 'Inner Triangles' Text

As we shall see, Richard's 'Inner Triangles' text, although similar in many ways to the work produced by a significant group of students, may nevertheless be considered to be aberrant in that it breaks many of the 'rules' about the kind of writing expected by teachers in the 'ideal' investigative report. This seemed to give rise to particular difficulties for teachers as they attempted to assess Richard's work — and hence to substantial differences in their evaluative responses. Indeed, of the six teachers asked to rank the three 'Inner Triangles' texts, three placed Richard's work first while the other three placed it last. In this section, I shall describe in some detail the way in which two teachers, Joan and Fiona, read and assessed two sections of this text, comparing and contrasting their reading practices. Joan ranked the three 'Inner Triangles' texts in the order: Richard (1), Steven, Clive, while Fiona's ranking was: Steven (1), Clive, Richard. A comparison of the entire texts of Joan's and Fiona's readings of Richard's work is given in Morgan (1995).

The first pair of extracts consist of Joan's and Fiona's responses to a single page of Richard's text (see Figure 9.1).

Figure 9.1:   Richard's (IT) text — extract 1 'Generalization'

Results

Top length	Bottom length	Slant length	Unit triangles
1	3	2	8
2	4	2	12
3	5	2	16
1	4	3	15
2	5	3	21
3	6	3	27
1	5	4	20
2	6	4	32
3	7	4	40
1	6	5	30
2	7	5	45
3	8	5	55

Formula

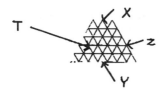

$$Z(X+Y) = T$$

This page contains a table of values with correct results[6] followed by a single diagram, labelled with letters, and a correct formula (making use of the same letters as variable names) expressing the relationship between the dimensions of a trapezium and the number of small triangles it contains. It followed a title page and two pages containing correct answers to questions about specific trapezia and a small number of rough diagrams of these trapezia.

Joan:

> *Gosh . . . he's leapt into a formula . . . so let's just see if it works . . . so he's given the top the bottom, the slant height and number of triangles, top plus bottom times the slant height . . . let's try one of these* [referring to the data in Richard's table] *. . . 3 and 5 is 8 . . . it seems to . . . yeah, so that seems to work just as a quick check. And he's explained it quite nicely with the diagram. What he hasn't done is given any sort of lead up as to how he arrived at it. Which he probably did orally in the group but, you know, it would be nice to have it written down . . . The presentation's nice on both of them by the way . . .*

Fiona:

> *He's gone on next to give results and a formula. Let's see what else he's done, working out here . . . one, three, two . . . Ok, well he's obviously been systematic*

here in his working out cos he's kept the slant height two to begin with then he's done it as three, then as four, then as five. So he's obviously got it ordered. Um
5 *let's just see how he's come up with these though . . . That's his working out for that bit. He's got a formula . . . Oh, so he's got an extension.* [Turning to the next page, then back again] *So it seems there's no justification and no working out at all on this is there. So that's a major draw back here because unless he's got it at the end, if he's included rough work and it's there then . . .* [looking through the re-
10 maining pages] *this is all extension though. His extension seems ok but this . . . This is a major problem because he's got these results but unless one is there in the class and you're a teacher you don't know whether this is his results or somebody else's. He hasn't shown any diagrams of where these results have come from. He hasn't done any drawings as far as I can see. He's come up with a formula which*
15 *is Z equals. Z must be the slant height. Is equal to X plus Y equals T. I assume that's right, I don't know.*

Interviewer: *Yes, I think that's right.*

Fiona:
That is right is it? Ok . . . but again even that's not, I mean he's given, one thing that I think they have to do is when they give a formula they should explain it using
20 *quite a few examples and show how it works. The thing that I always look for and I say to the kids is: you write it up as if you're writing it for somebody who's never seen this problem, who's never done that but would be able to understand it if they were to read it. And from this, somebody . . . I don't think it's clear enough for somebody to use it and then work out, I mean he hasn't done even one example of*
25 *how it works. So I think he's got a major problem here, he hasn't shown how he's got it. If you were in the class, obviously we can award marks when they've done something in class but it's not written down. If you're the teacher in the class and you knew that he's just omitted it by mistake um but also he hasn't included his rough work and that's, when this happens, often you find what you need in the*
30 *rough work and that can, you know. So none of his results are justified there at all. I think he could have problems with that.*

While reading this page of Richard's text, the practices of the two teachers are very different. Joan starts by making sense of the formula, interpreting the variables and then using the data in the table to check whether the formula works. The table is used as a tool for the reader to make sense of the mathematics. The diagram is also seen as a way of helping the reader to understand. Joan's initial position while reading this section of text is as an interested reader, seeking to understand the text. It is only once she has made sense of and validated the mathematics that she takes on an assessor role, evaluating the form and identifying missing features.

Fiona, by contrast, does not attempt to make mathematical sense of Richard's formula until after she has considered and evaluated other features of his work. While Joan used the values in the table to check the formula, Fiona demands that examples should be provided for her, taking on the role of a naive (and uncooperative) reader. For her, the table is not a means of communicating mathematics but an indicator of systematic working, i.e. fulfilment of an assessment criterion. Her reading is a search for evidence which leads her to read in a non-linear way, searching through the whole text for the 'working out' that she claims is missing. The diagram which Joan interpreted as an explanation is completely ignored by Fiona, who even states that 'he hasn't done any drawings' (line 14). As the drawing on this page is a generic diagram (labelled with variable names rather than with specific lengths) it cannot fulfil the 'working out' identity and is thus not significant for Fiona. After this search for evidence, she returns to the formula but even here does not appear to wish to make sense of it, apparently willing to assume it is right or at least to accept the authority of the interviewer.

The major issue in this section for both Joan and Fiona is the lack of any verbal explanation or elaboration of the formula. As examiners, both of them identify this as a problem but they resolve it in different ways. Joan takes on the role of teacher/advocate, suggesting that the necessary explanation probably took place in the classroom (although there is no suggestion of this in the text). Fiona recognizes the possibility of taking this position but rejects it in favour of an examiner role; the teacher role is apparently only acceptable to her 'if you're the teacher in the class'.

It is worth looking in some detail at this extract from Fiona's interview as it reveals the tensions that the teacher experiences and the complexity of her relationships to the text, to the (unknown to her) student-author of the text, and to the examination system. Several times Fiona identifies 'problems' with Richard's work. She is reading here in the role of an examiner looking for evidence that the results 'belong' to Richard (lines 10–13), for evidence of 'how he's got it' (line 25), and for justification of the results (line 30). Her discomfort in this role, however, is suggested by the repeated use of the word *problem*. There is a tension between the rigour of the examiner, for whom use of the assessment criteria determines unproblematically a decision about the value of a piece of work, and the wish of a teacher that a pupil should get as high a grade as possible. In this case, Fiona reading as teacher, acting as advocate on behalf of her pupil (although she did not have personal knowledge of Richard), feels, as Joan did, that the missing evidence might have been available in the classroom. When she reads as examiner, however, she cannot take account of this possibility. The problems are Richard's problems but they are also Fiona's problems in resolving her two roles.

This tension is expressed again (lines 18–19) when Fiona describes 'one thing that I think they have to do'; there is an ambiguity in this phrase which was also present in the intonation used: is this her own opinion of what is appropriate or is it her belief about what is expected by the examination board? I would suggest that this ambiguity serves the function of enabling Fiona to reconcile her different roles: when she (as teacher concerned to support a pupil) is uncomfortable with the severity of her judgment of the piece of work, she is able to shift the blame to an anonymous authority that lays down what 'they have to do'.

At lines 20–21, Fiona again expresses a dual role — this time a more comfortable one — as examiner and as teacher/adviser, looking for the specified characteristic of the writing as an assessment criterion and simultaneously advising the pupils of the criterion that is being used. The nature of the criterion she describes, however, forces her to adopt yet another reader position, as an imaginary naive

Figure 9.2: Richard's (IT) text — extract 2 'Extension'

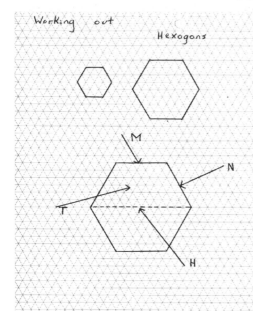

Working out
Hexagons

Length of sides	Unit triangles
1	6
2	24
3	54
4	96
5	150

Formula

$$N(M + H) \times 2 = T$$

Eg

$$2(2 \cdot 4) \times 2 = 24$$

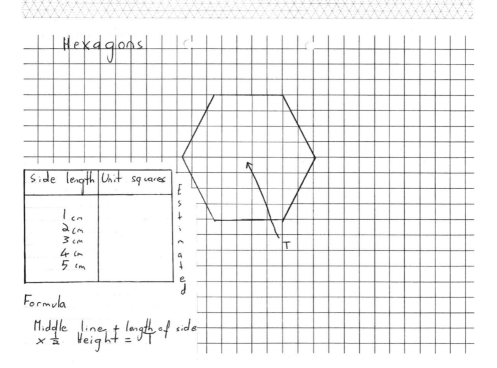

Hexagons

Side length	Unit squares
1 cm	
2 cm	
3 cm	
4 cm	
5 cm	

Formula

Middle line + length of side
× ½ Height = √T

reader 'who's never seen this problem, who's never done that but would be able to understand it if they were to read it' (lines 21–23). This invocation of an imaginary audience is presumably intended to provide the student with guidance about the level of detail required for assessment purposes. There is an assumption, however, not only that the student will understand the nature of this hypothetical audience and actually address it, but also that the teacher will successfully adopt the position of the specified audience when reading and judging the student's work. Neither of these assumptions is justified (see, for example, Gilbert, 1989; Redd-Boyd and Slater, 1989). Where, as in this case, the teacher is reading as an 'expert' examiner, judging the mathematical quality, and simultaneously attempting to read as 'somebody who's never seen this problem', the tension is less easily resolved. This is particularly the case where the characteristics of the specified imaginary audience are unclear; in Fiona's case it appears that 'somebody' has some degree of mathematical understanding as they 'would be able to understand it if they were to read it' and yet they are constructed as needing an example in order to be able to use a simple formula.

The next pair of extracts refer to a section of Richard's work labelled as an 'Extension'. On each of five pages, a similar pattern of work (diagram(s), table of results and formula) was repeated for triangles, hexagons, stars, squares (drawn on squared paper), and hexagons (drawn on squared paper). Figure 9.2 shows two of these five pages. On these pages Richard has posed his own problems, deciding on a selection of different shapes to investigate. This extension, though technically 'optional' for the student, forms a major proportion of Richard's submitted text and represents a substantial amount of work on his part. As was seen in Chapter 5, the notion of 'extension' and, in particular, the posing of 'creative' mathematical problems are highly valued within the discourse of mathematical investigations.

Joan:

> he's gone on to hexagons . . . Phew, that seems to be ok . . . I wonder . . . the fact that he's drawn that dotted line [across the middle of the hexagon] across the middle makes me think he was looking at it in terms of two trapeziums but he hasn't said that here, yet anyway unless it's further on, so that seems like a very sensible idea . . . but it would have been a good idea perhaps if he'd written in there . . . Ah the same sort of thing here . . . now this time he's looked at the perimeter, which seems to be jumping about. With the star I thought maybe he'd try and put it into triangles as he's already done a triangle one but . . . Now squares . . . no real overall conclusion . . . so perhaps . . . a table at the end showing all the different shapes he'd looked at . . . with some general conclusions . . . which would be, if he had done that, . . .

Fiona:

> And then hexagons. [The stars and squares are passed over; the next comment refers to the hexagons drawn on squared paper.] But he hasn't done his answers there, so that's not very good. He's put down some kind of a formula here but he

hasn't got any answers or anything to go with it. Right, his extension is much better than the actual investigation itself I would have thought. Even then it still lacks detail.

The contrast between the reading practices of the two teachers is again apparent in this section. Joan seems to be engaging with the mathematical problem, considering the connections between trapezia, triangles, hexagons and stars. She takes Richard's diagram of a hexagon as evidence that he has thought in a particular way and presents her own way of thinking about the star as a collection of triangles. During this passage, Joan shifts between a position of interested reader and a more assessment oriented position. Although she has inferred Richard's thinking from the diagram, a written explanation would have been 'a good idea'. Similarly, a summarizing table and overall conclusion would have been good. As well as identifying (as an examiner) what is missing from the text, the way in which Joan hypothesizes about what Richard could have done, in particular the hesitant modality of her advice that 'it would have been a good idea perhaps if', suggests that she is reading partly as a teacher/adviser, suggesting ways in which the pupil might improve his work rather than merely pointing to its limitations.

Fiona, on the other hand, has nothing to say about the pages on hexagons, stars and squares, each of which contained diagrams, a table of results and a formula. She passes quickly over these but stops at the final page of hexagons drawn on squared paper, commenting that there is a formula produced without any evidence in the form of 'answers' in the table. Her reading is only evaluative: criticizing what has not been done, making a comparison between the standard of the extension and of the earlier work and summing up the whole of Richard's work as lacking 'detail'. At no point does Fiona demonstrate any attempt to make sense of the mathematics or even to check the accuracy of Richard's work; her assessment of all parts of this text appears to be based on the presence or absence of formal features: diagrams, tables, examples, formulae, writing.

In contrast to her lengthy consideration of the previous single page, Fiona dealt perfunctorily with these five pages of Richard's extension work. This was consistent with her statement later in the interview that she believed the quality of the extension could only marginally affect her evaluation of the piece of work as a whole. She appeared concerned primarily with Richard's satisfactory completion of all parts of the directed task rather than with his problem solving and investigative skills in general.

Having read the complete piece of work, both Joan and Fiona summed up their evaluations of Richard's work. Both teachers picked out Richard's use of symbolic algebraic notation and his lack of 'justification' as significant to their overall evaluation of his work, praising the algebra as 'quite advanced' (Fiona) and at the same time condemning the lack of justification. The ways in which they resolved the tension between these two aspects again reflect different reading positions. While Joan identified aspects that are missing from Richard's text, she did so from the position of teacher/adviser suggesting what he might do to improve the level of his work and, in spite of her lack of personal knowledge of the pupil, stating as teacher/advocate that she was 'sure he'd have . . . got a level 8 if he'd have put things together at the end'. An unwillingness to take on an examiner role is suggested by the way in which she hedged her final evaluation, suggesting that she was 'maybe a bit generous' and that her assessment was in any case only 'a gut reaction'.

Fiona, on the other hand, summed up from an unambiguous position as examiner. Although she did say that 'it would have been nice' if Richard had shown his working, this was not a suggestion about how he might have improved his grade but a request for evidence that he has not cheated. She listed all the things that Richard had not done (or had not shown he had done) and dismissed what he had achieved 'by whatever method I don't know'. Unlike Joan, she was not prepared to hypothesize about Richard's potential or hidden attainment but would only consider what was written on the paper, measuring it against her 'norm product' (Rapaille, 1986) and finding it wanting.

To a large extent these two teachers identified the same features of Richard's text as significant both during their initial reading and when asked at a later stage to compare it with the other pupils' texts. However, the ways in which they interpreted and resolved the tensions between positive and negative features varied considerably, leading eventually to opposite rankings of Richard's text (Joan ranked it highest while Fiona ranked it lowest of the three texts they read). One of the sources of this variation seemed to be a difference in the definition of the 'investigation' task used by each of the two teachers. This led them to place very different values on the extension section of the text. I would suggest that this difference is closely related to differences in their reading practices. As has been seen, Fiona's dominant reading position throughout was as an examiner, tightly constrained by her perception of the requirements of the examination board. As well as searching for 'evidence' that the work belongs to Richard himself, she was concerned to determine whether or not he had fulfilled the assessment criteria. Her reading was thus a search for indicators that allowed her to compare his work to an imaginary ideal answer. This imaginary ideal was determined by the structure of the task set by the examination board, which not only included a number of closed questions but also specified processes to be demonstrated while 'investigating'. The extension was officially described as 'optional', which suggests that it was peripheral to the main task. It is hardly surprising, therefore, that Fiona attached little weight to Richard's extension when evaluating the whole piece of work.

Joan, on the other hand, appeared uncomfortable with the examiner role when forced into it by the demands of the interview and generally adopted reading positions which allowed her a less formal relationship both with the pupil-author of the text and with the task itself. Rather than seeking for performance indicators she appeared much of the time to be reading in order to understand what had been written; she thus accepted the definition of the task given by the student and did not refer explicitly to the questions set by the examination board. Her frequent adoption of a teacher role (adviser or advocate) led her to treat Richard as an individual with an existence outside the text. Although the text was the only evidence available to her, Joan's reading led her to make statements about what might have happened in class or what Richard might have done if he had been advised differently. The extent of the extension section of his work, therefore, caused her to make assumptions about Richard's understanding and about the existence of work that had been done but not recorded. Hence she evaluated the text as a whole highly, largely on the basis of the extension.

The two teachers whose readings of a single text have been compared here may be seen to differ both in the positions they adopted in relation to the student-author and in the general strategies they used in order to make sense of the text and of the assessment process. Similar varying positions and contrasting strategies were also found among the other teachers interviewed; in particular, each teacher's practice could be described predominantly either as comparing each student's text with an imaginary 'ideal' or as building up an imaginary picture of the student and his or her activity. While the small size of the sample of teachers does not allow us to speculate about the distribution of the various orientations and strategies among mathematics teachers as a whole (or, indeed, to be confident that there are no further significant types of strategies), it is clear that differences do occur and that the case study described here is illustrative and raises general concerns about teacher assessment of mathematics coursework.

Consequences of Differences in Reading Strategies

In the case of Richard's text, the aberrant nature of the text highlighted the possible differences in outcome of the various strategies. Thus, while Joan judged Richard to be an able mathematician and ranked his work first (of three), Fiona focused on the shortcomings of his text in comparison to her 'ideal' and ranked it last. It was also clear that all the teachers who read Richard's text found it difficult to assess and were, to some extent, uncomfortable with their ultimate evaluation of it. Where a student's text differs from the stereotypical, as Richard's does, this may give rise to difficulties for teacher-assessors and to variations in their evaluations.

In most cases, however, when asked to rank the student texts they had read, teachers gave very similar rankings whether their judgments had been based on a construction of the students' personal characteristics or on a search for the fulfilment of criteria or a comparison with an 'ideal' text. This might suggest that, except in a few unusual cases, the different approaches to reading and assessment identified here do not generally appear to have major effects on the outcome of the examination process. Nevertheless, a question must be raised about the validity of the assessment process: to what extent can any meaning in relation to the student's mathematical attainment be attached to its outcomes? It is unclear whether the grade achieved by an individual student may be taken to be a measure of some general impression of his or her 'ability' or an indication of the extent to which the text produced matches the teacher's image of an ideal response to the task. Where these measures coincide it seems likely that this will be because the form of mathematical thinking displayed is of a relatively routine and predictable kind.

Notes

1 Ranking is part of the standard procedure for grading sets of coursework texts. Some teachers did this spontaneously before being prompted to do so.
2 This passage from Dan's interview is also discussed in Chapter 10.
3 The general interpretation of such linguistic features is discussed more fully in Chapter 6.
4 An example of the use of similar linguistic signals in the study of teachers' assessment practice is provided by Rapaille (1986) who suggests that the obscuring of agency achieved by use of the indefinite pronoun 'one' instead of 'I' 'can be interpreted as an attempt of the teacher to protect himself from blame from others' (p. 138), where 'others' may include the researcher listening to the recording of the assessment event.
5 A narrative may be defined as involving temporality, causation and human interest, which 'determines whether the events and causes fit together in a plot' (Cortazzi, 1993, p. 86).
6 Richard's results do contain a single error, but this was not remarked upon by any of his teacher-readers.

Chapter 10

Teachers' Responses to Student Writing

In Chapter 6 I suggested some of the ways in which features of students' GCSE coursework texts might be interpreted by their readers. So far, this has been done from a largely theoretical perspective, drawing on analysis of the values expressed within the public discourse of investigation and on consideration of the examination context. In this chapter, the readers' point of view will be examined to identify which features of students' mathematical writing teachers attend to and the ways in which they interpret and evaluate them.

In the interviews described in the previous chapter, six experienced teachers (Amy, George, Andy, Dan, Fiona and Joan) read the 'Inner Triangles' texts by Richard, Steven and Clive while five (Charles, Harry, Grant, Jenny and Carol) read the 'Topples' texts by Ellen, Steven and Sandra. The teachers were not explicitly asked to comment on the ways in which the texts were written as the intention of the interviews was to elicit reading practices as close as possible to those used during the normal assessment process; questions related to the form of the writing would have substantially changed the nature of the teachers' relationship to the text. Nevertheless, there were frequent spontaneous evaluative comments on the form of a text, particularly in response to perceived weaknesses or absences of 'writing'; when such comments had been made by teachers it was sometimes possible to follow them up with further questions to encourage elaboration of the reasons for the judgments. The features that were commented on included the use of specific forms of representation or communication (e.g. words, tables, diagrams, algebraic symbolism) and more substantial structural elements of the text (e.g. the statement of the problem, passages relating what was done or explaining the results). There were also a few general references to the 'style' of the texts. In this chapter, the teachers' expressions of attitude towards such features are examined, together with the meanings that they appeared to ascribe to them.

A Generic Demand for 'Writing'

Coursework differs most obviously from the other kinds of written work carried out in the traditional mathematics classroom by being an extended text, possibly including substantial passages of verbal text (neither symbolic nor graphic). It seems that the presence of such passages has become one of the defining characteristics of the genre. Thus, there were numerous instances during the interviews when teachers expressed a wish to see more 'writing'. Grant, for example, stated explicitly in response to a general request to say what he was looking for when assessing students' work that he wished to see 'sentences' and repeated this demand several times during the course of his interview. When reading Ellen's text, however, he justified this by referring to the nature of the genre rather than to any difficulty in communication:

> *I suppose it's pernickety isn't it to look at short sentences like that or the way they said it but after all I think that investigations are a **report** on some work so they should be writing about what they done and not just going for an answer*

This attempt to justify his 'pernickety' judgments suggests that Grant experienced a tension between the normal value placed by school mathematics on correct answers, his evident ability to make coherent sense of Ellen's text, and his understanding of the genre of investigations. This tension was seen perhaps most strongly in the teachers' reactions to Richard's 'Inner Triangles' text which was almost exclusively non-verbal. Although Richard's conclusions were recognized to be correct, and some of the teachers suggested that they considered Richard more mathematically able than the other two students whose work they had read, his work was nevertheless universally criticized for its lack of 'writing'; two teachers' ways of dealing with this were discussed in the previous chapter.

In general, the absence of words was condemned even when the teacher was clearly able to make adequate sense of the non-verbal text (i.e. provided an interpretation of the meaning of the text and expressed no difficulty in understanding it). There were, however, a small number of cases in which it was admitted that a non-verbal form used without verbal accompaniment could be more effective in communicating meaning. Harry, for example, rather grudgingly admitted that Sandra's illustration of her extension problem was probably the best way to present it because 'I think something like that to explain in words would be quite difficult so that's a good use of an alternative method of presenting it'. Even in such cases, however, teachers appeared to struggle with the normal requirement to put things in words. There is a tension between the general rule that 'you must explain in words' and its application within a specific context in which words might be difficult to understand and other forms of text may be completely effective in communicating the required meaning.

While all the teachers interviewed made similar demands that the students' texts should contain 'writing', some appear less convinced of the justification for this demand. Dan, for example, repeatedly hedged his condemnation of the lack of 'writing' in the texts he read by appealing to the external authority of the examination board's requirements, relating an anecdote about a boy whose work was 'marked down' by the moderator because it was very 'blank'. This suggests that, for Dan, the requirement for writing was seen as an arbitrary (though unquestionable) assessment criterion rather than an essential part of the practice of doing investigations.

Some non-verbal forms were, however, valued in their own right. In particular, tables, diagrams and 'algebra' were frequently mentioned as being desirable in principle and were often commented upon positively when they occurred within students' texts.

Tables — A Sign of 'System'

Not only did all the students' texts used in this study contain tables at some point but all of the teachers also commented positively on the presence of tables. The table is clearly an important, if not essential, component of the investigation genre, frequently mentioned as one of the things that would be looked for when assessing and in several cases included in teachers' accounts of the advice they provided for their own students. The teachers' responses to the tables varied, indicating a number of different ways of reading and evaluating them. Some appeared to value the table for its own sake, without indicating any specific interpretation of its function within the text:

- merely marking the presence of the table — *He's tabulated the results.*
- non-specific approval of the presence of the table — *Then he came up with a table, I like that.*
- non-specific approval of the form of the table — *He's tabulated his results nicely.*

In some of these cases, it appeared that the presence of the table was being used simply as a mark of fulfilment of an assessment criterion. Other responses gave some indication of the role that the table played in the teacher's reading of the text:

- helping to communicate (in a non-specific way) — *I liked his table, I could read his table.*
- helping to communicate because it is an organized form — *A reasonable set of results. They're systematically laid out.*
- signalling that the student has worked systematically — *Tabulated results . . . she's done this systematically.*

The identification of the table with a systematic way of working was made explicitly and spontaneously by four of the eleven teachers. It seems that the organization of data into a table is taken as a sign that the student has 'controlled the variables' and collected the data itself in an organized way. Not every type of table will serve this function, however, and this raises an issue about the use of textual form as evidence of student activity.

In his report on the 'Inner Triangles' investigation, one student, Clive, presented the results of his data collection in a two dimensional array (Figure 10.1).

Figure 10.1: Clive's two dimensional table

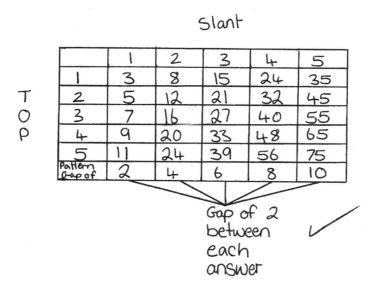

Given that the problem itself involved two independent variables (the top length and the slant height of isosceles trapezia) it could be argued that such an organization was mathematically appropriate and might even facilitate the search for patterns within the data. However, Fiona interpreted the form of his table rather differently:

> *at least he's tabulated his results and made some effort to, so that ... so there's some organization there. Um, he doesn't seem, he's gone one two three four five on the slant, one two three four five on the top. He hasn't kept anything constant, you know, at any point, and certainly there's no evidence of it here.*

She grudgingly acknowledges the table but evaluates it negatively. In particular, she focuses on the lack of evidence of control of the variables. 'Keeping something constant' is one of the indicators of 'working systematically' and hence contributes to the assessment of the student's problem solving processes within the Data–Pattern–Generalization format. A one dimensional table such as that provided by another student, Richard (Figure 10.2), by suggesting that the entries in the table are arranged in the order in which they were derived by the student, would appear to act as a sign that the student's chronological actions have taken place in a logical order. Clive's two dimensional table is, however, organized by a different logical principle that does not include any chronological aspect. It cannot, therefore, be read as a record of the order in which the work was done and, as Fiona says, provides no evidence that Clive 'kept anything constant'. Fiona thus judges his work to be lacking in this respect.

While deviation from the standard format makes Fiona's negative evaluation of Clive's two dimensional table possible, it is not a necessary reading. The

Figure 10.2: Richard's one dimensional table

Results

Top length	Bottom length	Slant length	Unit triangles
1	3	2	8
2	4	2	12
3	5	2	16
1	4	3	15
2	5	3	21
3	6	3	27
1	5	4	20
2	6	4	32
3	7	4	40
1	6	5	30
2	7	5	45
3	8	5	55

identification between a one-dimensional table and systematic way of gathering data assumes that the table contains a chronological record of the work carried out. While in some cases this may be true, there is no necessary connection. Even data gathered on an entirely random basis can be organized into a table of the conventional form. The 'systematic' nature of the student's work would in such a case reside in the organization of the data rather than the original collection. If this were recognized, the organization of the data into a two dimensional table could also be taken as a sign of a systematic way of working.

In contrast to Fiona's reading, Joan recognized and valued the relationship of the structure of the table to the structure of the situation:

> . . . *his tables are probably the best because he's put, you know, he's actually correlated two different things (. . .) I actually like these tables. (. . .) So he has actually looked for a relationship that way, you know, joining things together rather than just that it builds up in 2's or it builds up in 3's.*

Joan has taken the form of the table as an indication of the way in which Clive was thinking about the problem; the more complex form of table is taken as evidence of more sophisticated forms of thought. Joan's acceptance of Clive's table suggests that she is taking it as a sign of his way of thinking about relationships between the variables rather than a sign of his way of organizing his data gathering. As forming relationships between variables may be taken to be a more highly valued aspect of his work (demonstrating progress into the later stages of the DPG process), she is not concerned with the lack of evidence of systematic variation of the variables.

This variation in the ways in which these two teachers[1] interpreted the same table raises a dilemma for students. The conventional way to provide evidence to fulfil the assessment criterion related to 'working systematically' appears to be to include a linear table in which the value of the independent variable is increased in some consistent way. Where there is more than one independent variable, a non-linear representation may be more effective in arriving at a solution. Although this may be interpreted by a teacher-assessor as a sign of a higher level of thinking about the problem, it is also possible that the consequent loss of evidence of a 'systematic' linear approach will be penalized.

Diagrams — Not Too Much of a 'Good Thing'

As was the case with tables, diagrams were generally remarked upon positively by the teachers and frequently appeared to feature in the advice offered to students about what to include in their coursework. The specifications of both the 'Inner Triangles' task and the 'Topples' task include diagrams and this may also be seen at least to sanction and possibly to encourage the use of diagrams in students' responses to the tasks.

Where teachers commented on particular diagrams, their comments were almost always positive even when suggestions were made about how the diagram might be improved. The existence of a diagram thus appeared to be being used as a positive performance indicator, irrespective of the context in which the diagram is found. There was, however, considerable variation in the ways teachers read and interpret particular diagrams. These interpretations include:

- data gathered by the student
- working out
- the student's attempt to explain his or her activity or thinking
- evidence of the way the student was thinking
- evidence of student ownership of the results

They may also be seen to help the teacher's own reading process, either by supporting the verbal text or by providing a check on the accuracy of the results provided.

In spite of the value generally ascribed to diagrams, there were also a number of indications given in the interviews that in some cases diagrams might not be appropriate or might even be a sign of work done by a 'less able' student. Too many diagrams or diagrams which are not arranged according to an easily recognizable system may be taken as evidence that the student was working at a more concrete, practical level. The highest level of abstraction is characterized by an absence of the practical activity which is embodied in the drawing of diagrams. Thus Andy stated as one of the things he would look for when assessing that the student should be able to '*calculate the area of a triangle [sic] just by looking at the dimensions given for any particular trapezium without drawing them and counting*'. There comes a point in the assessment of a solution to the problem at which the *absence* of a diagram becomes a positive performance indicator.

Moreover, some types of diagrams may be read as indicators of 'low level' activity. In particular, Sandra's 'Topples' text contained naturalistic diagrams of piles of rods showing the use of several rods to make up lengths over twelve units (Figure 10.3).

Figure 10.3: One of Sandra's piles of rods, illustrating her 'practical' activity

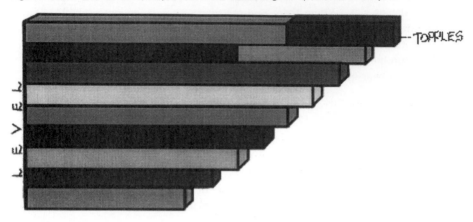

This seems to have contributed to the way in which Harry made sense of her mathematical activity, blaming her incorrect results on the story he constructed about her practical activity.

> *Now one of her illustrations here shows I think that she's used, she's actually using split rods. We haven't actually tried that but I'm sure that would have an influence on the result.*

While the constraints of the materials used for this task mean that the other students and Harry himself must have combined rods in order to build their piles, the effects of this on the results generated by the practical activity were only considered in Sandra's case and were used to explain why her results were different from those produced by the others. Moreover, although he suggested alternative sources for Sandra's errors — general inaccuracy in building the piles even when they are not split or blindly continuing a pattern of numbers — the remedy Harry eventually prescribed for her difficulties was still based on the persistent idea that the split rods were the key source of her errors.

> *I would — post investigation again I would try to see if I can get any — go down to CDT or whatever and get some blocks of wood and chop them up and see you know if it does make a difference. I would get actually longer lengths um to try and eradicate this. So that's what's done it I think. That's what's caused the damage.*

The naturalistic form of Sandra's diagrams so strongly presents her work as being of a very concrete nature that this overrides all the other possible interpretations that Harry had identified.

Similarly, while 'good presentation' is valued (although usually only 'by the way'), it is also possible that a teacher may interpret some forms of presentation as detracting from the mathematical content of the work. Thus Harry began by praising Sandra's presentation:

Three dimension illustrations to start with, very nice, nicely presented.

but quickly moved on to criticize its specific form:

Oh, she's colour coded anyway. She's used some sort of key. Um, not really necessary. She could have just put the numbers on, . . .

There is a suggestion here that the use of colour is an unnecessary elaboration. Using numbers to label her diagrams would not only have saved her time but might also be interpreted as a more abstract, and hence more highly valued, way of thinking about the problem. The presentation of Sandra's work was also commented upon by Charles in summing up his evaluations of all three Topples texts:

C: Then you've got Sandra, well, . . . got some nice diagrams [. . .]
I: You said that she had some nice diagrams.
C: Yeah, I mean, well, artistic ones [laughs] I think perhaps she probably went a little bit over the top but I mean . . . there's nothing wrong with that. Er nicely presented work. In fact they've all presented their work pretty well.

In both cases, the presentation was the first feature of Sandra's text to be commented upon; in both cases the initial praise is then qualified. Being 'artistic' or using colour seem not to be considered appropriate to the genre.

These qualifications of teachers' reactions to the presence of diagrams and elaborate presentation in students' texts imply that the context free approval given to diagrams does not reflect the way in which the teachers actually read. Their advice to their students to 'draw diagrams' may not be helpful to students as it does not provide any means of distinguishing between those uses of diagrams which will be approved and those which will be taken as signs of a low level of mathematical achievement or will be judged to have been a waste of time.

Algebra — With or Without Words

Because of the high status of generalization and algebra within school mathematics and in the assessment of coursework within the Data–Pattern–Generalization paradigm, I anticipated that this would be a significant theme in teachers' reading and assessing of the coursework texts and the nature of generalizations was thus one of the features I took into account when choosing the student texts for teachers to read. In addition, at the end of each interview, teachers were asked to compare a further set of extracts containing generalizations in different forms. All of the student texts included a generalization expressing a relationship between the variables of the task situation or describing a procedure for generating the dependent variable from the independent variables. The way in which this relationship was expressed varied from a sentence describing the procedure without algebraic symbolism, through a formula with descriptive variable names, to an entirely symbolic equation relating single letter variables.

The most easily identified difference between the various generalizations the teachers were given to read was probably the presence or absence of an expression involving single letter variables. The use of symbols as variable names in the expression of generalizations is stated as one of the assessment criteria for achieving higher grades in GCSE coursework in both the general criteria and the task specific performance indicators issued by the examination board. It has, moreover, become part of the folklore that, in order to achieve one of the top grades (A – C) for an investigation in GCSE coursework, it is necessary to have used 'algebra'. In this context, 'algebra' normally appears to be interpreted as the use of symbols rather than verbal variable names. Although not all the teachers made explicit use of grades or official criteria, in all cases symbolic algebra appeared as a key indicator in forming teachers' assessments both when making decisions about ranking actual student texts and when stating the general principles of their assessment practice. Some teachers even appeared to be led to overlook other aspects of a student's text in their search for algebraic expressions.

In spite of this general recognition of the role of algebra as a decisive assessment tool, its application appears problematic; it was often stated hesitantly, modified with 'hedges' like *perhaps* as in the following example:

> *This one perhaps may come towards the bottom, maybe the third one, because they've just shown a couple of examples and then written it out in words whereas the other two have used the letters.*

In other cases, the importance of algebra was seen to conflict with other assessment criteria, causing apparent discomfort. Charles, for example, found it difficult to resolve the tension between his assessment of 'understanding' and the use of the algebra criterion. Thus, having identified the lack of algebra in Ellen's text, he initially claimed that it was irrelevant, but, when pushed to rank the set of texts, decided that algebra was nevertheless crucial to the assessment process:

> *Well I don't know cos I think these two are very similar. I think probably Ellen understands it a bit better than Steven does but the Steven's got his little bit of algebra in there which . . . I mean you're always looking for your algebra aren't you so* [laughs]

His nervous laughter was symptomatic of the difficulty he appeared to be experiencing in coming to an assessment and the use of *you* in the final sentence served to distance himself from his decision by passing responsibility to an external (but unspecified) authority.

Several teachers, like Charles, indicated some degree of conflict with the authority of the criteria provided by the examination board, but claimed themselves to be unconcerned by the difference between verbal and symbolic variable names. For these teachers, the key distinction between algebra and not-algebra appeared to be between a relational or equation format and an explicitly procedural generalization, whereas they perceived the examination board to be distinguishing according to the use of verbal and symbolic variable names. Dan, for example, saw little difference between the formula:

(TOP LENGTH + BOTTOM LENGTH) × SLANT LENGTH = No. OF TRIANGLES

and one expressed using algebraic symbols and suggested that he might interpret the examination board's criteria (perceived by him to demand such notation) flexibly:

> *If every other criteria [was fulfilled] and the only thing that was stopping it being a particular grade was the fact that it wasn't expressed algebraically I wouldn't mind. To me, the difference between that and sticking letters in instead is so minimal that it doesn't really matter.*

The opposite problem was experienced by Carol who saw Steven's (Topples) text to be lower in quality than might be expected from the fact that it contains symbolic generalizations:

> *It's strange because this student has in a few places tried to use algebra which would make you think well people who try to use algebra are generally sort of the good Ds and the Cs but other things that you're looking for in good Cs and Ds don't seem to be there so there seems to be a sort of inconsistency when I'm assessing this as a teacher. Um . . . I'm wondering if it's not so much using what you'd call real algebra but just using a letter in place of a phrase*

Having identified a mismatch between the 'algebra = good grade' criterion and her other, unspecified and probably less easily identifiable criteria, she resolves it by devaluing Steven's symbolic generalizations, suggesting that they are not really algebra at all. It is not clear what she would consider to be 'real algebra'; it is possible that this is a context-bound concept and that her reading of a section of text as algebra or not-algebra would depend on her reading and evaluation of the rest of the text within which it is embedded.

Where there is tension between presence or absence of symbolic algebra and the evaluation of the rest of the text, some teachers will resolve the tension by appealing to the authority of the examination board, while others will respond by redefining the nature of 'algebra' in order to fit their overall evaluation. These two methods of resolving tension are associated with different positionings in relation to the activity of assessment. Deferring to authority suggests a position as examiner/employee with relatively little power, using externally determined criteria. Redefining the terms of the criteria suggests a more autonomous position for the teacher as a professional able to determine the criteria herself. The different resolutions are also likely to give rise to different ultimate evaluations of the student's work.

In the examples provided above, no reasons were given for the importance accorded to the use of algebraic symbolism by the teachers or by the examination board. Algebra appears as an unquestioned and unjustified 'good thing'. A few of the teachers did, however, indicate reasons for preferring generalizations expressed symbolically. These included:

- it is easier to read (for the teacher him or herself)

  But I found this, you know it took me a second to understand what he meant, slant and top.

- it is easier to read in general

  Ellen has got to the stage of finding a formula but hasn't tried to put that in a more easy way for people to use.

- it is sign of high mathematical ability

  I mean I think that people with a reasonable mathematical brain ought to be able to think algebraically a bit.

- it is a sign of a higher level of attainment

  letters shows you that they're comfortable with that, even at that sort of reasonably low level. So it's something that you know I'd definitely recommend at this next stage.

Reasons for valuing symbolic generalizations over those expressed in words were not addressed deliberately during the interviews with teachers; the reasons listed above were given by the teachers spontaneously as justifications for their judgments. A more explicit inquiry into teachers' beliefs about algebra might well discover a variety of different rationalizations for its value, including ones which related more to the place of symbolism within mathematics itself. In particular, the distinction between procedural and relational generalizations that was used in ana-lysing the student texts did not arise explicitly in the teachers' discourse. Although those generalizations identified as potentially relational were more highly valued, the reasons given for this seemed to be associated with the use of symbols rather than with the structure of the statement. It is not possible to determine whether the teachers were reading generalizations in the form of equations as statements of relations between variables or as procedures for performing calculations.

Whatever the reasons for valuing algebra, the apparent close association between use of algebra and teachers' perceptions of ability is significant in the coursework assessment context. As was seen in the previous chapter, some teachers seem to form their assessments of a piece of work by building up a picture of the personal characteristics of the author. A perception that a student is 'able', based on the existence of symbolic algebra within her text, would thus be very influential in forming a final assessment.

In spite of the value placed on a symbolic generalization, however, it is not considered to be adequate in the coursework context without some verbal elabora-tion. Richard's 'Inner Triangles' text was a particularly extreme case of a lack of words. Most of the teachers took this to be a sign of relatively high achievement or ability. For example, Fiona praised the algebraic notation as 'quite advanced', while Dan, who had at one time taught Richard, described him as 'quite an intuit-ive mathematician'. It is interesting to note that both Fiona and Dan hedged their praise with the qualifier *quite* as they, like all the teachers who read these 'Inner Triangles' texts, also criticized Richard for not including more 'writing'.

The reasons given by the teachers for requiring words as well as algebraic notation were multiple, arising from their simultaneous occupation of a number of (potentially contradictory) positions in relation to the activity. Teachers, in their role as examiners and as teachers responsible to a range of external authorities, are naturally concerned that their judgments of students should be seen to be valid. They feel the need, therefore, to find evidence within a student's script that the work 'belongs' to the student. For example, Dan commented on Steven's text that:

> *the formula . . . did sort of appear out of nowhere as though he did have a sly look round somebody's arm or something.*

It is not clear why a symbolic formula should be considered more likely to be copied from another student than any other part of the text. It is, however, true that Steven's 'Inner Triangles' formula is not integrated into the rest of his text either by a narrative of its provenance or by an argument for its validity.

Andy's reading of Richard's text is particularly interesting because of the multiplicity of reasons he provides for demanding a generalization in words. Andy acknowledged the lack of evidence in his text but was prepared to act as teacher/advocate on his behalf:

> *I'm very confident that, although there's no evidence of it, what he's produced is right and he's done it. It definitely wouldn't be a copy. . . .*

Interestingly, Richard was given the benefit of the doubt on this point by most of the teachers. Demonstrating ownership is not, however, the only function of a generalization in words. While satisfied that the formula was Richard's own, Andy nevertheless went on to give a number of other reasons for wanting to see the generalization expressed in words:

> *I would like to see that he can generalize in words first of all. It kind of gives the understanding, I think, putting it into words the patterns which they see. Then I think it underpins the algebra which they produce later.*

Initially, Andy claims that he wants to see that Richard 'can generalize in words'; he is looking for evidence of a skill. In the next breath he is suggesting that this would also provide evidence of 'understanding'. The expression that he uses is, however, ambiguous — 'It kind of gives the understanding' to whom? Do the words give evidence to an examiner who needs to know that the student understands, or is the understanding given to the student himself by the process of expressing the generalization in words? This ambiguity marks a shift in Alan's reading between an examiner role, looking for evidence, and a teacher/adviser role, suggesting ways in which students can be helped. In the final sentence of the extract above, the role of generalization in words has clearly shifted from being evidence towards assessment of the student to being a pedagogic device for helping the student to gain understanding. At the same time Andy has shifted from referring specifically to Richard to using a non-specific *they*; he is now stating general pedagogic principles. He went on to describe the assessment methods used by the teachers in his school:

> *When we moderate, we usually do it as a group in the same room usually working in different corners on the scripts that we're moderating and frequently we ask across the room to the teacher concerned 'where did this come from, is that alright?', and . . . on we go. But there's usually a check of that kind. We try very hard to tell the children generalize in words first of all and we say if you know a pattern, can you tell us about it, tell your friend about it. When they can explain the pattern in words and they write those words down then they're ready to produce the algebra.*

Again, he moves from a description of the way the teachers behave as examiners looking for evidence to a description of the pedagogical device they use to help the students to become 'ready to produce the algebra'.

Andy and the other teachers interviewed appear to be using an unwritten criterion that any algebraic generalization appearing in a piece of coursework should be preceded by a verbal statement of the same generalization. Stated like this, it is a simple matter to judge whether or not a student has fulfilled the criterion. The justification for its use, however, is not so simple but takes a number of forms: it is evidence that the student has the skill to write a verbal generalization; it shows that the student understands the algebra; it proves that the formula 'belongs' to the student; it provides evidence of the processes that the student has gone through in order to arrive at the formula; it helps the student to understand the pattern; it prepares the student to 'produce the algebra'. The discourses of assessment and of pedagogy are intertwined here.

Advising students to generalize in words as a step towards using algebraic symbols is a common pedagogic strategy. The process is described by Mason (1987) as 'a necessary part of the struggle towards meaning along the spiral [of symbolizing]' (p. 80) and has been incorporated into the official discourse of the mathematics curriculum in statements such as this from the Inspectorate:

> It is damaging to pupils' mathematical development if they are rushed into the use of notation before the underlying concepts are sufficiently developed and understood. At all stages the teacher needs to stress the translation of words into mathematical symbols, and the reverse, so that pupils may develop a facility in the use of symbols and an understanding of the meanings attached to them. (HMI, 1987, p. 10)

It seems for these teachers, however, that a principle related to facilitating children's learning has been transformed into a prescriptive algorithm for 'doing investigations'. Regardless of the individual student's actual facility with symbolizing, she or he is expected to have gone through the entire 'struggle towards meaning'. As Amy put it, criticizing Richard's (correct) symbolic generalization: *'He needs to explore. There's something needed before he could generalize'*. Although Richard is clearly able, at least in the context of this problem, to generalize symbolically without such aids, because he has failed to comply with the conventions of the coursework genre he is judged harshly; the 'need' is a requirement of the examination, expressed in the language of pedagogy.

The primary, and in most cases only, use made of symbolic notation in the set of coursework scripts examined was to express a generalization. This generalization appeared to be seen by both students and teachers as the end point or solution of the task and was in many cases underlined, presented on a separate page under a heading *FORMULA*, or otherwise signposted as the 'answer'. While forming such symbolic generalizations is an important mathematical process, outside the school context it would not normally be seen as an end in itself. Symbolization is not merely a process of translation from one language into another but is the starting point for developing new ways of looking at a problem and for enabling manipulations that may lead to new discoveries and further generalizations. As Mason (1987) points out, 'Classification is for the purpose of formulating theorems, not simply to achieve superficial classification' (p. 77).

In the few cases where evaluation or manipulation of a formula was found in a coursework text, it appeared to be used by both students and teachers as a means of demonstrating proficiency in decontextualized algebraic skills rather than as part of the investigative or problem solving process. While the formation of a generalization may be seen as part of the investigative process and the use of symbolism may be seen as assisting communication, other algebraic aspects, including substitution and manipulation of algebraic expressions appear to be valued primarily as demonstrations of 'content' skills. The manipulation of an algebraic expression was particularly highly valued by some teachers, perhaps as a sign of even higher ability. There appeared to be some conflict, however, between this perception of the value of manipulative skills and a recognition that performing such manipulation was not relevant within the given problem solving situation. Algebra is clearly one area which gives rise to tension between the value placed on process within the discourse of investigation and that placed on content in traditional modes of curriculum and assessment.

Statement of the Problem — Copying vs. 'Own Words'

An initial statement of the task being undertaken by the student appears to be an expected and approved part of a coursework text. The general attitude of the teachers, however, appeared to be that merely copying the task from the question sheet was a waste of time and might even be taken as a sign of laziness or lack of thought, while a statement in the student's own words was highly approved. While in some cases the 'own words' introduction was merely stated to be a 'good thing' in itself, there are some indications that other functions are ascribed to it, in particular that it may demonstrate that the student has understood the nature of the task or provide evidence that the student has worked through the examples provided. Thus Carol remarked:

> And the pupil has carried out the initial task that's given . . . done the initial task as was given on the sheet and checked that the information as given on the sheet was correct as they were supposed to do.

It is interesting to note that the section of Sandra's text that Carol was commenting on was actually copied verbatim from the question paper. This was not, however, recognized; the copied words were taken as a sign of material activity and of engagement with the task.

Carol was not alone in mis-identifying introductory statements of the problem as copied or written in the student's own words. Of the 15 occasions on which teachers commented on whether the student had copied or not, only 8 correct identifications were made. Although in some cases the differences between the statement of the problem on question paper (which was available throughout the interviews) and the student's version were subtle and might not be noticed or considered significant by the reader, it appeared that even substantial differences between the versions might be neglected while, conversely, verbatim copies were sometimes read as original. Although there were hints that different teachers had consistently different reading practices in respect to the problem statements, the number of texts read was too small to allow such generalizations to be made. However, it does appear either that there are different standards of what counts as 'copied' or that some of the teachers, in making their judgments about these sections, are using other aspects of the text as well as or instead of the actual words.

The relatively consistent readings of Sandra's introduction is particularly interesting; four of the five teachers who read her text commented that she had used her own words while the fifth made no reference to this section. Sandra had omitted the first part of the first sentence of the question paper 'In this task you will be asked to', starting her introduction with the next words 'Balance some rods of different length . . .' and continuing subsequently to copy both the words and the diagrams of the rest of the statement of the problem exactly. It is possible that some of the teachers judged this to be in her own words merely on the basis that the first sentence started in a different way. However, Grant actually looked more carefully at the whole introduction, suspecting that it might be copied, yet still concluding eventually that it was not:

> *Now this is a good introduction. This is the type of thing that would put me in a good mood before I started to mark it I think in terms of whoever it is just described what they got to do with pictures which always help. It's in fact a copy of that isn't it? Almost? No it's not. They've rewritten this in their own words which is fairly good I think.*

The positive impression made by Sandra's immaculate presentation, using colour, elegant handwriting and a well-balanced layout of the page, may be a stronger influence on the reader than the actual words she has used. One explanation for this might be that the interpersonal effect of the presentation is such as to suggest a great deal of effort and personal engagement in the task, which is then interpreted by the teacher-readers as personal 'ownership' of the task.

The inconsistency (and inaccuracy) of the teachers' readings of these sections of text raises a problem for the student who wishes to demonstrate that she has 'understood the problem' or performed the required material actions. While paraphrasing the words given on the question paper may be the best strategy, this does not in itself guarantee that the teacher-assessor will recognize that it has been done. Where an introduction was missing, its absence was generally not remarked upon; it may, therefore, be possible to persuade a teacher-assessor that one has 'understood the problem' by other means.

Narrative — Telling the Right Story

The value placed on processes in the discourse of investigation leads to a requirement that students should demonstrate those processes in order that they may be assessed. As Charles remarked, however: 'It's very difficult to judge what's going on in somebody's head'. In order to attempt to overcome this difficulty, the processes have to be externalized in some concrete form that may be observed and interpreted by the teacher-assessor. One of the main forms this externalization appears to be expected to take is the writing of a narrative of the student's actions and/or thought processes. Indeed, the absence of such a narrative may be taken as a sign that the required processes have not taken place and sometimes even raises the suspicion that the student has copied the results from a colleague rather than obtaining them through her own efforts.

Clearly there are logical objections to such an identification of the existence of actions and thoughts with their written description. Moreover, it is possible for a student to achieve a result in an intuitive way that could not easily be described in words. The requirement to provide a narrative to authenticate such an intuitive result must be problematic for the student-author. This problem with the use of narrative as an indicator of activity was recognized by several of the teachers but such recognition did not appear in practice to lead to any less demand for narrative in the students' work.

Not all narratives, however, are seen to be equally acceptable as indicators of processes. For example, the passage in Figure 10.4 contained a personal narrative aspect that was strongly criticized.

The temporal themes in this extract (*Once . . .* , *First . . .* , *In a very short time . . .*) and the use of the past tense serve to structure it as a story of what the author and her collaborator did. This did not, however, satisfy its teacher-readers' expectations. There appeared to be several sources of dissatisfaction with the text. The expression 'in a very short time' was remarked upon negatively by several teachers although they did not on the whole articulate the reasons for their disapproval. For example, Andy commented that he had seen it 'a thousand times' in students' work and that it 'always rings alarm bells'. It is possible that the thematization of this claim is considered inappropriate, suggesting over-confidence or a lack of care. On the other hand, it may also be that it contributes to an overall lack of specificity in the narrative. We are told that the two girls 'discovered a relationship' and 'were able to put this into a formula' but are not told how this was achieved. When the teachers provided examples of the sort of narratives they would prefer to see, these tended to involve mental processes with a fairly restricted reference (e.g. 'recognized' or 'predicted' rather than 'saw' or 'thought') and

Figure 10.4: An 'inappropriate' narrative — 'Inner Triangles' Extract No. 1

Once Suzanne and I had completed tasks 1 and 2, we set out to discover if there was any connection between the triangular area and the lengths of the sides. First we lettered the sides: —

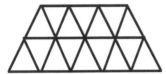

$a = slant\ line$
$b = base\ line$
$c = top\ line$
$d = area$

In a very short time we had discovered a relationship between the lengths of the sides and the area (triangular). We were able to put this into a formula: —

$ab + ac = d$

This simplified becomes:-

$a(b + c) = d.$

To make sure this worked, we checked it out:

---

referred to the specific nature of relationships rather than just to 'a relationship'. For example, Andy suggested a narrative framework for the stages leading to the discovery of a formula, using the deictic 'this' to indicate where the details of the particular situation should fit:

> *Once he's found, he's got the data say 'I've noticed* this *pattern and I predict that* this *is going to happen or* this *is the pattern which I can see'*

Another feature of some of the teachers' examples was a relatively complex structure, often expressing causal relationships between the actions, for example:

> *I then looked carefully at the results to see if there was a pattern, a pattern I recognized and this was . . . and so I eventually came to this formula*

This contrasted with the simple structure of many of the students' examples the teachers had condemned: often a string of clauses linked by 'and' or merely declaring the existence of a pattern or formula.

In spite of the importance that all the teachers seemed to attach to such narratives and the general consensus that students find such writing difficult and often do it inappropriately, it appears that the teachers themselves, although able to give examples of the kind of narratives they would like to see, may be less than successful in communicating their specific expectations to their students. It may even be the case that general advice given to students can give rise to the very forms the teachers reject. Joan gave her students written advice on writing coursework reports, including the admonition to 'Write down what you did in the order that it happened', yet condemned the temporal approach in the extract in Figure 10.4, parodying its anecdotal nature:

That's one of my pet hates. It's the sort of, you know, 'Miss put this task on the board and we copied it down' but not quite that bad.

Although the teachers tended to express their demand for such narrative writing in terms of wanting to see what the student did, a closer examination of the types of writing that were approved and of the more elaborated reasons that were given in response to probing during the interview suggest that there are actually several different functions that such writing is expected to fulfil:

- it should provide not only description of the student's actions but also the reasons for taking them;
- it should provide a basis for conclusions made in the text;
- it should give enough detail to be taken as evidence that the results are the student's own work;
- it creates coherence to make the text easier to read;
- its existence fulfils an examination requirement.

Although there was general agreement that narrative was required and a certain amount of similarity in the forms which were approved by the various teachers, some expressed concern about the relevance of the requirement. While expressing his unease with the examination board requirement for 'writing', Dan identified the source of his discomfort as a perception that students who are good at mathematics may not have matching competence in writing:

'Explain your strategies' is one they find quite difficult, cos they know what they're doing and they do it quite efficiently. To actually put down on paper . . . the strategies they're using. I think sometimes they find it too — especially with an intelligent child — they find it too mundane to actually say well this is what I did and so on. And some children have very good mathematical skills and can see through things but actually their English skills don't match it in terms of explaining what they do to go on.

As well as suggesting that the requirement to include a narrative of the process of solution is perhaps not relevant for the 'intelligent child', he is making a clear separation between mathematical competence and 'explaining', suggesting that he places more value on the 'product' of the investigation than on the processes. Carol also appeared to experience difficulty in resolving her judgment of the mathematical value of a piece of text with her judgment of the language used in it:

As I say we're not supposed to be assessing their English skills but it does help with marking it if they tell you what they've been doing, even if their spelling is awful and their English is awful, but the trouble is the ones with English are awful are reluctant because they've got hang-up about that.

She does, however, acknowledge the role that the narrative of 'what they've been doing' plays in influencing her own understanding and assessment of the text and recognizes an interaction between achievement in the two fields. Those teachers who questioned the requirement to provide a narrative of the student's processes appeared to be placing greater value on the mathematical 'content' that may be displayed in lists of results and formulae than on the 'processes' that are displayed through narrative. This is perhaps in tension with the more general value placed on processes within the discourse of 'investigation'.

Explanation — For Some

Although development of 'investigations' in the mathematics curriculum has been blamed for an alleged decline in students' appreciation of the role of deductive reasoning and proof in mathematics (see, for example, LMS, 1995), it is generally recognized that explanation, justification and proof[2] are important. This importance is reflected in the discourse of GCSE coursework in the assessment criteria, in the instructions included in set investigation tasks to 'explain' the results achieved, and in the frequent mention of the presence or absence of such explanation by teacher-readers. However, it is clear that, although all students are *asked* to explain their results, it is only expected that the highest achievers will actually succeed in doing so:

> The ability to explain or prove these generalizations, relate the generalized form to the geometry of the experimental mode (a proof) should *always* be deemed to be an *extension* and — if correct — worthy of a very top grade A. (ULEAC, 1993, p. 21; original emphasis)

This identification between explanation and high achievement was also made by the teachers, as may be seen in Fiona's description of her assessment practice:

> *For the really, the more able, if they found a formula can they explain why it works, and then I would have given probably an A, certainly an A grade.*

The 'Inner Triangles' student texts read in the interviews contained very little that could be considered explanation in this sense. Its absence was remarked upon in only a few cases, suggesting that it is not a general expectation of all students. However, two of the 'Topples' texts, by Ellen and Steven (see Figures 10.5 and 10.6), attempted to address the instruction:

> e) Explain your result. (Well argued explanations based on intuition and insight will gain at least as much credit as those based on the principles of Physics.)

The mention of the 'principles of Physics' in the instruction makes it clear that this demand for explanation is expecting the student to make connections between the numerical results and inductive generalizations achieved through practical experimentation and the nature of the physical phenomena involved. There is a tension here between the value that is being laid on the form of the argument and

Figure 10.5: Ellen's explanation of the 'Topples' result

> The smaller the unit at the bottom the more likely the load will fall quicker. i.e. a one unit rod can't even balance a 2 unit rod, yet a 3 unit rod can balance 8 units.

Figure 10.6: Steven's explanation of the 'Topples' result (extract)

> The reason that the pile topples could be because the weight over the starting pile becomes too much and gets pulled down by gravity. . . .

the physical validity of the content of the argument. The capitalization of 'Physics' confers a status that seems at odds with the apparent valuing of 'intuition and insight'. This tension was also apparent in the teachers' interviews, both in their readings of students' attempts to provide such explanations and in their general comments about their expectations. Of course, the explanations for the results achieved in this task cannot be expected to be mathematical proofs. Nevertheless, the teachers' readings raise some general issues about the ways in which language of explanations and proofs may affect the value placed upon them.

Ellen's explanation (Figure 10.5) was largely ignored or dismissed by the teacher-readers. Although the fact that she had made an attempt to provide an explanation was appreciated, those teachers who commented on it at all suggested that they would not lay much importance on it, dismissing it as 'intuitive' and, in the case of Grant, suggesting that it was only worthy of a 'low ability pupil'. Ellen was credited with effort but not with any degree of understanding.

Steven, on the other hand was judged more highly. His explanation (Figure 10.6) not only uses a vocabulary that identifies it as 'Physics' (i.e. 'weight', 'gravity'), but also makes it explicit that he is answering the question 'why', starting with a statement of a causal relationship. Those teachers who spent time reading his explanation appeared to find it difficult to make sense of it. Thus Grant, for example, struggled to quantify the explanation in order to make it fit in with the numerical results achieved through experiment and in an attempt to understand the physics of the situation himself:

> *'There's too much weight on the right hand side so the pile topples over'. Um, he could have gone a bit further into it. He could have counted the units of weight and perhaps given an example for this one being perhaps, what would that be — two — so that would be eight on one side and er seven on that side, so is that going to topple? Two three four five. It will won't it, so it doesn't work in that one but it should do shouldn't it? Am I right? No, cos it would depend on how much was above the base, it wouldn't depend on the base one so much, yeah. So he could perhaps have gone into that a little bit more. He's obviously quite a good pupil in terms of his thought processes about it, but could have explained more.*

Although Grant judged the explanation itself to be inadequate, he nevertheless credited Steven with being a 'good pupil'. It appears that the form of the explanation as well as the validity of its content contribute to the evaluation of the argument; this distinction between form and content was made explicitly by Charles:

> *I think any argument would be good so long as they got a good explanation and a good argument as to why it might be the case. I'm not too worried about it necessarily being correct but I would be more interested in them whether they could actually argue the point for themselves. So I would be looking more in the assessment on the strength of the argument than actually what they're trying to put across.*

The explanations provided by Ellen and Steven differ in both form and content. While Steven's is clearly in the form of an argument, stating a causal relationship, Ellen's statement describes a general association between two states without making any explicit claims about causality. At the same time, Steven makes use of the vocabulary of physics, suggesting that he is searching for explanations outside the confines of the task itself, while Ellen has confined herself to terms used within the question paper itself. The data available is too limited for it to be possible to determine which of these factors plays the greater role in influencing the teachers' judgments of the value of the argument. It does, however, appear that students would be well advised to use linguistic forms that clearly signal that they are making claims about causality, whatever the validity of the explanation they are attempting to provide.

The roles of 'explanation' of the reasons for the results are two-fold:

- it is a sign of high mathematical achievement (on the way to 'proof');
- it shows ability to construct a coherent argument.

There is a tension between these two roles that is related to the tension between content and process in the 'investigation' discourse as a whole. In many of the coursework tasks with which students engage, a mathematical proof of the result is likely to be beyond the capability of the vast majority of the students. On the other hand, a substantially larger group of students is expected to be able to produce some form of argument in an attempt to 'explain'. For most students (and their teachers), therefore, the production of an argument in an acceptable form is of greater importance than producing a 'correct' explanation.

Use of a Conventional Mathematics Register

As I argued in Chapter 2, the aspects of mathematical language most commonly recognized are its use of symbols and its specialist vocabulary. It might be anticipated, therefore, that teacher-readers would remark on whether student texts made use of these features and would value those texts which did so. In fact, while there was clearly an expectation that students should use conventional forms of mathematical vocabulary, this expectation was not strongly enforced. Only one teacher, for example, identified Clive's use of the term 'conversion table', commenting that it didn't convert anything. Similarly, Jenny was the only teacher who objected to the way in which the word 'unit' was used in the Topples texts, complaining that it was not used 'in a very mathematical way'. Jenny also objected to Sandra's use of the equals sign as an operator (Sandra had several statements of the form $50 - 2 = 48 \div 2 = 24$).

The use of succinct descriptors for variables was desired by several teachers; for example, Steven's variable name was read disparagingly by Andy as 'the distance along the bottom, as he describes it'. There appears to be a hierarchy of ways of denoting variables: while a single letter variable name was, as we have already seen, clearly preferred by all the teachers, labels such as 'top length' were also acceptable. One feature, apart from its shortness, that might distinguish the acceptable 'top length' from the less acceptable 'top of the trapezium' or 'distance along the bottom' is the objectification of the measurement. This distances the quantity from the physical object that gave rise to it, thus placing it at a slightly higher level of abstraction.

Specialist vocabulary and symbolism are not, however, the only characteristics of conventional mathematical writing. As was seen in Chapter 2, an impersonal, formal style is a recognized characteristic in academic texts, especially in mathematics and science, and, although such a high degree of abstraction and formality might not be expected in coursework, teachers reacted with what appeared to be affectionate humour to some of the more informal and personal aspects of students' texts. Ellen's heading 'THE REAL FORMULA' was marked by laughter from Carol, while Jenny laughed at Steven's expression of confidence: *Well I like his enthusiasm that he thinks 'with such a definite pattern a formula should be easy to find'*.

Such expressions of attitude are not a common part of most other forms of mathematical writing. Similarly, statements about the way in which the student worked (in a group or individually) were greeted with laughter by Fiona and with rather condescending approval by Dan: *It's quite nice when they say things like that as well 'a formula that our group worked out'*. Unlike the expected narrative of the student's processes, this mention of the group provides the reader with access to the context within which the student's activity took place. The reaction of laughter suggests that the teachers saw such inclusion of the personal and contextual as incongruous (or at least unusual).

There were occasional general comments on 'style' of the writing. These suggest that, even where the teacher cannot articulate the nature of the stylistic incongruity they experience, this is likely to affect their assessment. Dan, for example, commented repeatedly on his discomfort with Steven's text, stating in a non-specific way that 'the writing's not all that marvellous' and eventually linking his evaluation of the standard of the writing to a more general evaluation of Steven's ability: *'He writes perhaps not at the same level as the others ... on intellectual terms'*, and concluding that Steven, although he had produced 'a good sound piece of work' was a 'not particularly able mathematician'. It is possible that the use of concrete variable names such as 'the distance along the bottom', discussed above, may have been one of the features which contributed to Dan's discomfort with Steven's writing. Similarly, Dan compared two of the extracts from Inner Triangles texts (Figures 10.7 and 10.8):

Figure 10.7: 'Inner Triangles' Extract No. 2

If you add the top length and the bottom length, then multiply by the slant length, you get the number of unit triangles.

For example:

$3 + 5 = 8$ and $2 + 4 = 6$
$8 \times 2 = \underline{16}$ $6 \times 2 = \underline{12}$

This, therefore is the formula:

(TOP LENGTH + BOTTOM LENGTH) × SLANT LENGTH = No. OF TRIANGLES

Figure 10.8: 'Inner Triangles' Extract No. 3

If you add together both the top length and the bottom length and times it by the slant length, you will end up with the number of unit triangles in that trapezium.

You can write this as $S(T + B)$

> *Number 2 gives me the impression they obviously know what they're talking about whereas this one [No. 3], although it says almost exactly the same thing in different words, er, it doesn't give me the same impression.*

The comparable parts of the two texts, as Dan said, say almost the same thing in slightly different words.

Obvious differences between the two texts include the fact that No. 2 had included two examples and had used verbal variable names, while No. 3 had used algebraic symbols for her formula. Dan had commented on these differences earlier, claiming that they did not greatly affect his assessment of the students although he would wish to advise each of them to include the features found in the other's text. His 'impression' appears to be based rather on the verbal descriptions of the procedure which, as he says, appear very similar in form. An analysis of the two texts suggests a number of aspects which may have affected Dan's reading:

> *Processes and participants* No. 3's procedure uses *add together* rather than simply *add*, and *times it by* rather than *multiply by*. The number of unit triangles is also qualified as being *in that trapezium*. These additional words include reference to the concrete lengths, numbers or shapes. The procedure may thus be read as being at a lower level of abstraction.
>
> *Causal relationships* No. 3's introduction of the final formula by *You can write this as* . . . presents the symbolic formula merely as an alternative to the verbal procedure. No. 2's announcement *This therefore is the formula*, on the other hand, displays the formula as a product in its own right which follows logically from the procedure rather than merely being equivalent to it. Mathematics is thus presented as an autonomous system rather than being dependent on human action. It may also suggest that No. 2 has a better understanding of the importance of the relational formula in mathematics, even though she has not used algebraic symbols to express it.

Specialist vocabulary   The use by No. 3 of *times* rather than *multiply* is less formally 'mathematical' and the use of such vocabulary may be read as a remnant of the early years of mathematics schooling and hence a sign of immaturity.

Modality   The modality of the phrase *you will end up with* (No. 3) suggests an authority over the reader's activity rather than over the mathematics, whereas *you get* (No. 2), being in the present tense, focuses on the universal generality of the mathematical statement. The contrasting modality of the two statements introducing the final formulae, *You can write this as* . . . (No. 3) and *This therefore is the formula* (No. 2), also suggests that the two students differ in their levels of confidence.

Expression of reasoning   No. 2's use of *therefore* clearly signals that her text is presenting a logical argument whereas No. 3 merely juxtaposes statements and does not, therefore, force the reader to read her text in this way. Such juxtaposition, being characteristic of spoken rather than written language, may also be taken as a sign of immaturity.

Cohesion   No. 2 presents the variables and operations in the same order in both procedure and formula, whereas No. 3 changes her order from $(T + B) \times S$ in the verbal procedure to $S(T + B)$ in the symbolic formula. This disjunction further reinforces the lack of logical structure in No. 3's text and may even be taken by a teacher-assessor as a suggestion that the symbolic formula was copied from another source rather than 'belonging' to the student herself.[3]

Any of these features might have contributed to Dan's impression that No. 3 is less competent mathematically. While it is not possible to say precisely which aspects contributed to his assessment, there is clearly a mismatch between her text and Dan's expectations which appears to have affected his evaluation of the whole of No. 3's performance and even of her general level of intellectual 'ability'. As Dan himself was unable to identify the features of the text which gave rise to his impressions it seems unlikely that he would be able to provide advice to a student on how to produce an acceptable text. Moreover, his identification of the style of writing with 'intellectual level' and with 'knowing what they're talking about' suggests a view of language as the transparent representation of thought. It is a logical consequence of such a view that 'improvements' to the text can only follow (and will necessarily follow) developments in the students' thinking about the mathematics. A teacher holding this view of language may not consider it necessary or useful to address the form of writing with his students.

Coherence: A Case Study

In the discussion above, the teachers' readings of features of students' texts have been largely isolated from the rest of the text. This is justified to some extent in that it reflects the way in which many of the features were read; they were remarked upon as data or 'evidence' or as performance indicators in their own right rather than being seen as part of a coherent argument. However, teachers read and assess whole texts. In this section, I intend to look at a teacher's strategies for reading rather longer sections of text and the way in which these strategies depend both on

Figure 10.9: Clive's solution and explanation

Below is a formula that our group work out, here it is.

The top + The bottom × The slant

Also my formula is the one above but mine is below.

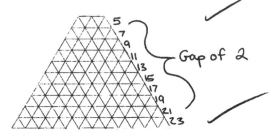

Gap of 2

The numbers can be added together to get the next row of numbers. It can also tell you the answer from a 2 top, 2 slant and 4 bottom as well as a 2 top, 10 slant and a 12 bottom to get ~~this~~ add all the numbers together.

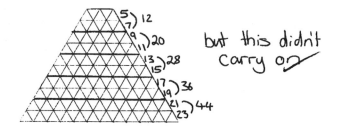

but this didn't carry on

the text itself and on the teacher's expectations. Two sections of coursework text, both containing diagrammatic forms, will be considered, together with the readings made of these sections by an experienced teacher, Andy (who had taught both the student-authors, Clive and Richard, and had actually marked their coursework the previous summer).

Clive's text (Figure 10.9) has integrated diagrams and verbal text using several cohesive devices. The section considered here starts with the words 'Also my formula is the one above but mine is below' and continues to the bottom of the page. These first words link the section to the previous one, indicating that it should be read as a 'formula' and that it forms an alternative or an addition to the previous section.

In the verbal text between the two diagrams, references to 'the numbers' and to 'the next row' make explicit links between diagrams and verbal text; the words do not have any reference without the diagrams to provide context. Similarly, the use of the pronoun 'It' must refer to one or both of the diagrams as there is no previous verbal subject for it to refer to. The final verbal statement 'but this didn't carry on' also appears to refer to some aspect of the pattern of numbers displayed in the diagram next to it. This statement, moreover, brings the section to a close; the echoing of the beginning statement 'but mine is below' by 'but this didn't carry on' forms a frame around the two diagrams and the intervening verbal text which further marks this as a self contained coherent section of the whole text.

The second diagram is a copy of the first one with the addition of further annotations in the form of lines separating out pairs of rows (thus forming trapezia of slant length 2) and brackets with numbers showing the sums of the numbers of triangles in each pair of rows. The addition of numbers is referred to in the intervening verbal text, as is the trapezium of '2 top, 2 slant and 4 bottom' which is formed by the top two rows of the diagram. It thus appears that Clive is presenting both his solution (or 'formula'), in the form of a diagram that 'can also tell you the answer', and an explanation in writing of how this solution is constructed, deriving the second diagram from the first.

This analysis of the cohesion of this section of text was achieved by paying explicit attention to cohesive devices used within the verbal part of the text and to similarities and differences between the two diagrams. In doing this, not only is the formal linguistic cohesion of the text described but also the logical coherence and textual function of the section is clarified. It is not, however, an easy section of text to read and make sense of. Factors contributing to this difficulty include: the ambiguity of the reference of 'row' and 'next row'; the discontinuity between the sentence which describes a pattern within the diagrams and the next one which makes connections between the diagrams and the original trapezium problem; some technical errors in punctuation and lack of capital letters; the elliptic 'but this didn't carry on', which suggests a weakness in Clive's mathematical solution without making it obvious what 'this' might be. Rather than merely reporting what he has done, Clive has attempted to describe both a pattern and a general procedure. The task that he has undertaken is thus a complex and perhaps a difficult one and this may account for a greater difficulty for a reader in making sense of it.

The lack of control of the written language displayed in Clive's verbal text may contribute to the way in which his teacher, Andy, reads and assesses it.

He's illustrated the difference in the area — a nice attempt to show that as you increase the slant height by one so the area increases by two each time. He's tried to do that all on one diagram. It's not easy but it's er, I can understand what he's getting at there. And he's tried that then for a . . . a second occasion.

Figure 10.10: Richard's 'stars' extension

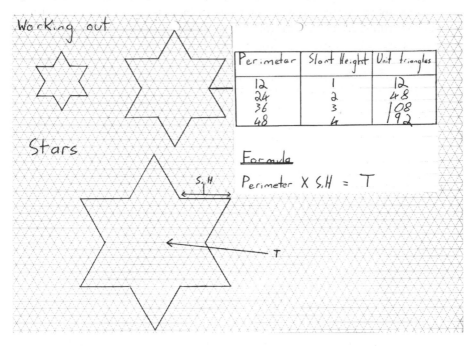

Working out

Perimeter	Slant Height	Unit triangles
12	1	12
24	2	48
36	3	108
48	4	192

Stars

Formula

Perimeter X S.H = T

S.H

T

Andy is not reading this section as an integrated text. While the first diagram is analysed and identified as a form of communication, providing an illustration of an observation about the trapezia, he makes no reference to the verbal text and the second diagram is interpreted as a repetition or variation rather than a further step in the argument. The brevity of this extract from Andy's interview indicates the speed with which he passed over the whole section. Given the difficulties that might be involved in reading the verbal part, he is unlikely to have followed the logic of Clive's text in this time. This fragmented reading is paralleled by the ticks with which he had originally marked Clive's work. The page containing this section is structured visually as four parts of almost equal size: writing, diagram, writing, diagram. Each of these parts has a tick next to it, suggesting that Andy was originally validating the form of each part rather than the content. While he expresses approval of the first diagram, this approval is qualified by the modality of the whole passage. Clive has made a 'nice attempt' and he has 'tried'. By repeating this theme of 'trying', Andy suggests that Clive has not been very successful. He is getting credit for effort rather than for the quality of his work. It appears that Andy is imposing his own generalization onto Clive's text ('as you increase the slant height by one so the area increases by two each time') and criticizing Clive for not stating this more clearly.

Richard's section of text (Figure 10.10) differs in a number of ways from Clive's. Firstly, the section is more clearly defined than Clive's: it is on a separate page with a heading (although there is some ambiguity about whether the heading for the page is 'Working out' or 'Stars'). There is no explicit reference in this section to any other part of the work although when seen within context its structural similarity to other pages contributes to the coherence of the text as a whole (see also Figure 9.2). Also unlike Clive's text, there are few explicit cohesive ties within the section; the labels on the large star, S.H and T, are repeated in the formula but apart from that it is left entirely to the reader to make sense of the connections between the various parts of the page. There is a line drawn apparently connecting one of the 'working out' star diagrams to the table which might be interpreted as a cohesive link suggesting that the table contains data taken from the diagram; it might also, however, be read as a line drawn in error that has been partially covered by the paper containing the table that has been stuck over it.

As in the rest of Richard's text there is a lack of any verbal language other than disconnected headings and labels. While this characteristic of his work was heavily criticized by most of the teacher-readers, it does not seem to have detracted from the ease with which Andy made sense of this section.

A: *Oh, some stellations here! What have we got for this? . . . Slant length times perimeter . . . aha! Yeah, now here he's made a jump which needs to be made clear because the unit triangles have now changed. The actual size of the unit triangle has now changed from . . . the unit is now a two by two by two triangle*

I: *Oh, is it? I hadn't noticed that.*[4]

A: *We've got, on this one here, the perimeter's twelve, he's counted that as being one here*

I: *I see, yes*

A: *And the slant height as well, it's just the length of one side*

I: *Yes*

A: *And so he's actually taken different size unit triangle which I think he should make clear about. Whoever's marked this should have made a comment about it* [said with irony as Andy himself was the original marker]

I: *So do you think that this star corresponds to the first one rather than to that*

A: *I think he's done that. That's my first [. . .]. Because the perimeter's twelve and it's, and I think he's taken that as one unit so that would seem . . .*

In contrast to his fragmented reading of Clive's text, Andy is making strong connections between the diagrams and the table. In particular, he is making inferences about the nature of the correspondence between the smallest diagram and the first entry in the diagram. In assuming that the first entry (perimeter 12 and slant height 1) refers to this diagram (perimeter 24 and slant height 2) he is forced to conclude that Richard is using a different scale for his diagrams. The necessity of this assumption might be questioned: there is no labelling on the diagrams to indicate such a change of scale; there are no explicit links between the diagrams and the table. While there are four entries in the table, there are only three diagrams and two of these diagrams could be taken to correspond directly to the second and fourth entries while the third could be read as a generic star being used to demonstrate the reference of the variable names (a device that had been seen to be used earlier in Richard's text) rather than as a specific example. However, the information structure provided by the left to right orientation of the page (Kress and van Leeuwen, 1996) may contribute to the assumption that the diagrams (left hand side of the page, hence 'given' as fundamental data) have given rise to the table and formula (right hand side of the page, hence 'new'). They are thus read as different, perhaps progressively more sophisticated, representations of the 'same' data.

This section of Richard's text, while lacking the 'writing' expected by the general assessment requirements, is nevertheless consistent with the conventional expectations about the investigation process. Its three parts (diagrams, table, and formula) may easily be identified with the DPG investigation algorithm: generate data, tabulate it to look for a pattern, generalize. The page can thus be read within this structure as a narrative of what Richard did, i.e. he drew three examples, he put the values derived from these examples into a table, he formed a fourth set of values based on the pattern he observed in the table, he derived a general formula from the pattern. As the text appears to conform to this algorithm it is not surprising that Andy should make sense of it within this convention.

In reading both these sections of text, Andy constructed a story about what the author was attempting to communicate, identifying in each case a difficulty or lack in the text but expressing no doubt about his own interpretation of the student's thinking. The amount of use he made of the text, however, differs considerably between the two texts. In the case of Clive, the first diagram was interpreted by itself while the verbal text and the second diagram were passed over with little comment; apparently no attempt was made to use the diagrams to make sense of the verbal part or vice-versa. When reading Richard's text, in contrast, Andy clearly made an assumption that the diagrams and the table were intimately connected and, indeed, worked hard to establish that connection himself. The degree of integration of diagrams into their context during the reading of these two sections actually appears to be in inverse proportion to the amount of integration in the form of explicit cohesive links provided by the authors.

I would suggest that the coherence that Andy constructed in Richard's text arose from its close adherence to the form of the Data–Pattern–Generalization investigation algorithm. This itself provides cohesion in a student's text by providing a conventional assumption that the juxtaposition of the various parts implies equivalence in their content and provides both chronological and logical progression. Thus the table was read as a representation of the information contained in the diagrams and the formula as a representation of the pattern formed within the table. The section of Clive's text does not conform to this convention either in the mathematical processes he was writing about or in the relationship between the various parts of the section. His verbal text does not merely repeat and reorganize information provided in the diagram; rather it attempts to explain how the diagram may be used to gain further information. Andy's reading, however, firstly assumed that Clive was only trying to describe a pattern (which is an appropriate thing to do within the conventions of the genre) and then identified the second diagram as a repetition of the first. There appears to be a mismatch between what Clive was attempting to do in his writing and the way in which his teacher read it. In spite of the fact that Andy and the other teachers who read Richard's text criticized his lack of writing or 'explanation', none had any difficulty in making coherent sense of his work. He was given credit for mathematical understanding, achievement and even ability. Clive's work, on the other hand, appeared to be more difficult to read and he was given credit for effort rather than achievement.

As we have seen in this chapter, it is relatively easy to identify the major features (i.e. tables, narrative, statement of the problem, etc.) that teachers pay attention to during their reading of student texts, and hence to construct a picture of the gross form of an 'ideal' coursework text. This is essentially what some of the teachers interviewed had done in providing advice to their own students to, for example, draw tables and explain what they had done. The evidence discussed here, however, suggests that the detailed form of these features significantly affects the interpretations that teachers make of them and may consequently affect their assessments of the students' achievement. Moreover, the contrast between Andy's readings of two longer sections of text suggests that the extent to which the text as a whole conforms to the stereotypical 'investigation' format may have an important effect on a teacher's ability to make coherent sense of the text.

Notes

1   The contrast in this example between Fiona's search for signs of 'system' and Joan's acceptance of the mathematical value of Clive's table is consistent with the variation between these two teachers that was discussed in Chapter 9.

2   I am aware that these terms are not easily distinguishable and am not attempting to distinguish them here. In this section, however, 'explaining' refers to explanation of *why* rather than explanation of how the results were achieved.

3   I am grateful to participants at the Birmingham meeting of the British Society for Research in the Learning of Mathematics in 1995 for bringing this point to my attention.

4   Although the interviewer's interventions lead Andy to expand on and clarify his interpretation of Richard's method, his first utterance clearly indicates that he had already formed his belief that the size of the unit triangle had been changed.

Chapter 11

Assessing Difference: 'Creativity' and Error

The introduction of investigational work in school mathematics and of assessment by coursework had as one of its aims to encourage students 'to create their own mathematics: actively taking part in mathematical thinking rather than passively receiving mathematical thought' (Pirie, 1988, p. 7). At the same time, however, the discourse of assessment in mathematics[1] is dominated by ideas of unique answers and 'correctness'. As we saw in Chapter 5, there is a tension between the aim of encouraging creativity and the traditional values of assessment practices which aim to make the final grade appear valid and 'objective'.

Early in her interview, when asked what she would look for in students' answers to the 'Inner Triangles' investigation, Joan, a head of department, described her attempt to resolve the tension between a perceived need for standardization and a recognition of variation in students' work by producing sets of exemplar materials for each investigation to guide the teachers' assessment.

> *Now the big problem with that of course is that before you've actually seen the children's work you're not always sure what you're going to come up with and they do sometimes surprise you, come up with something brilliant or just something that you haven't thought of. [. . .] Um the reason we started doing it really was for standardizing because that's been the biggest problem.*

The fact that Joan chose to describe this general process before addressing the specific question she had been asked, together with the repeated statement that this is a 'big problem', point out the importance of this issue for her.

While creativity or coming up with 'something brilliant' in coursework may be rare (and how indeed may it be recognized?), the nature of extended, relatively independent work ensures that there are many variations between students' responses to the same starting point. These variations include different lines of inquiry (including 'extensions'), strategies, interpretations of results and forms of communication; some variations may also be identified as errors. In this chapter, teachers' identifications of and responses to such variations in the students' texts they were asked to read and assess will be examined.

How Is 'Difference' Identified?

The texts which were read by the teachers during their interviews were originally selected to be different from one another in a number of ways related to their linguistic and other textual features, but to be relatively similar in the extent of their progress through the tasks set. When the teachers read the texts, however, there was generally little direct comparison made between the texts read and few of the pre-selected textual differences were commented on explicitly. Rather, comparisons were made between each individual text and an imaginary norm. For those teachers who were familiar with the tasks this norm may have been based either on their general expectations related to the specific task or on their recollections of other students' work on it, including knowledge of particular common results or ways of working. Joan's collection of exemplars described above suggests a formalization of such norms. Most of the teachers interviewed, however, had not used the tasks with students, yet were still able to identify some aspects of the students' texts as being 'different' and thus worthy of comment. In these cases, the identifications cannot have been made on the basis of concrete knowledge of what students usually produce in response to these particular tasks but rather on the basis either of their own work on the task or of more general expectations and experiences of how 'typical' students respond to this type of task.

When the teachers were reading the students' texts, much was read quickly and either passed over without comment or evaluated by applying a common category. This was often done by making a comment about the ways in which students or teachers work in general rather than by referring in detail to the characteristics of the individual student's text. Much of the students' work thus appeared to be read in a routine way as typical non-problematic examples of the type of work usually produced by students. Where a teacher did deal in an individual way with a feature of a specific text, this has been categorized as an instance of identification of 'difference'. These instances were identified in the interview transcripts by one or more of the following indicators: an explicit statement that this student's work is different or unusual; a statement that the student has had an idea or has thought about the problem; an expression of interest, surprise, or difficulty; an effort to make sense of the mathematics involved; the construction of a narrative to explain how the student might have arrived at a result; a statement that the student has made an error.

Difference Is Desirable but Difficult

In accordance with the general value placed on 'creativity' in the discourse of investigation, doing something that is different may be judged to be good in itself, even without examination of the details of the difference. For example, George's approval of Clive's work seems to reflect a common attitude:

He's done it in a different way. That's good, they can see it in a different way [. . .] I might give him credit for doing it in a different way.

The switch between the singular *he* and the plural *they* suggests that George's approval is not specific to this single case but is a general approval of any 'different way' of seeing or doing. The quality of the specific case is not significant in making this judgment.

Composing an Explanatory Narrative

Differences and unusual behaviour do, however, cause problems for teachers. One way in which this may be seen is in the teachers' struggle to compose stories to explain how the differences might have come about. These narratives were based on evidence in the student texts but also appeared to draw on other experiences and expectations of individual teachers. Different teachers may thus compose different explanatory narratives, and hence arrive at different evaluations of the same student's work.

Extract No. 1 (Figure 10.4 — see page 166) contained a generalization for the number of inner triangles in a trapezium in the form $ab + ac$ rather than the more commonly found $a(b + c)$ (where a, b and c are the dimensions of the trapezium). Although the performance indicators provided by the examination board actually gave the formula in this form, both Andy and Dan, who had used the Inner Triangles investigation with their students, commented on this form as unusual. Andy's reaction was complex:

> *It seems the formula which they produced where they multiply the top by the slant and multiply the base by the slant and add them to find the area. It's perfectly correct. It's an unusual way of finding the area. It's more common to add top and bottom first of all. From a geometrical point of view it's easier to do it that way. These things happen, and it's nice that children do work in different ways and I'm not at all surprised that somebody's found that way of doing it from the geometry angle.*

He first interprets the formula by reading it using the full referents of the variables rather than the single letter variables used in the student's text, thus marking the formula as non-routine and in need of interpretation. He then validates the formula; the qualification of his judgment of its correctness with the word *perfectly* indicates that there is a particular need to validate this formula because of its unusual format. The usual formula would be more likely to be passed over either without comment or with a bare 'that's right' — the verbal equivalent of a tick. His validation of the student's work is then elaborated: not only is the formula correct but it is given some additional value because it is in general 'nice that children do work in different ways'. In using several bases — both specific to this case and general principles — for judging the unusual formula to be acceptable, Andy appears to be displaying some discomfort with his judgment which needs to be resolved by creating an extended narrative to justify himself. He elaborates further by suggesting an explanation of how the student might have found the formula. There is no evidence in the extract of the student's text presented to Andy of how the formula was arrived at or, in particular, that any consideration was given to the geometry of the situation; he appears to have constructed this explanation from his own understanding of the 'Inner Triangles' problem and from his need to justify his judgment of the work.

Dan, on the other hand, was not able to construct the same narrative as he appeared not to have considered the possibility that students might work on this problem 'from the geometry angle'. Nevertheless, he too composed a story of how the student might have arrived at the formula, stressing the unusual nature of the result. The agency for the discovery this time was 'curiosity' rather than geometry

> *I mean I think it's unusual that it's that way round . . . I actually think that most children anyway would see that way round first* [pointing to the form $a(b + c)$] *and see those two added together multiplied by that far easier than they would see . . . I mean unless there was a table there that existed before that actually did that* [ab] *and did that* [ac] *and then did that* [$ab + ac$] *just by curiosity and saw that it came out like that*

Unlike Andy, however, Dan treated his explanation as merely hypothetical and was not satisfied that it establishes the validity of the student's result.

> *I mean I find this a very difficult thing. I think I'd have to talk through this . . . I find this an odd way round of doing it and I don't think I'd give them straight advice would be difficult I'd have to actually talk to the children involved and discover why they did that and how they came across that, so I'm a bit curious about how that comes up. They never explained how it works but anyone can get a formula as long as they understand algebra and they can get a formula and show how it works but that's the wrong way round. You want to know how it's actually derived. If there wasn't enough information I'd be a little bit worried about that.*

The unusual structure of the formula makes him 'a bit curious' and 'a little bit worried' and he finds the interviewer's request to give the student advice about how to improve her work 'difficult'. The modality of this passage suggests the conflict that Dan was experiencing in attempting to deal with unusual student behaviour.

The other two extracts presented to the teachers simultaneously with No. 1 gave the formula in the more usual structure (although using different notations). Although neither of these two extracts contained any real evidence of the origins of the formulae, this was not commented upon by either Dan or Andy; in these cases they were prepared to accept the formula as given without questioning or attempting to justify its validity. The 'usual' way of doing things is thus naturalized by these teachers. Although explanation even of the usual method is desired and even required for its own sake, the usual result or formula is likely to be accepted as valid and unproblematic even without any explanation. The unusual, on the other hand, is suspect and needs further validation and the construction of a narrative to explain its origin.

Another example of different teachers constructing different explanatory narratives is found in the various responses to Steven's 'Topples' text. In this text, Steven presented an alternative method for finding results for large lengths of rods by scaling up his results for small lengths (Figure 11.1).

Figure 11.1: Steven's alternative method

2　Imagine that you start with a rod length of 100 units and build up the pile using rods of lengths 101, 102, 103, ... units.

What will be the length of the rod that makes the pile topple?

$$(100 + 100) = 200 \quad \left(\frac{100}{2}\right) = 50$$

$$200 + 50 = 250$$

250 would be the one at which it would topple

An alternative way to do this would be to take the result of a pile starting at 10 and multiply it by 10. e.g.

$$(10 + 10) = 20 \quad \left(\frac{10}{2}\right) = 5$$

$$20 + 5 = 25$$

$$25 \times 10 = 250.$$

or you could even take the basic result of 1 without rounding it up and you could to multiply it by 100.

e.g.

$$(1 + 1) = 2 \quad \left(\frac{1}{2}\right) = 0.5$$

$$2 + 0.5 = 2.5$$

$$2.5 \times 100 = 250.$$

No further justification of this method was provided in the text. In particular, there was no indication of how it was derived. A number of different, and even contradictory, readings and evaluations of the student's understanding and competence were made by the teachers and different stories were composed to explain how Steven had achieved his results.

Charles, for example, recognized the mathematical validity of the alternative method and took this as a sign of that the student had 'come up with' the formula as a result of understanding the linearity of the situation:

> *Um ok so I mean he's found the rule and he's quite successfully used it from what I can see to make predictions about what's going to happen for things that he obviously can't set up. So that shows that he understands the formula which he's come up with quite well, I think. There's also found some sort of linearity in the results whereby he can just multiply up numbers which again shows quite a good understanding of the problem I think.*

Grant, on the other hand, appeared less confident with the mathematical validity of the formula, expressing some uncertainty about whether the method would work in general.

> *It's interesting that the next part works, I don't know if it works for everything or it just works for this but he's spotted it and again he hasn't really looked into it any further. He's done it for one case but whether it would work for any other case is er I don't know, he hasn't looked into it . . . And he's used it in the next part er used the this multiplying section in the next part and it's just a knowledge of number that's got him there I think intuition whatever. He may have guessed at a few and found one that works for it.*

Perhaps because of this uncertainty, his narrative explaining how Steven might have arrived at the method devalues the student's achievement, suggesting that the processes involved were not really 'mathematical': 'spotting' the method, not looking into it properly, guessing, using 'just a knowledge of number' or 'intuition'. Steven is clearly not being given credit either for the result itself or for the processes he may have gone through in order to arrive at it.

Like Grant, Harry seemed to have some difficulty in making sense of this method and did not appear to recognize the equivalence between the original formula and the alternative method. In spite of this, he was able to compose yet another narrative to explain the student's intentions, stressing by repetition the suggestion that Steven has been 'trying' (possibly with the implication that he has not succeeded).

> *and he's got another formula here . . . I don't really understand what he's done here . . . So he's produced another formula where . . . he's taken the result of a pile starting at ten and multiplying by ten and I don't understand what he's done there . . . I would have asked him to explain a bit further. He's — the initial formula with two hundred and fifty is proved to be correct and he's trying to*

extend it, he's trying to look for other ways, maybe he has realized that two hundred and fifty could be the exact answer or maybe not. So he's trying other ways to explain some of the inconsistencies that he's seen but I think greater explanation needed here.

Harry locates the responsibility for his own failure to understand in the inadequacies of the student's text.

The differences between the various readings lie not only in different interpretations of the mathematical content of the text but in different interpretations of the student's level of understanding and different hypotheses about the methods that the student might have used in order to achieve his results. There may be a connection between these two aspects; it is Charles, expressing the clearest understanding of the relationship of the alternative method to the linearity of the situation, who makes the most positive evaluation of Steven's understanding, while Grant and Harry, apparently uncertain of the general validity of the method, both construct pictures of the student working in relatively unstructured or experimental ways. In composing their explanatory narratives, each teacher must draw on the resources available to them. These resources include common expectations of the general nature of investigation and investigative reports, but also include more personal mathematical understanding and experiences. Where the student text diverges from the 'usual' to the extent that it is not covered by the established common expectations, each teacher must resort to their more personal resources, thus creating the possibility of divergence in the narratives they compose.

While the teacher reading as mathematician or as a teacher personally interested in the student may express pleasure and interest in novel student behaviour, this causes tension with the teacher's role as assessor, both in deciding what credit to award and in the effort required to validate a non-standard result, particularly if it is not accompanied by extensive verbal elaboration. Different teachers, composing different narratives of student behaviour to explain the text, will resolve these tensions in different ways.

'Good Mathematics' v 'Good Coursework'

The tension between the value placed on difference and the difficulty in validating it is also reflected in conflict between teachers' expressions of what is good mathematics or good mathematical behaviour and their judgments of what is good coursework. For example, while all those interviewed regarded evidence of working systematically and explaining how results were achieved as important criteria for assessing coursework, there were several indications that these were not necessarily considered to be sufficient criteria for identifying good mathematicians. Steven's work on 'Inner Triangles', for example, was recognized as systematic and 'sound' work but its routine nature appeared to lead Dan to judge Steven to be 'a not particularly able mathematician'. Abiding strictly by the explicit coursework rules may not be enough to gain a high evaluation of one's mathematical ability.

Another characteristic of 'good coursework' seems to be the presence of written narrative of the processes gone through and verbal elaboration of graphical and symbolic components. Richard's text, as we have seen earlier, lacked this characteristic, and so clearly failed to fulfil the criteria for good coursework. At the same time, however, its author was nevertheless judged by several teachers to be an able mathematician.

Richard's text provided one of the few instances of student's work which provoked interest in the mathematics from the teacher readers. He extended the 'Inner Triangles' problem to look at the areas of six pointed stars drawn on isometric paper. Andy's detailed analysis of the mathematics of this section was discussed in Chapter 10. Dan also spent time on this section:

Now this one he's gone on to stars and he's sort of gone on to stars hasn't he? I don't quite know what he means by this . . . Perimeter times slant height . . . mm! . . . Blimey, I would definitely have liked a bit more explanation of that, cos that's quite interesting isn't it. The perimeter multiplied by the slant height gives you the area inside, that's quite an interesting find which I doubt if many other people did so it's quite innovative and something a bit different but given us absolutely no . . . not even 'oh gosh look at this' would have been . . .[2]

His approval of the interesting and unusual is stressed by repetition but is simultaneously qualified (*quite* interesting; *quite* an interesting find; *quite* innovative; *a bit* different) as if to reconcile this approval with the simultaneous disapproval of Richard's lack of explanation. It is interesting to note that the 'explanation' required does not appear to be any form of mathematical proof but is merely a commentary on the surprising nature of the finding.[3] The tension that Dan is apparently experiencing may be seen in the variation in his relationship with the text while reading this passage. The modality of the exclamations, the repetition of 'interesting', and the statements that it is 'innovative' and 'different' suggest a personal involvement with the subject matter. At the same time he is evaluating Richard's work as an examiner, comparing it to other students' work and then criticizing it because no evidence or comment has been given to 'us'. Use of the first person plural here marks Dan's shift from reading as an interested individual to reading as an examiner acting as part of a group with common expectations. The suggestion that 'oh gosh look at this' would be an appropriate comment is an evaluative suggestion also from a position as examiner; such a comment would not help an interested reader to understand the mathematics.

Good mathematical behaviour may thus include working in a non-systematic way and providing little in the way of verbal explanation as well as setting oneself unusual and interesting tasks. These behaviours, however, all cause problems for teachers as assessors. The first two are explicitly disapproved of in coursework, while the setting of unusual and interesting tasks appears to demand further elaboration in order to be valued. The challenge for the student is to recognize for herself just how 'unusual' her task might seem to a teacher-reader.

Figure 11.2: Sandra's first extension: Two piles of rods

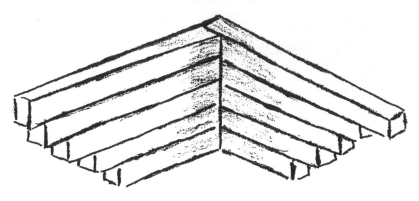

'Interesting' Extension

As was seen in the analysis of the 'practical' discourse of investigation in Chapter 5, one way in which 'creativity' may be operationalized in coursework is through suggesting and/or carrying out an 'extension' of the task set. The statements of both the 'Inner Triangles' and 'Topples' tasks asked students to do an 'Optional Extension', extending the investigation in a way of their own choosing, providing some opportunity for originality on the part of the student as neither a task nor ways of working are specified. Of the student texts used, Richard and Clive included extensions of 'Inner Triangles', considering several different shapes each, while Ellen and Sandra extended 'Topples', building piles of rods according to different rules.

Neither of the extensions of 'Inner Triangles' were remarked upon as unusual, apart from Richard's stars which were discussed above. Andy, who was familiar with this task, commented that 'extending it is fairly limited I think on this one'. The restricted nature of the context of this task means that teachers are likely to find the extensions predictable and hence are unlikely to consider them interesting. In contrast, the 'Topples' extensions were remarked on frequently, either as being interesting or because the teacher appeared to have difficulty understanding what had been done by the student. Indeed, the very fact that the teachers had difficulty in making sense of Ellen's extension seemed to be associated with the interest they displayed.

Sandra's first extension, which was illustrated by a diagram showing two piles of rods set at right angles against each other (Figure 11.2), also gave rise to difficulties for the teachers in understanding the nature of the problem. This extension seems, moreover, to be judged to be inappropriate. Harry labelled it as physics rather than mathematics, while Carol appeared relieved to find Sandra's second extension which returned to building a single pile with the rods increasing by two's (Figure 11.3):

> *Yeah this second extension is more what I'm, is the more predictable sort of extension where instead of going up in unit at a time decided to go up two units at a time.*

Figure 11.3:   Sandra's second extension: Going up in twos

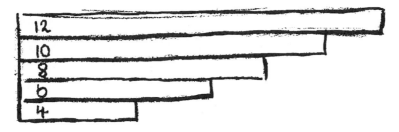

Similarly, Jenny found Sandra's first extension 'interesting' but simultaneously dismissed it in favour of her own idea of what an extension ought to be.

There is a tension here between the value placed on originality within the discourse of investigations and these teachers' apparently clear ideas about the ways in which an investigation may be appropriately extended. The 'predictable' extension is applauded, although it may not be seen as 'interesting'. Jenny's expectation that 'anybody who was going to get anywhere' would pose the same extension question as she would herself suggests a view of the nature of problem solving that allows little room for alternative lines of inquiry. Moreover, given that Jenny admitted to having spent very little time working on the problem herself, it seems likely that she had not pursued her expected extension and seen it to be useful in some way, but was judging its appropriateness on the basis of general expectations about the formation of extension problems. In general, little effort appeared to be made to make sense of the problems posed by the students, suggesting that value is placed on their existence rather than on their content or possible solution.

Expectations and Tensions in Valuing 'Creativity'

In reading students' coursework texts, teachers seem to have clear expectations about what a text is likely to contain. The individual text is compared with this imaginary norm and deviations are noted. The characteristics of such a 'typical' text seem at least in part to be related to the characteristics of standard ways of working, including in particular the stereotypical Data–Pattern–Generalization process. This leads to expectations about the order of presentation of work and the type and form of results. For example, inspecting values in a table arranged in a standard way is likely to give rise to a formula expressed in a standard format; deviations from that order or format (e.g. placing a table after the formula or using different bracketing in the expression of the formula) may be seen as unusual. Teachers' expectations relate both to the content of the work and to the way in which it is written. Deviations from the 'ideal text' constructed by expectations about the form of the writing, as seen in Chapter 10, are likely to be condemned. In contrast, deviations from expectations related to the results achieved, questions posed and paths followed may be read more positively and may even be taken as signs of high mathematical ability.

The assessment context brings with it assumptions about the importance of standardization and 'fairness' that are in tension with the valuing of 'difference'. Standardization of the assessment of students' work is sought through the use of criteria and performance indicators such as those provided by the examination board and through the use of exemplar material. The use of exemplars, as described in the extract from Joan's interview at the start of this chapter, does not address the problem of how to assess unusual work; it is likely, however, to contribute towards the construction of imaginary 'typical' texts. Similarly, performance indicators for individual tasks contribute towards teachers' specific expectations of student behaviour on the task without providing guidance for dealing with unusual work. The general criteria, while stated in terms which could in principle be applied to any piece of work, appear in practice to be associated with particular features of a 'typical' text. Teachers, therefore, experience some difficulty in applying them to more unusual texts.

While the difficulties experienced by teachers in reading and assessing unusual student texts have been considered in some detail, there are also difficulties for students in attempting to produce a text that will be valued by its readers. It is clear that, although any evidence of originality is likely be welcomed by teachers, the amount of value placed on it will vary according to the ease with which the teacher is able to make sense of it, the extent to which the processes are communicated, and the extent to which characteristics which fulfil standard criteria such as 'working systematically' are displayed. In reading the 'normal' coursework text, teachers are able to make assumptions about meanings and about the student's processes; similar assumptions are not available when reading the 'unusual' text. The student is thus required to support unusual work with additional elaboration of the question they have posed and of the processes they have undertaken in achieving their results. The problem for the student, of course, is in knowing what is likely to be identified as unusual.

Dealing with Error — Is 'Practical' Different?

It might be expected that those 'unusual' features of students' work that are identified as errors would be easier for teachers to deal with as they would not give rise to the tension experienced between 'creativity' and the assessment requirements.[4] Three main issues related to error that caused concern for the teachers may be identified in relation to both the 'Inner Triangles' and the 'Topples' tasks: the accuracy of the data arising from the initial stage of the task; the correspondence between this data and the formula or other description of patterns within the data; and compliance with the conventions of algebraic notation. There are also indications that the ways in which teachers deal with their recognition of student errors may be different for different types of task.

The two tasks 'Inner Triangles' and 'Topples' may be distinguished from one another by reference to the nature of their subject matter, although the structures of the tasks and the processes that students are expected to undertake are very similar.

The subject matter of 'Inner Triangles' is essentially 'pure' in the sense that all numerical results and relationships between variables (if correct) are entirely determined by the definitions of the basic objects (although variations may of course occur in the forms in which results and relationships are expressed and in the particular relationships pursued by individual students). In 'Topples', on the other hand, because the basic objects are physical and the student's initial activity is experimental, numerical results may be affected by factors other than the defined lengths of the rods (e.g. other properties of the rods, the stability of the surface on which the piles are built, the student's manual dexterity); the nature of the resulting relationships will be affected correspondingly by the quality of the experimental data. 'Topples' may thus be seen to be a 'practical' or 'scientific' activity rather than a 'pure' mathematical activity.

One area in which mathematical and scientific activity vary significantly is in the attitude to error. In pure mathematics, errors do not arise if procedures are followed correctly; scientific activity, in contrast, when making use of experimental data, must take account of the possibility of error arising from uncontrolled variables in the experimental situation. It might be expected, therefore, that the teachers' readings of the two tasks would differ in respect to the ways in which they respond to students' errors. While the differences between teachers' readings of 'pure' and of 'practical' tasks are of interest here, the fact that none of the teachers read complete student texts on both tasks means that direct comparisons based on the practice of individual teachers reading both types of task are not possible.

Accuracy of Data Gathering

For some of the teachers who read the 'Inner Triangles' texts, checking the accuracy of the answers to the initial questions was an important first step in their process of forming a judgment of the student's text. (These two questions require only that the student should give numerical answers to questions about the dimensions of specified trapezia.) While they appeared to feel that accuracy was 'obviously' important, its role was relatively limited, according to Fiona, 'moving' the student 'up to a grade F'.

A further function that Fiona ascribed to this level of accuracy was as a sign of understanding of the nature of the problem, drawing the conclusion:

So he's got question one done correctly. He obviously understands the problem

She commented on this aspect when starting to read each of the three texts. 'Understanding the problem' is one of the general assessment criteria proposed by most published assessment schemes for investigational work. The criterion is not usually, however, elaborated in a way that makes it immediately applicable. In the context of this task at least, Fiona operationalized the criterion by relating it to the more familiar (and more easily identified) idea of giving correct answers.

In practice, all three 'Inner Triangles' texts gave correct answers to this data-gathering section of the task; it is not possible, therefore, to see how these teachers would have reacted to errors in this section, although the priority that Andy gave to accuracy and his suggestion that errors would indicate 'particular problems' suggests that he at least would not find them acceptable.

In contrast, the teachers reading the 'Topples' texts presented a very different attitude towards the accuracy in the data gathered. Thus Harry, although expressing a belief that Sandra's results were wrong, simultaneously claimed that this should not affect the evaluation of her work:

> *So I'm not sure that that's — I'm not sure that it would topple then. But if she's convinced that it did topple — again we said about the accuracy of the actual modelling of it the setting up of it. If it toppled it may be something to do with it but she's convinced that it toppled. Then we have to accept that.*[5]

The practical nature of the task is explicitly seen to change the nature of teachers' judgments of error, making some variation acceptable. Indeed, having data that appears 'too' accurate may cause the teacher to be suspicious, Ellen's original set of data could be fitted exactly to a linear formula:

> **H:** *Um, I'm not convinced that will be right, I don't know . . .*
> **I:** *Why not?*
> **H:** *Um, I think the real working, from our when we were working out, we produced a table and it wasn't always constant. It wasn't always two point five. Um, sometimes it actually came out to be more than that. It was reasonably consistent. It's hard to actually work it in practice in ideal conditions because sometimes the way that you've set up the blocks and so it needs really some constant sort of method of putting it into practice. But I mean I, I mean she's used, she's formulated her own theory in her mind and she's made a prediction which I think is, which is all valid to be honest about it.*

For Harry, being 'right' in this context involves having the messy sort of data that arises from a scientific experiment. The absence of error leads him to suspect that Ellen may have worked backwards in order to produce a 'clean' set of data. On the one hand, accuracy is valued, while at the same time it may be taken as a sign of inappropriate problem solving strategies. Harry's discomfort with this is resolved by the 'hedge' at the end of the above extract which allows him to accept Ellen's data without penalty, although he went on to suggest that commenting on the inconsistencies in her data (for whose existence there is no evidence in the text) would have allowed her to be assessed at a higher level. Charles suspecting a similar 'working backwards from the theory' strategy in Sandra's work, resolved the problem in the opposite direction. In this case, however, Sandra's data did not even coincide with Charles' beliefs about the correct results; this seems likely to have influenced his decision to 'mark it down' rather than declare the strategy valid.

The student working on such a practical task is thus placed in a situation in which she is expected to gather data that is accurate but not *too* accurate. She must then comment on, and preferably explain, inconsistencies in her data (even if there were none). It appears that these teachers are looking for an ideal level of accuracy appropriate to a practical task. It is likely that many students do not share a knowledge of this ideal level or an appreciation of the differences in teacher expectations of accuracy between pure and practical tasks. While working backwards from the formula in order to generate data may be a successful (if not teacher approved) strategy in a pure task it may be detected and hence condemned more easily in the practical task. The way in which both pure and practical tasks have been fitted into the same 'investigation' format may make it more difficult for students to distinguish between them and between the different sorts of expectation that teachers may have.

Correspondence between Data and Formula

Whether or not the original data were seen to be correct, teachers reading both tasks expressed concern that the formulae produced should 'work', fitting the data gathered at the beginning of the task. Some spent time checking the formula with the data provided. Others were prepared to take the correctness of the formulae on faith or to make a more rapid judgment. Interestingly, both Andy and Fiona, who had expressed most concern about the accuracy of the original (Inner Triangles) data, were willing to accept the resulting formulae without thorough checking.

As was seen above, teachers reading the 'Topples' texts were faced with the dilemma of what to do with Sandra's work, which was based on a set of data which they all believed to be wrong but which contained a formula which fitted the data set reasonably well. Charles, before reading the texts, identified this as a potential issue:

> *I think I'd be looking for some kind of statement based on their observations and their tables of results. So even if the table of results may be wrong, if they could generalize their own table of results, so long as it wasn't too trivial, I'd be quite happy to actually give them something for that . . . Um . . . how important is it that they get the right result? I think it's . . . I think it's more important that they go through the right thought processes that **they** achieve the right result than actually get the right result itself as long as they're aware of how they should be tackling the problem, or aware of strategies that they can use to tackle the problem rather than actually getting the right answer would be more important.*

His focus on process rather than content allows him to take a relativist position towards the accuracy of results. Thus, he decides that consistency between the generalization and the data is more important than correctness, although he tempers this with the caution that the generalization must not be too 'trivial', indicating that the process–content distinction is still problematic for him. The difference between the degree of complexity of Sandra's relationship (of the form $2n + 2$) and that of the relationship found in the other students' text (of the form $2.5n$) seems hardly significant enough to make such a profound difference to the evaluation of the work overall. This degree of 'triviality' was, however, sufficient to provide grounds for several teachers to justify their low assessment of Sandra's work without making overt use of the fact that her results were wrong. The tension between the assessment discourse valuing of 'correctness' and the investigation discourse valuing of 'creativity' and student 'ownership' was thus side-stepped by using the value placed on mathematical sophistication that is found within both discourses.

Conventional Use of Algebraic Notation

The students' texts on both tasks included examples of formulae expressed in algebraic forms which did not conform to conventional norms. Teachers reading both sets of texts commented on these formulae, suggesting that there is some tension between the notion of 'correct' use of algebraic notation and the idea that such notation is useful for communication.

Speaking in general terms, Joan identified 'working' as the primary criterion for assessing the validity of a generalization, suggesting that conforming to conventional forms of notation was not important to her assessment (although unconventional forms might make it more difficult). At the same time, however, she identified this as an area in which 'the less able ones' are likely to have difficulty; an unconventional form might thus serve to mark a student as 'less able' and hence affect Joan's judgment of the whole text. In practice, this ambiguity about the value to be placed on convention was reflected in her discomfort about Steven's formula for the number of 'Inner Triangles' in a trapezium ($y + x \times z = $ Unit No.) which fails to include brackets to indicate the correct order of operations:

> *the use of the algebra unfortunately is still not absolutely brilliant as he hasn't used the brackets in the right place but* [it could] *have just been an error so . . . that's probably not a fair thing to say . . . The use of um, how could I put it, the symbolic communication isn't quite there.*

It is interesting that she hedges her condemnation of Steven by suggesting that he may have 'just' made an error. A judgment that he had made an error would presumably be considered more lenient than a judgment that his use of algebra suggests him to be one of the 'less able'. In contrast, Andy seems to have read the same formula in a rather different way:

> *The formula is accurate needs a bracket in it but it's quite clear that his intention and he's given a nice example which clarifies his thinking, so although algebraically it's not that strictly correct, it's quite clear he knows what he's doing.*

Unlike Joan, who condemned Steven's 'symbolic communication' and hence his ability, Andy judges Steven to have communicated his intention and his competence effectively, taking into account the example accompanying the formula as well as the formula itself. I would suggest that these two teachers are both resolving (in their different ways) a tension between valuing the student's self-consistent solution and valuing the use of conventional algebraic forms — a tension which once again seems to arise from the process–content dilemma in the investigation discourse.

The question of conventional use of brackets was raised again in readings of the 'Topples' texts by Steven's formula: $(a) + (a) + \left(\dfrac{a}{2}\right)$. Although this formula is technically 'correct', it is not conventionally concise,[6] making unnecessary use of brackets and failing to simplify the whole expression by 'collecting like terms'. Teachers' readings of this formula echoed the tensions described above in the 'Inner Triangles' context. It seems that such 'errors' give rise to similar tensions and possible resolutions for teachers reading both types of task.

Despite the lack of direct comparability between the sets of texts used and the teachers' readings it is clear that there are differences between the issues related to error and accuracy that arise in the contexts of the 'pure' and the 'practical' tasks. In the practical situation there is a tension between the value placed on accuracy both in the data and in the formulae arising from the data and the simultaneous belief that data arising from a practical situation is likely to be inaccurate. This gives rise to problems in assessing students' texts both in cases where the experimentally derived data is 'incorrect' and in cases where it is too perfect. A valuing of 'process' over 'content' suggests that the relationship between data and formula is more important than the relationship between either and any sort of objective reality. It appears that 'incorrect' data and formulae may thus be acceptable in the practical setting. If the resulting formula is perceived to be too simple, however, this conflicts with the value that is placed on demonstrating mathematical skills. At the same time, while there is a concern in both types of task that the formulae should 'work' for the data, if the correspondence is too perfect in a practical task this may raise suspicions that the student has used an inappropriate method, working backwards to generate her data from the formula rather than generating the data experimentally. While the data available here has not provided evidence of teachers' reactions to inaccurate numerical results in a 'pure' setting, it does appear likely that a student producing a perfect set of results would be given credit for working in an appropriate way. From the student's point of view, the general similarity in the structure of investigational tasks and in the forms of reasoning expected may make it difficult to distinguish those tasks which the teacher-assessor may designate as 'practical' and hence to know what levels of accuracy and of match between data and formula is desirable.

In almost all the cases in which errors were identified by teachers, there was a suggestion of anxiety on the part of the teacher in deciding how to judge the student's work. There was repeated shifting between condemnations of the errors and playing down their importance in coming to an assessment of the student. Part of this shifting may be related to the multiple roles that the teacher has in relation to the student and the student's text, in particular the potentially incompatible roles of examiner and advocate on behalf of the student. I would suggest, however, that an important role is also played by the tensions that exist within the discourse of investigation and coursework and between this and the traditional discourse of external examination. The discourse of investigation and coursework within which the teachers and students are situated (including the publications of the examination boards) officially values diversity and, in particular, places emphasis on the use of general mathematical processes rather than specific pieces of content knowledge. Simultaneously, however, the discourse contains ambiguous messages about the importance of accuracy. On the one hand, there is stress on the idea that investigative work does not have single right answers and that there is even positive benefit for students in being wrong while, on the other hand, students producing coursework for examination purposes are also expected to demonstrate mathematical skills and knowledge. In this respect, the examination of coursework is not clearly distinguished from the traditional paradigm of assessment in mathematics in which great emphasis is laid on accuracy and hence great significance on the identification of error. It is hardly surprising, therefore, to find such tensions and evidence of anxiety reflected in the way the teachers read students' texts containing errors.

Notes

1 Some other areas of the school curriculum have a longer tradition of assessing more nebulous aspects of students' work (e.g. 'personal response' to literature in English). While this probably does not avoid all the tensions identified here for mathematics teacher-assessors (Dixon and Brown, 1985), it is likely that the problems are somewhat different in different subject areas.

2 The way in which Dan shifts between a position as interested reader and a position as examiner in this passage was discussed in Chapter 9.

3 The suggestion that Richard might have written 'Oh gosh look at this' assumes that his ideas of what is interesting and unusual must coincide with the teacher's ideas. This suggests a stereotyped idea of the nature of the problem and even of mathematics. Stars (unlike trapezia, triangles and parallelograms) are not figures whose areas are normally considered in school mathematics; they are thus interesting. This does not take into account the fact that, when working on isometric paper as these students were, stars are highly regular and easy to draw. They might thus be considered by the student to be a normal and natural variation rather than an innovation. Using the perimeter as one of the variables in an area formula may also be considered as unusual but this could only be identified by someone with a knowledge of a wide variety of standard area formulae and a general view of their common features.

4 The incidence of error in the student texts was not one of the factors taken into account in selecting the texts and was, overall, quite low. Only one of the 'Topples' texts (Sandra) contained substantial errors that gave rise to comments from all the teachers reading it.

5 Harry's reading of Sandra's diagrams as a sign of the nature of her practical activity is discussed in Chapter 9.

6 As Pimm (1987) remarks, the mathematician's 'aesthetic for symbolic expressions' includes valuing 'brevity over clarity' (pp. 126–7).

Chapter 12

Towards a Critically Aware Mathematical Writing Curriculum

The analysis of student texts and teachers' reading practices within the discourses of investigation and assessment has identified a number of problems for both teachers and students related to the written communication of mathematical activity. It has raised questions about the validity of the assessment process and about the ways in which the assessment context may distort the activity of mathematical investigation. Many of these problems and questions arise, I believe, from the nature of the beliefs and knowledge about language, especially written language, embodied in the discourse of investigation and in teachers' practices. In this chapter, I intend to explore these beliefs and knowledge and to consider what sort of curriculum might help to address these issues for teachers and students of mathematics.

The Myth of 'Transparency'

Firstly, the whole process of assessment appears to be based on an assumption that writing is 'transparent'. In other words, the written (or oral) text is assumed to convey the intentions of the author, without distortion or alteration, into the mind of the reader. This has been the traditional assumption of the positivist assessment paradigm (Galbraith, 1993): there is an objective reality — the student's 'understanding' — that is observable by means of reading or listening to the student's linguistic production. But many mathematics educators, whose philosophies have led them to reject positivism in other areas, have also adopted this assumption without substantial question in the context of assessment. Thus, for example, many of those advocating the greater use of writing as a way for students to construct personal mathematical knowledge simultaneously claim that students' writing provides the teacher with insight into student thinking.[1]

Such an assumption is based on a 'common sense' or naive transmission view of the nature of communication. The examples of teachers' readings discussed in Chapters 9 to 11, however, demonstrate clearly that, as Hodge and Kress (1988) argue, 'transparency' is not a viable theory of the relationship between thought, writing and reading. Different teacher-readers made different interpretations of the meanings of the same passages of texts. Influences on these interpretations included the teachers' expectations about the investigative process itself; parts of the students' texts were interpreted in terms of their fit with the stereotypical investigation process or, where this was difficult to do, the section of text was likely to be neg-lected or evaluated unsympathetically. Teachers' interpretations were also affected by their understandings of the mathematics involved and the various roles they adopted as teacher-assessors with consequent differences in their relationships to the student-authors.[2] There is thus no necessary simple correspondence between a piece of text and the meanings its various readers construct. Rather, the meanings constructed will depend on the interaction between the text and the resources brought to bear on it by individual readers, varying according to the discourse within which the text is read and the positions adopted by a particular reader within that dis-course, as well as the reader's previous experience.

Alongside the 'common sense' assumption of transparent communication, it is simultaneously widely believed that many students do not have the linguistic skills or judgment necessary to represent their thinking adequately in written form and that there may be a mismatch between assessments formed solely on the basis of written work and those which take other sources into account (MacNamara and Roper, 1992; NCTM, 1995). This acknowledgment of problems in taking written texts as evidence of thinking, however, is not based on an appreciation of the potential diversity of teachers' readings but locates the responsibility for any short-comings in communication with the students and in the text itself: if the student's language skills or judgment about what to include in the text were better then the written evidence could be taken as unproblematic. It is thus assumed that there exists a notional 'perfect' text that *would* provide the teacher with a transparent representation of the student's intended meanings if the student's skills were ad-equate. Where the student's text fails to match the teacher's expectations, the teacher, acting within a discourse of school mathematics in which she is an authority (and hence entitled to define what is acceptable within the discourse), is likely to inter-pret the failure of communication either as a failure on the part of the student to understand the mathematical subject matter in the desired way or as a general lack of writing skills. As Clark and Ivanic (1997) argue, the idea that writing is a set of skills 'rests on an unproblematised view of sociolinguistic appropriacy and an acceptance of the existing sociolinguistic order' (p. 84) and hence leads to a deficit view of the learner.

An alternative interpretation of the situation is that the perceived weaknesses in a student's text result from a mismatch between, on the one hand, the resources the teacher-reader brings to bear on the text and the position she adopts in relation to it and to its author and, on the other hand, the student's knowledge of and beliefs about those resources and relationships together with her own available resources. For example, Sandra, who produced multiple coloured diagrams for the 'Topples' task, may have believed that her teacher would value such evidence of meticulous, carefully presented work (which is indeed often highly valued in other school mathematics contexts), being unaware that it might be taken as a sign of a failure to progress beyond the routine and hence act as an indicator of 'low ability'. While most 16-year-old students will have been thoroughly inducted into the routine discourse of the traditional mathematics classroom, the relatively small amount of time devoted to investigative work means that students are less likely to learn this rather different discourse 'naturally' and may not be able reliably to distinguish its expectations and conventions.

If the student writer is to convey her intentions most effectively to her teacher-reader it is necessary for her to share a knowledge of the teacher's resources and most likely reading position. If students are to achieve the highest possible evaluations of their investigative coursework (or in other forms of 'authentic' assessment that involve extended or non-traditional written responses), attention must be paid to the forms of written language they use in order to ensure that these are likely to be read positively by teachers as signs of high achievement or at least to match teacher expectations about the genre. In spite of wide spread awareness of the difficulties that some aspects of mathematical language may cause for many learners as readers and listeners, far less attention has been given to the ways in which students may learn to produce mathematical language themselves, particularly written language. While 'Writing-to-Learn Mathematics' has many advocates, few have addressed 'Learning-to-Write Mathematics'.

Teachers' Lack of Language Awareness — and Its Consequences

Studying mathematics teachers' reading practices in the discourse of investigation has revealed both the ways in which their judgments about a student may be influenced by the form of the student's text and their apparent lack of a means of talking about the forms that influence them. It seems that, like teachers of many other curriculum subjects (Langer and Applebee, 1987), most teachers of mathematics do not have adequate explicit vocabulary available to characterize the language of their subject domain. Mathematics teachers' language for describing text is dominated by the names of highly visible features such as diagrams, algebra, introduction, explanation, etc. but appears very limited when it comes to identifying the characteristics that determine how they will judge the quality of these features. This has two consequences: firstly, the naming of highly visible features places emphasis on these in ways that may distort the character of the activity students are expected to undertake. Secondly, the lack of explicit ways of knowing and talking about forms of language means that teachers are likely to be unable either to diagnose the ways in which their own judgments are influenced by various styles of student writing or to provide adequate guidance to their students on how to produce texts that are likely to create more positive impressions.

Over-emphasis on the Highly Visible

It is, perhaps, unsurprising that teachers' talk about mathematical writing should emphasize features such as algebraic symbolism, tables, and diagrams and structural components such as introductory statements of the problem. Not only are these easily recognizable and very noticeable within a text, but their presence is also characteristic of a very wide range of types of mathematical texts. They may thus play a major role in helping readers to recognize that a text *is* mathematical. Within the context of the assessment of investigative coursework, however, they appear to have taken on a further role as indicators of student achievement. In particular, written forms that students might be advised to use in order to help them to achieve particular learning objectives or to make progress in a particular problem situation have themselves became assessable outcomes. The essential duality of the teacher-assessor's role is reflected in this conversion of pedagogic knowledge into assessment guidelines. At the same time, the identification of such textual features as signs of particular types of achievement lessens their potential as means of communication; they are likely to be read only in stereotypical ways.

Words before algebra

As we have seen, although the teachers valued algebraic symbolism highly they also expected any symbolic generalization to be preceded by a verbal description of the generalization. A number of reasons were given for this demand, including the suggestion that it would help the student to achieve the symbolization. This idea of a progression towards algebraic symbolization, characterized as 'see-say-record' (James and Mason, 1982; Mason, 1987), is intended, both by its original advocates and by the subsequent curriculum materials which incorporated it into pedagogic sequences, as a support for learners, making symbols meaningful. At the same time, it must be stressed that gaining such a comfortable familiarity with algebraic symbolism is intended to lead the student to an ability to manipulate symbols freely, independent of their reference. In the coursework assessment context, however, this pedagogic *support* has been transformed into an *algorithm* for forming generalizations and hence into an assessment *requirement*, demanding that the student include a verbal description of any generalization before symbolizing. The pedagogic intent is thus negated: the student is never able to operate symbolically because she must always reconstruct the concrete referents in order to demonstrate that she has gone through the required processes. The student who is capable of operating entirely symbolically may be penalized for failing to demonstrate processes that she did not need to go through in order to achieve her generalization. The inclusion of both 'words' and algebra in this context has become a ritual fulfilment of assessment requirements rather than a genuine means of communicating the nature of the student's mathematical activity.

Tables and diagrams

The presence of tables in student texts was generally approved by the teachers and was included in their lists of desirable features of coursework and in their reports of the advice provided to their students. In some cases, tables appeared to be used by teachers as a way of operationalizing the assessment criterion 'works systematically'. The presence of a table in a student's coursework text has thus become highly significant. As observation of the processes used by individuals working within a class is likely to be difficult, the table is taken to be a written sign that data has been collected systematically. In those cases where a student has followed the routine inductive path through the problem, this may be a valid inference. By making the table the *only* acceptable sign of system, however, other ways of working are devalued. In particular, those students who seek insight into the structure of the situation and hence achieve a generalization without gathering large amounts of data or spotting number patterns are disadvantaged. Although teachers may recognize that such students are 'more able' and are working in a valid mathematical way, they are nevertheless seen to be failing to fulfil the assessment criteria. A table in an acceptable format needs to be included even if it serves no purpose in helping the student to achieve a solution to the problem. In the words of one teacher, 'The system says they should jump through hoops'.

Like the advice to describe a generalization in words before attempting to symbolize it, the advice to students to make a table is intended to play a role in helping them towards an algebraic generalization. From a pedagogic point of view, the table serves to encourage the student to organize her data while simultaneously providing visual cues to assist pattern spotting, in particular through the use of difference patterns. The table is, however, firmly allied to an inductive mode of reasoning and is unlikely to support a structural analysis of the situation being investigated. The institutionalization of investigative work subsequent to the Cockcroft report and the introduction of GCSE coursework has been associated with the routinization of such an inductive approach, strongly criticized by, among others, Wells (1993) and Hewitt (1992). From being a tool to be used for helping to solve some problems but not for others, making a table has become part of a routine algorithm for 'doing investigations'. By becoming a routine fulfilment of an assessment requirement, the table may cease to be a useful tool in the student's problem solving repertoire, particularly in the light of the possible rejection by some teachers of more complex tables which organize data in ways which, while possibly helping the student to form a greater understanding of the relationships between the variables, do not demonstrate a systematic varying of the variables during data collection.

Similarly, in the inductive investigation approach, data is often gathered by drawing diagrams and counting or measuring. Diagrams in students' texts that appear to serve this purpose are likely to be recognized and, in general, approved; the absence of such data-generating diagrams may also be noted. Diagrams that cannot be read in this way, however, may be ignored completely or dismissed as inappropriate or insignificant. The identification of diagrams with data within the inductive investigation paradigm rejects the important functions that diagrams can serve in many other mathematical texts as means of examining structures, as tools for looking at geometric properties and relationships, and as a means of communicating about these aspects. In relation to both tables and diagrams, the term *appropriate* in the assessment criterion 'uses . . . appropriate visual forms' (LEAG, 1989), must be read as 'appropriate to the teacher's view of the standard investigative process' rather than 'appropriate to the student's approach to the problem' or 'appropriate to the effective communication of the mathematics'.[3]

Introduction

Where a text includes an introduction to the problem that is identified as being written in the student's 'own words' this appears to be interpreted by some teachers as a sign of the student's 'understanding the problem' and hence as fulfilment of one of the general assessment criteria specified by the examination board (LEAG, 1989) and by the practical discourse of investigations, coursework and their assessment (e.g. Pirie, 1988). Where an introduction is identified as copied from the question paper, however, this is likely to be dismissed as irrelevant and a waste of the student's time.

A pedagogical reason for linking a written introduction to 'understanding the problem' may be found in the arguments of those concerned with using writing to support learning across the curriculum. The initial stages of making sense of an unfamiliar problem may involve rewriting the question, identifying what is given and what is wanted, or trying a small number of specific examples. Even copying the question may play a role in providing the problem solver with time and a structure within which to make sense of the words. This role for writing in organizing thought is recognized by some of those concerned with 'Writing-to-Learn' (e.g. Emig, 1983) although the specific role of copying does not appear to have been explicitly addressed. In the assessment context, however, the role of such tactics as tools for the problem solver has been transformed into a role as signs of the extent to which she 'understands the problem'. In doing this, the concept of 'understanding the problem' is itself trivialized. Moreover, the communicative function of such writing is again minimized. If the student were genuinely attempting to inform her reader about the problem she had worked on, copying the words of the given question might be a very effective way of communicating the purpose of the student's subsequent mathematical activity. The teacher-readers of introductions, however, appear not to be interested in being informed about the mathematical subject matter but adopt a position solely as examiners.

Writing plays many different roles for writers and for readers. The proponents of 'Writing-to-Learn' stress the role that the process of writing can play in helping writers to organize, reflect on and revise their thinking. In mathematics education, specific forms of writing such as tables and diagrams and the formulation of symbolic generalizations are seen to play important roles in the problem solving process. We must also not forget that writing is a means by which a writer may seek to inform, influence and communicate with her readers. In this assessment context, however, the role of specific forms of writing as 'performance indicators' appears to have precedence over other purposes. Those students who focus on the problem solving and communicative aspects of their writing and do not take into account the roles that the features identified here may play in the assessment process are likely to be disadvantaged.

Unspoken Language Expectations — Reading a Student's 'Ability' from the Text

At least some teachers appear to make judgments about a student's general level of mathematical 'ability' on the basis of their reading of features of a single coursework text. This judgment of 'ability' may have an effect on the teacher's ultimate judgment of the piece of work, allowing the teacher, for example, to ignore errors or missing 'evidence' on the basis that they are merely 'slips' by a 'high ability' student. The way in which the judgments are formed, however, is generally implicit and unarticulated. Subtle differences in the language used may lead to differences in the 'impression' of a student's level of understanding achieved by a teacher-assessor. Indeed, the teachers interviewed occasionally even commented on their inability to describe what it was that influenced their judgment. The features identified here are thus, on the whole, unspoken, identified through my own analyses of the student texts and the teachers' readings.

Features of texts which seem to be associated with judgments of 'high ability' include:

- the presence of 'algebra' — in particular the use of single letter variable names and any manipulation of algebraic expressions;
- 'abstractness', including an absence of deixis, the use of the present tense, an absence of reference to practical apparatus or diagrams;
- the use of 'correct' terminology;
- the presence of 'unusual' forms of representation or posing 'unusual' problems;
- the absence of evidence of process (seen to be characteristic of some 'high ability' students, though not approved).

Several of these features (algebra, abstractness, 'correct' terminology) are similar to those identified in Chapter 2 as characteristic of academic mathematics texts. There is, however, no simple connection between identifying a student as 'more able' and valuing his or her text highly. Although errors in these texts may be treated indulgently, some teachers will not be tolerant of a text which lacks evidence of processes, despite identifying the author as 'more able'. There is a tension within the discourse of investigation between the value placed on 'real mathematics' and 'advanced' mathematical behaviour and the conventions of the investigation report genre. However able a mathematician a student is judged to be (and breaking the rules may be taken as one sign of such ability), she must still conform to the rules of the assessment game.

Features that seem to be associated with judgments that a student is 'less able' include:

- 'concreteness', including the use of concrete variable names, the use of tenses other than the present tense, and naturalistic diagrams;
- the use of unconventional vocabulary or other forms of communication;
- writing that is difficult for the teacher-reader to make sense of (extensive deixis may contribute to this).

The unconventional or unusual appears in both these lists and may be interpreted either as a sign of originality (and hence high ability) or as error or lack of facility with conventional forms (and hence low ability). The way in which a specific instance is interpreted is likely to be dependent on other signs of the student's 'ability' within the text. While the student judged to be 'more able' may be indulged to the extent of excusing some errors and the absence of a narrative of processes, the student judged to be 'less able' is likely to be given less credit for her achievements — her errors will reinforce the low evaluation of her 'ability'.

In addition, features that are interpreted by the teacher as not contributing to the problem solution, including copying the question (or at least being perceived to have done so) and elaborate presentation, may be taken as an indication that the student, who might have been capable of better work, has wasted her time, diverting her energies to aspects which would not contribute to her grade. Some of the teachers interviewed remarked that such features were typical of girls' work. The sample of texts used, however, was not wide enough to allow comparison with teachers' reactions to similar features occurring in texts written by boys, although Spear's (1984; 1989) studies of teachers reading student texts in science suggests that there are likely to be differences in the ways teachers respond to similar texts attributed to girls or to boys. Such readings of 'good presentation', while not contributing directly to the teacher's perception of the student's 'ability', nevertheless form part of the teacher's characterization of the student; this again appears likely to affect the ultimate assessment of the student's achievement.

Previous studies that have observed teachers' use of a general construct of a student's 'ability' to affect their assessment of achievement (e.g. Broadfoot, 1995; Filer, 1993; Ruthven, 1987) have considered only cases in which the teachers had personal knowledge of the students and hence made use of 'evidence' beyond that offered by the particular piece of work being judged. In the cases I have described, the teachers had, in most cases, no personal knowledge of the student-authors involved and no evidence beyond that presented to them in the coursework texts. Any judgments about the students' 'ability' must therefore have been made entirely on the basis of the texts in front of them. The use of a construct of 'ability' in teachers' assessments of coursework cannot, therefore, be located solely in the bias or preconceptions that might arise from familiarity with the previous achievement or behaviour of known individual students. It is clear that characteristics of the text itself affect the ways in which teachers will read and interpret it and the weight that will be accorded both to negative aspects such as errors and to apparently positive aspects such as 'good presentation'. It seems likely, however, that there would be some interaction between personal knowledge of students and the textual features associated with 'ability' and other personal characteristics identified above.

The lack of adequate vocabulary for describing and thinking about the characteristics of student writing means that teachers are likely to be unaware of the ways in which they are influenced by the form of the writing. They thus lack tools that might enable them to examine their own reading and assessment practice more critically; to consider the validity of their use of performance indicators such as tables, diagrams and algebra; or to reflect on what causes them to identify a text as the product of a 'more able' or 'less able' student. Furthermore, they lack a means of communicating with their students about their writing in a way that could usefully empower the students to make more effective use of language themselves.

How May Students Learn to Write Mathematically?

Given the influence that the forms of writing used appear to have on teachers' interpretations and evaluations of students' work, it must be important to consider how students may best come to learn ways of writing that will be likely to be highly valued. Some possibilities are considered here.

Natural Development

In order to look informally at the possibility that students might develop forms of writing within the discourse of investigation reports 'naturally', without explicit instruction in writing, I analysed a set of five texts produced by one of the students, Steven, written over the two year period of the GCSE course. Steven's texts showed no obvious change over time that might have been the result of interaction with a teacher. For example, the set of five texts consistently included the use of the phrase 'I have found a formula' without any further elaboration of the student's mental processes. This suggests that Steven was not aware that this phrase and a general lack of a more specific narrative of mental processes were specifically condemned by teacher-readers or, if he was aware of this, that he did not have adequate resources to construct a more acceptable text. Any feedback he may have received about his writing had not effectively addressed this aspect. As we saw in Chapter 3, most of the literature related to writing in the mathematics classroom does not pay attention to forms of language and appears to assume that effective forms of communication develop 'naturally' through experience. This view of natural development of writing is challenged by Martin et al. (1987) who argue that writing, unlike speech, is unlikely to develop 'naturally' because of the lack of the possibility of 'immersion' in a written language environment. While curriculum developments involving continuous, long-term written interaction between teacher and students may show some development in students' writing, it seems unlikely that the present UK mathematics curriculum allows enough time and space for such development to take place in the writing of reports of investigative work. Indeed, for any programme to have a chance of allowing such development would demand considerable commitment on the part of both teacher and institution

Implicit Structure

It is sometimes argued (e.g. Andrews, 1992) that the used of highly structured tasks is likely to help both students and teachers to develop ways of working independently.

It is thus worth considering whether structuring can also play a role in developing students' independent use of language. The differences between Steven's responses to relatively highly or weakly structured tasks, however, suggest that 'desirable' characteristics of the language used in structured tasks may not be adopted. For example, the more structured tasks encouraged the formal naming of mathematical objects and consistent use of such names. This way of naming is one of the characteristics of much high status mathematical writing; moreover, there is some evidence from the teachers' readings that they particularly value concise, abstract types of names. But, while Steven used a very consistent vocabulary when responding to the structured tasks, where he was allowed more independence he devised and used multiple names for the same mathematical objects. This sort of overlexicalization may be interpreted as 'fluency' in some other genres of writing (including much of the 'creative' writing encountered in English assignments) but is not likely to be valued in mathematical text. The structure provided by some of the tasks clearly did not help this student to develop this particular aspect of conventional mathematical language as part of his independent repertoire. In general, it is unlikely to be clear to students which characteristics of the structure provided by a particular task are likely to be valued if transferred to other contexts unless these characteristics are deliberately attended to in the classroom.

Interaction with Readers

There are indications that interaction between student-authors and their readers can help students towards greater awareness of the ways in which their writing will be read and of features that will be more highly valued. For example, a Year 9 student, Kelly, was encouraged to show her writing about her investigation to some of her classmates before submitting her final report. She commented on her readers' response to the introduction to the problem she had worked on:

> *. . . some people didn't understand it so I thought of a better way to do it cos I didn't put the tens and units on it and it was all squashed up together and people couldn't really read it . . .*

She even showed an awareness that her own familiarity with the problem meant that she was not an impartial judge of the readability of her work:

> *Because I knew the problem I didn't really notice it because I knew.*

Later, while discussing another piece of work, Kelly used the criterion suggested by the earlier criticism of her own writing:

> *Well I would have spreaded it out more so it would make sense cos I . . . here where it says results and prediction it's more cramped and you can't really understand some of it.*

Interaction with other students appeared to have some success in enabling Kelly to have a more intersubjective view of readability, to adapt her own writing to the needs of her readers and to identify explicitly some of the characteristics that might affect a reader's response to the writing. The expectations and responses of other students as readers, however, may not match the ways in which teachers are likely to read and evaluate the same texts. Peer reading and feedback, therefore, may not be sufficient to help students towards effective mathematical writing. Unlike situations involving communication in spoken language, students do not usually receive immediate feedback from the teacher about the appropriateness of their writing. Moreover, the response that they do eventually receive may well be very general: evaluating the whole piece of work without attention to the details of the form. Learning from interaction with an audience may thus be useful but is unlikely to be sufficient.

One device used by some teachers during their assessment of student texts and apparently offered as advice to their students is the invocation of an imaginary naive reader. This appears to be a means of attempting to communicate to students the expectations of their future readers, acting as a guide to the amount of detail that needed to be included and trying to overcome the problems for student-writers of addressing a teacher-as-examiner audience (Britton et al., 1975). Research on the effects of 'audience' on student writing (see Chapter 3), however, suggests that such advice to imagine a non-expert reader is not guaranteed to be helpful to students, particularly as their lack of experience of non-teacher readers in mathematics may leave them with little awareness of the needs or preferences of such an audience. Indeed, Gilbert (1989) suggests that the most successful student-writers may be those who ignore such advice and focus on their experience of the preferences of their teacher-reader.

Teaching Mathematical Writing

If, as seems likely, mathematics students are not likely to learn how to write effectively solely through experience, structured tasks or interaction with readers, should mathematics teachers be teaching writing explicitly? Marks and Mousley's (1990) study of the limited range of writing undertaken by students in Australian primary and secondary schools led them to conclude that, in order to learn to write mathematically, students need to learn the features of the various genres of mathematical writing (including, for example, reports and explanations) 'through pointed discussion about language and through activities using models of appropriate genres' (p. 133). In other words, they argue that teachers need to pay explicit attention to language both in their planning of lessons and in their interactions with students, ensuring that students are introduced to a wide variety of genres of mathematical writing.

There is some debate in the domain of literacy education about whether students should be taught the characteristics of specific genres of writing explicitly (see, for example, Reid, 1987). On the one hand, teaching the features of a genre is seen to be prescriptive and restrictive, curbing students' opportunities for creativity and self-expression. On the other hand, it is seen as empowering, enabling students to participate in high status forms of discourse. Most of the examples drawn upon by both sides in this debate seem to be from the earlier years of education when, it might be argued, the consequences of deviations from the expected genre may not be so significant. Moreover, it appears to be largely assumed that this is an issue for language teachers, concerned with general language development, rather than for teachers in other curriculum areas, concerned with communication within their subject area. An exception to this (on both counts) is Kress (1990), who illustrates his argument in favour of teaching specific genres with examples of teacher assessments of student writing in school leaving examinations in economics. Here, as is the case in GCSE mathematics coursework, the use of forms of language that will be judged 'appropriate' by the teacher and that will construct meanings that conform to the expectations of the particular academic discipline has great significance for the individual student, for whom success or failure in the examination may have life-long effects. As Kress points out, subject teachers are unlikely to be aware of the ways in which their judgments are affected by students' use of particular forms of language. If teachers were more explicitly aware of the forms that are highly valued within their discipline and of the effects that may be achieved by various linguistic choices and could pass this awareness on to their students, this would not only help students to conform to the conventional expectations of the genre but would also empower them to make informed choices to break the conventions in order to achieve deliberate effects, including to demonstrate 'creativity'.

The analysis of teachers' responses to students' writing that I have offered in this book has suggested that, while a simple list of highly visible features of writing appears to be the only language available to mathematics teachers to describe the language of coursework texts, such a list is not adequate to describe the characteristics of a text that will be highly valued in the assessment process and is thus unlikely by itself to help students to produce such highly valued texts. Indeed, one of the effects of using such a list to guide the writing of investigation reports is likely to be to reinforce the hold of the stereotypical 'investigation', stifling any possibilities of creativity, as Dixon (1987) argues in his attack on the idea of 'teaching genre'. Knowledge of official assessment criteria might be thought to provide some guidance about teacher's expectations, but Love and Shiu's (1992) study of GCSE students' awareness and understanding of the criteria for assessing mathematics coursework suggests that, while some students who already have a relatively sophisticated understanding of the discourse and of the power of manipulating language will be able to make use of such lists of criteria, others are unlikely to find them helpful. These authors also remark on the tension between the provision of explicit lists of criteria which may result in the 'routinization of producing work for assessment' (p. 356) and the attempt to 'elicit' the required behaviour in less explicit ways, which may result in some students failing to discover what behaviour is required.

Critical Language Awareness

So far I have highlighted the areas in which student-writers may fail to communicate their mathematical achievements in ways that influence their teacher-readers to evaluate their work positively. I have also argued that the opportunities offered to students within the dominant pattern of mathematics education in the UK are generally inadequate to help students to write extended mathematical texts more effectively. Of course, there are some groups of students who *are* able to make use of the available opportunities and experiences, who *do* learn to write effectively and mathematically. These students, however, are likely to be those who, as Clark and Ivanic (1997) argue, arrive at school with the 'cultural capital' (Bourdieu, 1991) that is valued and built on in the school, including reading and writing experiences in the home, attitudes towards literacy and implicit knowledge about language. Explicit attention to language in the mathematics classroom could enable more students, including those from less privileged backgrounds, to participate in the discourse on an equal basis.

The idea of 'Critical Language Awareness' in education proposed by, among others, Fairclough (1992b) and Clark and Ivanic (1997) provides an approach to teaching and learning writing (and other aspects of language use) that, by looking critically at the ways in which language may be used in texts, draws attention to the characteristics of language in particular genres while avoiding the prescription, restriction and consequent disempowerment of students that is associated with traditional approaches to teaching 'standard' and 'appropriate' use of language (Fairclough, 1992a). It is not just about *knowing* the characteristics of the language considered appropriate in a particular genre but also about understanding the ways in which writers can make choices between different forms of language in order to adopt more powerful positions within the discourse. Knowledge about the different effects that various linguistic choices can achieve can provide students with the power to manipulate their own use of language to produce such effects deliberately, for example, to name their variables consistently or to use the present tense in order to be seen to be 'more able'.

It is clear, however, that the language commonly available within the discourses of school mathematics to describe the features of extended mathematical texts is inadequate to characterize those forms that are likely to be considered 'appropriate' within a given mathematical genre. Hence it must also be inadequate for enabling students to recognize and produce such high status forms. I would like to suggest that the tools for analysing mathematical writing that I have offered in Chapter 6 provide ways of describing the language of mathematical texts, while taking account of the contexts within which the texts are embedded, at a level of detail that could be empowering. By focusing on the choices that are available between different forms of language and the influence that different choices may have on the meanings readers construct from a text, this forms a starting point for teachers, students and researchers to use to begin to develop ways of thinking and talking about mathematical genres.

Within the particular genre of reports of investigative work, I have identified some of the features that may be significant to teachers' interpretations and evaluations of students' texts and some of the forms that are particularly likely to lead to high or low evaluations of the student's achievement or ability. This provides a basis for explicit discussion with teachers and students about what can be achieved by choosing to use various forms of language and the ways in which both verbal and non-verbal forms of communication may be used most effectively to produce reports that are likely to be judged to display highly valued mathematical processes. Further investigation is likely to be needed, however, in order to produce knowledge about language at a level that may be useful for teachers and students, particularly in other genres of mathematical writing. Moreover, in order to make use of this knowledge, teachers will need support to develop more explicit awareness of the characteristics of the genre and of the effects that may be achieved by various choices.

Knowledge about language is, however, unlikely to be enough by itself. Any attempt to attend to language in the mathematics curriculum is likely to have to contend with teachers' and students' existing beliefs not only about writing in mathematics but also about what sorts of activities are appropriate within the mathematics classroom. As Langer and Applebee's (1987) case-studies of science and social studies teachers show, writing activities are only likely to be successfully introduced into the classroom when they fulfil 'important pedagogic functions' (p. 87) that are either familiar or obvious to the teachers themselves. It may be instructive to consider the place of spoken language within mathematics education. In the 1980s, serious attention began to be paid to the place of 'discussion' and the importance of oral language in the mathematics classroom. This was accompanied by the publication of a wide range of advice for teachers about the genres of mathematical talk that might be encouraged, the reasons for encouraging use of such genres (usually related to mathematical learning in general as well as to the development of the genre itself), and the types of tasks they might use with their students in order to enable the development of their oral mathematical language. It seems likely that similar extensive guidance needs to be provided in the case of writing. First, however, it is necessary to establish the importance of learning to write mathematically as part of students' mathematical education. I would hope that my study goes some way towards providing the evidence and arguments needed to make a case for this importance.

Notes

1   This naive view of language as transparent is not restricted to assessment practices. While mathematics educators have widely accepted some version of a constructivist epistemology in relation to the ways in which children make sense of their experiences, including the verbal and non-verbal texts available to them, much research methodology still tends to work within a traditional positivist paradigm in which meaning resides within the text, independent of the reader, carrying the author's intentions exactly. The

researcher's role is thus to 'extract the meaning' from the text (interview, transcript of classroom discourse, children's written work, etc.).

2 It is possible to pose an alternative explanation of differences between teachers — at least one of the teachers is 'wrong' or is reading inadequately or unskilfully. Given the extent and frequency of alternative readings and the fact that all the teachers were experienced and recognized as 'competent' within their schools, however, this explanation does not seem adequate or appropriate.

3 See Fairclough (1992a) for a critique of the use of 'appropriate' as a descriptor of forms of language used in similar criteria within the English National Curriculum.

References

ABBOTT, D., BROADFOOT, P., CROLL, P., OSBORNE, M. and POLLARD, A. (1994) 'Some sink, some float: National Curriculum assessment and accountability', *British Educational Research Journal*, **20**, 2, pp. 155–74.

ABEL, J.P. and ABEL, F.J. (1988) 'Writing in the mathematics classroom', *Clearing House*, **62**, pp. 155–8.

ABRAMS, F. (1991) 'GCSE fails to eliminate inequality', *Times Educational Supplement*, 15 February.

AHMED, A. and BUFTON, N. (undated). *Getting Started* (vol. 4): West Sussex Institute of Higher Education.

ALIBERT, D. and THOMAS, M. (1991) 'Research on mathematical proof', in TALL, D. (ed) *Advanced Mathematical Thinking*, Dordrecht: Kluwer Academic Publishers pp. 215–30.

ALTENBERG, B. (1987) 'Causal ordering strategies in English conversation', in MONAGHAN, J. (ed) *Grammar in the Construction of Texts*, London: Frances Pinter, pp. 50–64.

ANDERSON, R. (1988) 'Overwriting and other techniques for success with academic articles', in ROBINSON, P.C. (ed) *Academic Writing: Process and Product*, Hong Kong: Modern English Publications (in association with the British Council), pp. 151–8.

ANDREWS, P. (1992) 'Train spotters have feelings too', *Mathematics Teaching*, **142**, pp. 20–2.

APPLEBEE, A.N. (1981) *A Study of Writing in the Secondary School*, Urbana, IL: National Council of Teachers of English.

APPLEBEE, A.N. (1984) *Contexts for Learning to Write: Studies in Secondary School Instruction*, Norwood, NJ: Ablex.

ATM. (1984) *Teaching Styles: A Response to Cockcroft 243*, Derby: Association of Teachers of Mathematics.

AUSTIN, J.L. and HOWSON, A.G. (1979) 'Language and mathematics education', *Educational Studies in Mathematics*, **10**, pp. 161–97.

AUSTIN, K. (1981) 'Busprongs', *Educational Studies in Mathematics*, **12**, pp. 369–71.

BACKHOUSE, J., HAGGERTY, L., PIRIE, S. and STRATTON, J. (1992) *Improving the Learning of Mathematics*, London: Cassell.

BALACHEFF, N. (1987) 'Processus de preuve et situation de validation', *Educational Studies in Mathematics*, **18**, pp. 147–76.

BALL, B. and BALL, D. (1990) 'How do you cheat at coursework?' *Mathematics Teaching*, **133**, pp. 9–12.

BANWELL, C. (1987) 'A GCSE inservice day', *Mathematics Teaching*, **121**, pp. 26–27.

BARCLAY, T. (1990) 'Connectany: Telecommunications and mathematics', *Hands On!*, **13**, 1, pp. 8–9.

BAUERSFELD, H. (1992) 'Integrating theories for mathematics education', *For the Learning of Mathematics*, **12**, 2, pp. 19–28.

BAZERMAN, C. (1981) 'What written knowledge does: Three examples of academic discourse', *Philosophy of the Social Sciences*, **11**, pp. 361–87.

BELL, A. (1984) 'Language style as audience design', *Language in Society*, **13**, pp. 145–204.

BELL, E.S. and BELL, R.N. (1985) 'Writing and mathematical problem solving: Arguments in favour of a synthesis', *School Science and Mathematics*, **85**, 3, pp. 210–21.

BERLINGHOFF, W.P. (1989) 'Locally original mathematics through writing', in CONNOLLY, P. and VILARDI, T. (eds) *Writing to Learn Mathematics and Science*, New York: Teachers College Press, pp. 88–94.

BILLINGTON, J. and EVANS, P. (1987) 'Levels of knowing 2: The handshake', *Mathematics Teaching*, **120**, pp. 12–19.

BIRKEN, M. (1989) 'Using writing to assist learning in college mathematics classes', in CONNOLLY, P. and VILARDI, T. (eds) *Writing to Learn Mathematics and Science*, New York: Teachers College Press, pp. 33–47.

BLOOMFIELD, A. (1987) 'Assessing investigations', *Mathematics Teaching*, **118**, pp. 48–9.

BOLON, J. (1990) *Jeux de Communication*, Versailles: Institut Universitaire de Formation des Maîtres de l'Academie de Versailles.

BOLON, J. (1991) *Des Exercise D'Ecriture Mathématique*, Versailles: Institut Universitaire de Formation des Maîtres de l'Academie de Versailles.

BORASI, R. (1992) *Learning Mathematics Through Inquiry*, Portsmouth, NH: Heinemann.

BORASI, R. and ROSE, B.J. (1989) 'Journal writing and mathematics instruction', *Educational Studies in Mathematics*, **20**, pp. 347–65.

BORASI, R. and SIEGEL, M. (1994) 'Reading, writing and mathematics: Rethinking the "basics" and their relationship', in ROBITAILLE, D.F., WHEELER, D.H. and KIERAN, C. (eds) *Selected Lectures from the 7th International Congress on Mathematical Education, Quebec 17–23 August 1992*, Sainte-Foy: Les Presses de L'Université Laval, pp. 35–48.

BOURDIEU, P. (1974) 'The school as a conservative force: Scholastic and cultural inequalities', in EGGLESTON, J. (ed) *Contemporary Research in the Sociology of Education*, London: Methuen, pp. 32–46.

BOURDIEU, P. (1991) *Language and Symbolic Power*. Cambridge, MA: Polity Press.

BRANDAU, L. (1988) 'The power of mathematical autobiography'. Paper presented at the The Canadian Mathematics Educators Study Group, Winipeg.

BRIGGS, D. (1980) 'A study of the influence of handwriting upon grades using examination scripts', *Educational Review*, **32**, pp. 185–93.

BRISSENDEN, T. (1988) *Talking About Mathematics*, Oxford: Basil Blackwell.

BRITTON, J., BURGESS, T., MARTIN, N., McLEOD, A. and ROSEN, H. (1975) *The Development of Writing Abilities (11–18)*, London: Macmillan Educational.

BRITTON, J., MARTIN, N. and ROSEN, H. (1966) *Multiple Marking of Compositions*, London: HMSO.

BROADFOOT, P. (1995) 'Performance assessment in perspective: International trends and current English experience', in TORRANCE, H. (ed) *Evaluating Authentic Assessment*, Buckingham: Open University Press, pp. 9–43.

BROWN, T. (1990) 'Active learning within mathematical tasks', *Mathematics Teaching*, **133**, pp. 15–18.

BULL, R. (1990) *Mathematics Coursework: A Student's Guide to Success*, London: Macmillan.

BURKHARDT, H. (1988) 'National testing — liability or asset', *Mathematics Teaching*, **122**, pp. 33–5.

BURTON, L. and MORGAN, C. (forthcoming) 'The writing of mathematicians'.

BUTT, G.W. (1991) 'An investigation into the effects of audience centred teaching on children's writing in geography'. Unpublished MA dissertation, University of London.

References

CAMERON, D. (1992) *Feminism and Linguistic Theory* (2nd ed.), Basingstoke: Macmillan.

CARTON, K. (1990) 'Collaborative writing of mathematics problems', *Mathematics Teacher*, **83**, 7, pp. 542–4.

CAVALLERO, J. (1991) 'The effects of selected text features on teachers' judgements of student writing', *Dissertation Abstracts International*, **52A**, p. 826.

CAZDEN, C.B. (1988) *Classroom Discourse: The Language of Teaching and Learning*, Portsmouth NH: Heinemann.

CHAPMAN, A. (1997) 'Towards a model of language shifts in mathematics learning'. Paper presented at the British Society for Research into Learning Mathematics, Oxford.

CHARLES, R.I. and SILVER, E.A. (eds) (1989) *Research Agenda for Mathematics Education: The Teaching and Assessing of Mathematical Problem Solving*, Reston VA: National Council of Teachers of Mathematics and Lawrence Erlbaum Associates.

CHERRYHOLMES, C. (1988) *Power and Criticism: Poststructural Investigations in Education*, Columbia: Teachers College Press.

CLARK, R. and IVANIC, R. (1997) *The Politics of Writing*, London: Routledge.

CLARKE, D.J., WAYWOOD, A. and STEPHENS, M. (1993) 'Probing the structure of mathematical writing', *Educational Studies in Mathematics*, **25**, 3, pp. 235–50.

COCKCROFT, W.H. (1982) *Mathematics Counts*, London: HMSO.

COLLIS, K.F. (1992) 'Curriculum and assessment: A basic cognitive model', in LEDER, G. (ed) *Assessment and Learning Mathematics*, Victoria: Australian Council for Educational Research, pp. 24–45.

COOPER, C.R. (1977) 'Holistic evaluation of writing', in COOPER, C.R. and ODELL, L. (eds) *Evaluating Writing: Describing, Measuring, Judging*, New York: National Council of Teachers of English, pp. 3–31.

COQUIN-VIENNOT, D. (1989) 'Le discours justificatif en mathematique: L'implication du locuteur selon la representation du referent', *Proceedings of the Thirteenth Conference of the International Group for the Psychology of Mathematics Education*, Paris, pp. 188–95.

CORTAZZI, M. (1993) *Narrative Analysis*, London: Falmer Press.

CROWHURST, M. and PICHÉ, G.L. (1979) 'Audience and mode of discourse effects on syntactic complexity in writing at two grade levels', *Research in the Teaching of English*, **13**, 2, pp. 101–9.

CRYSTAL, D. and DAVY, D. (1969) *Investigating English Style*, London: Longman.

DAVIS, P.J. (1993) 'Visual theorems', *Educational Studies in Mathematics*, **24**, 4, pp. 333–44.

DAVISON, D.M. and PEARCE, D.L. (1988) 'Teacher use of writing in the junior high mathematics classroom', *School Science and Mathematics*, **88**, 1, pp. 6–15.

DELANEY, K. (1986) 'Vestigating', *Mathematics Teaching*, **114**, p. 16.

DES (1985) *GCSE: The National Criteria — Mathematics*, London: HMSO.

DES/WO (1988) *Mathematics for Ages 5 to 16: Proposals to the Secretary of State for Education and Science and the Secretary of State for Wales*, London: HMSO.

DFE (1995) *Mathematics in the National Curriculum*, London: HMSO.

DIFFEY, J., DONALDSON, J., HAWLEY, D. and KNOX, D. (1988) 'How to avoid frogs', *Mathematics Teaching*, **123**, pp. 6–7.

DIXON, J. (1987) 'The question of genres', in REID, I. (ed) *The Place of Genre in Learning: Current Debates*, Geelong: Centre for Studies in Literary Education, Deakin University.

DIXON, J. and BROWN, J. (1985) *Responses to Literature — What Is Being Assessed?* London: Schools Council Publications.

DOHENY-FARINA, S. and ODELL, L. (1985) 'Ethnographic research on writing: Assumptions and methodology', in ODELL, L. and GOSWAMI, D. (eds) *Writing in Nonacademic Settings*, New York: Guildford Press, pp. 503–35.

DONIN, J., BRACEWELL, R.J., FREDERIKSEN, C.H. and DILLINGER, M. (1992) 'Students' strategies for writing instructions: Organizing conceptual information in text', *Written Communication*, **9**, 2, pp. 209–36.

DOSSEY, J.A. and SWAFFORD, J.O. (1993) 'Issues in mathematics assessment in the United States', in NISS, M. (ed) *Cases of Assessment in Mathematics Education: An ICMI Study*, Dordrecht: Kluwer Academic Publishers, pp. 43 57.

DOWLING, P. (1991) 'A touch of class: Ability, social class and intertext in SMP 11–16', in PIMM, D. and LOVE, E. (eds) *Teaching and Learning School Mathematics*, London: Hodder and Stoughton, pp. 137–52.

DOWLING, P. (1992) 'Textual production and social activity: A language of description', *Collected Original Resources in Education*, **16**, 1.

DRISCOLL, M. and POWELL, A. (1992) 'Communicating in mathematics', in HEDLEY, C., FELDMAN, D. and ANTONACCI, P. (eds) *Literacy Across the Curriculum*, Norwood, NJ: Ablex, pp. 247–65.

DUNCAN, E. (1989) 'On preserving the union of numbers and words: The story of an experiment', in CONNOLLY, P. and VILARDI, T. (eds) *Writing to Learn Mathematics and Science*, New York: Teachers College Press, pp. 231–48.

DURKIN, K. and SHIRE, B. (eds) (1991) *Language in Mathematical Education: Research and Practice*, Milton Keynes: Open University Press.

DUVAL, R. (1989) 'Langage et representation dans l'apprentissage d'une demarche deductive', *Proceedings of the Thirteenth Conference of the International Group for the Psychology of Mathematics Education*, Paris, pp. 228–35.

DYE, R.H. (1991) 'Hexagons, Conics, A_5 and $PSL_2(K)$', *Journal of the London Mathematical Society*, **2**, 44, pp. 270–86.

EDWARDS, D. and MERCER, N. (1987) *Common Knowledge: The Development of Understanding in the Classroom*, London: Methuen.

EISNER, E.W. (1993) 'Reshaping assessment in education: Some criteria in search of a practice', *Journal of Curriculum Studies*, **25**, 3, pp. 219–33.

ELSHOLZ, R. and ELSHOLZ, E. (1989) 'The writing process: A model for problem solving', *Journal of Mathematical Behaviour*, **8**, pp. 161–6.

EMIG, J. (1983) 'Writing as a mode of learning', in GOSWAMI, D. and BUTLER, M. (eds) *The Web of Meaning: Essays on Writing, Teaching, Learning, and Thinking*, Upper Montclair, NJ: Boynton/Cook Publishers, pp. 123–31.

ERNEST, P. (1987) 'A model of the cognitive meaning of mathematical expressions', *British Journal of Educational Psychology*, **57**, pp. 343–70.

ERNEST, P. (1991) *The Philosophy of Mathematics Education*, London: Falmer Press.

ERNEST, P. (1993a) 'The culture of the mathematics classroom and the relations between personal and public knowledge: An epistemological perspective'. Paper presented at the Cultural Context of the Mathematics Classroom Conference, University of Bielefeld, Osnabruck, Germany.

ERNEST, P. (1993b) 'Mathematical activity and rhetoric: A social constructivist account', *Proceedings of the Seventeenth International Conference for the Psychology of Mathematics Education* (vol. 2), Tsokuba, Japan, pp. 238–45.

ERNEST, P. (1994) 'The dialogical nature of mathematics', in ERNEST, P. (ed) *Mathematics, Education and Philosophy: An International Perspective*, London: Falmer Press, pp. 33–48.

ERVINCK, G. (1992) 'Mathematics as a foreign language', *Proceedings of the Sixteenth Conference of the International Group for the Psychology of Mathematics Education* (vol. 3), Durham, NH, pp. 217–33.

EVANS, J. (1994) 'Quantitative and qualitative research methodologies: Rivalry or cooperation?', *Proceedings of the Eighteenth Conference of the International Group for the Psychology of Mathematics Education*, Lisbon, pp. 320–27.

FAIGLEY, L. (1985) 'Nonacademic writing: The social perspective', in ODELL, L. and GOSWAMI, D. (eds) *Writing in Nonacademic Settings*, New York: Guildford Press, pp. 231–48.

FAIRCLOUGH, N. (1989) *Language and Power*, Harlow: Longman.

FAIRCLOUGH, N. (1992a) 'The appropriacy of "appropriateness"', in FAIRCLOUGH, N. (ed) *Critical Language Awareness*, Harlow: Longman, pp. 33–56.

FAIRCLOUGH, N. (ed) (1992b) *Critical Language Awareness*, Harlow: Longman.

FAIRCLOUGH, N. (1992c) *Discourse and Social Change*, Cambridge: Polity Press.

FAIRCLOUGH, N. (1995) *Critical Discourse Analysis: The Critical Study of Language*, Harlow: Longman.

FAUVEL, J. (1991) 'Tone and the teacher: Instruction and complicity in mathematics textbooks', in PIMM, D. and LOVE, E. (eds) *Teaching and Learning School Mathematics*, London: Hodder and Stoughton, pp. 111–21.

FIELKER, D. (1982) 'Editorial', *Mathematics Teaching*, **99**, pp. 2–3.

FILER, A. (1993) 'The assessment of classroom language: Challenging the rhetoric of "objectivity"', *International Studies in Sociology of Education*, **3**, 2, pp. 193–212.

FLENER, F.O. and REEDY, J. (1990) 'Can teachers evaluate problem solving ability?' *Proceedings of the Fourteenth Conference of the International Group for the Psychology of Mathematics Education* (vol. 1), Oaxtapec, pp. 127–34.

FORD, M.I. (1990) 'The writing process: A strategy for problem solvers', *Arithmetic Teacher*, **38**, 3, pp. 35–8.

FOWLER, R. and KRESS, G. (1979) 'Critical Linguistics', in FOWLER, R., HODGE, B., KRESS, G. and TREW, T. (eds) *Language and Control*, London: Routledge and Kegan Paul.

FOXMAN, D., MAY, R. and THORPE, J. (1986) 'Assessing investigations', *Mathematics Teaching*, **118**, pp. 44–8.

FREEDMAN, S. (1979) 'How characteristics of student essays influence teachers' evaluations', *Journal of Educational Psychology*, **71**, 3, pp. 328–38.

FREUDENTHAL, H. (1978) *Weeding and Sowing: Preface to a Science of Mathematical Education*, Dordrecht: Reidel.

GALBRAITH, P. (1993) 'Paradigms, problems and assessment: Some ideological implications', in NISS, M. (ed) *Investigations into Assessment in Mathematics Education: An ICMI Study*, Dordrecht: Kluwer Academic Publishers, pp. 73–86.

GILBERT, G.N. and MULKAY, M. (1984) *Opening Pandora's Box: A Sociological Analysis of Scientists' Discourse*, Cambridge: Cambridge University Press.

GILBERT, P. (1989) *Writing, Schooling and Deconstruction: From Voice to Text in the Classroom*, London: Routledge.

GILL, P. (1993) 'Using the construct of "levelness" in assessing open work in the National Curriculum', *British Journal of Curriculum and Assessment*, **3**, 3, pp. 17–18.

GILLMAN, L. (1987) *Writing Mathematics Well: A Manual for Authors*; The Mathematical Association of America.

GIPPS, C. (1992) 'National Curriculum assessment: A research agenda', *British Educational Research Journal*, **18**, 3, pp. 277–86.

GIPPS, C., BROWN, M., MCCALLUM, B. and MCALISTER, S. (1995) *Intuition or Evidence? Teachers and National Assessment of Seven-Year-Olds*, Buckingham: Open University Press.

GOPEN, G.D. and SMITH, D.A. (1989) 'What's an assignment like you doing in a course like this? Writing to learn mathematics', in CONNOLLY, P. and VILARDI, T. (eds) *Writing to Learn Mathematics and Science*, New York: Teachers College Press, pp. 209–28.

GOSDEN, H. (1992) 'Discourse functions of marked theme in scientific research articles', *English for Specific Purposes*, **11**, 3, pp. 207–24.

GRAVES, D.H. (1983) *Writing: Teachers and Children at Work*, Portsmouth NH: Heinemann Educational Books.

GREENES, C., SCHULMAN, L. and SPUNGIN, R. (1992) 'Stimulating communication in mathematics', *Arithmetic Teacher*, **40**, 2, pp. 78–82.

GREIMAS, A.J. (1990) *Narrative Semiotics and Cognitive Discourses* (P. PERRON and F.H. COLLING, Trans.), London: Pinters Publishers.

GUILLERAULT, M. and LABORDE, C. (1982) 'Ambiguities in the description of a geometric figure', in LOWENTHAL, F., VANDAMME, F. and CORDIER, J. (eds) *Language and Learning Acquisition*, New York: Plenum, pp. 151–5.

GUILLERAULT, M. and LABORDE, C. (1986) 'A study of pupils reading geometry', in LOWENTHAL, F. and VANDAMME, F. (eds) *Pragmatics and Education*, New York: Plenum, pp. 223–38.

HAINES, C.R. (1991) 'Assessing mathematical science projects', *International Journal of Mathematics Education in Science and Technology*, **22**, 1, pp. 97–101.

HAINES, C.R. and IZARD, J. (1994) 'Assessing mathematical communications about projects and investigations', *Educational Studies in Mathematics*, **27**, 4, pp. 373–86.

HAKE, R. and WILLIAMS, J. (1981) 'Style and its consequences: Do as I do, not as I say', *College English*, **43**, 5, pp. 433–51.

HALLIDAY, M.A.K. (1966) *Grammar, Society and the Noun*, London: University College London.

HALLIDAY, M.A.K. (1973) *Explorations in the Functions of Language*, London: Edward Arnold.

HALLIDAY, M.A.K. (1974) 'Some aspects of sociolinguistics', *Interactions between Linguistics and Mathematical Education Symposium*, Paris: UNESCO.

HALLIDAY, M.A.K. (1985) *An Introduction to Functional Grammar*, London: Edward Arnold.

HALLIDAY, M.A.K. (1989) *Spoken and Written Language*, Oxford: Oxford University Press.

HALLIDAY, M.A.K. and MARTIN, J.R. (1993) *Writing Science: Literacy and Discursive Power*, London: Falmer Press.

HANSEN, K. (1988) 'Rhetoric and epistemology in the social sciences: A contrast of two representative texts', in JOLLIFFE, D.A. (ed) *Writing in Academic Disciplines: Advances in Writing Research*, Norwood, NJ: Ablex, pp. 167–210.

HARRIS, W. (1977) 'Teacher response to student writing', *Research in the Teaching of English*, **11**, pp. 175–85.

HATFIELD, M.M. and BITTER, G.G. (1991) 'Communicating Mathematics', *Mathematics Teacher*, **84**, 8, pp. 615–21.

HAVENS, L. (1989) 'Writing to enhance learning in general mathematics', *Mathematics Teacher*, **82**, 7, pp. 551–4.

HAYES, J., SCHRIVER, K.A., HILL, C. and HATCH, J. (1992) 'Assessing the message and the messenger', *The Quarterly of the National Writing Project and the Centre for the Study of Writing and Literacy*, **14**, 2, pp. 15–17.

HAYLOCK, D. (1985) 'Conflicts in the assessment and encouragement of mathematical creativity in school children', *International Journal of Mathematics Education in Science and Technology*, **16**, 4, pp. 547–53.

References

HAYLOCK, D. (1987) 'A framework for assessing mathematical creativity in school children', *Educational Studies in Mathematics*, **18**, 1, pp. 59–74.

HAYS, J.N., DURHAM, R.L., BRANDT, K.S. and RAITZ, A.E. (1990) 'Argumentative writing of students: Adult socio-cognitive development', in KIRSCH, G. and ROEN, D.H. (eds) *A Sense of Audience in Written Communication* (vol. 5), Newbury Park CA: Sage Publications, pp. 248–66.

HERRINGTON, A.J. (1985) 'Writing in academic settings: A study of the contexts for writing in two college chemical engineering courses', *Research in the Teaching of English*, **19**, 4, pp. 331–59.

HEWITT, D. (1992) 'Train spotters' paradise', *Mathematics Teaching*, **140**, pp. 6–8.

HIRIGOYEN, H. (1997) 'Dialectical variations in the language of mathematics', in TRENTACOSTA, J. and KENNEY, M. (eds) *Multicultural and Gender Equity in the Mathematics Classroom: The Gift of Diversity*, Reston, VA: National Council of Teachers of Mathematics, pp. 164–8.

HMI (1985) *Mathematics from 5 to 16*, London: HMSO.

HMI (1987) *Curriculum Matters 3: Mathematics from 5 to 16* (2nd edition ed.), London: HMSO.

HODGE, R. and KRESS, G. (1988) *Social Semiotics*, Cambridge: Polity Press.

HODGE, R. and KRESS, G. (1993) *Language as Ideology* (2nd ed.), London: Routledge and Kegan Paul.

HOFFMAN, M.R. and POWELL, A.B. (1989) 'Mathematical and commentary writing: Vehicles for student reflection and empowerment', *Mathematics Teaching*, **126**, pp. 55–7.

HOFFMAN, M.R. and POWELL, A.B. (1992) 'Writing as a vehicle to promote sense-making in mathematics and a learning community'. Paper presented at the 7th International Congress on Mathematics Education, Working Group 7: Language and Communication in the Classroom, Québec.

HOGE, R.D. and COLARDACI, T. (1989) 'Teacher-based judgements of academic achievement: A review of the literature', *Review of Educational Research*, **59**, 3, pp. 297–313.

HON, Y.C. (1992) *Children Writing Investigation Reports: A Linguistic View*; English Language Unit, University of Liverpool.

HORSELLA, M. and SINDERMANN, G. (1992) 'Aspects of scientific discourse: Conditional argumentation', *English for Specific Purposes*, **11**, 2, pp. 129–39.

HOUSTON, S.K. (ed) (1993) *Developments in Curriculum and Assessment in Mathematics*, Coleraine: University of Ulster.

HUBBARD, R. (1992) 'Writing humanistic mathematics', *HMN Journal*, **7**, pp. 81–8.

HURWITZ, M. (1990) 'Student-authored manuals as semester projects', *Mathematics Teacher*, **83**, 9, pp. 701–3.

JAMES, N. and MASON, J. (1982) 'Towards recording', *Visible Language*, **16**, 3, pp. 249–58.

JAWORSKI, B. (1994) *Investigating Mathematics Teaching: A Constructivist Enquiry*, London: Falmer Press.

JENSEN, K.B. (1989) 'Discourses of interviewing: Validating qualitative research findings through textual analysis', in KVALE, S. (ed) *Issues of Validity in Qualitative Research*, Lund, Sweden: Studentlitteratur, pp. 93–108.

JOHNSON, L.A. (1991) 'Effects of essay writing on achievement in algebra', *Dissertation Abstracts International*, **52A**, p. 833.

JOHNSON, M.L. (1983) 'Writing in mathematics classes: A valuable tool for learning', *Mathematics Teacher*, **76**, 2, pp. 117–19.

JOHNSON, P.E. (1990) 'Enhancing learning by using writing in history of mathematics', *International Journal of Mathematics Education in Science and Technology*, **21**, 2, pp. 259–63.

KANE, R.B. (1968) 'The readability of mathematical English', *Journal of Research in Science Teaching*, **5**, pp. 296–8.

KAPUT, J. (1987) 'Towards a theory of symbol use in mathematics', in JANVIER, C. (ed) *Problems of Representation in the Teaching and Learning of Mathematics*, London: Lawrence Erlbaum Associates, pp. 159–95.

KEITH, S. (1989) 'Exploring mathematics in writing', in CONNOLLY, P. and VILARDI, T. (eds) *Writing to Learn Mathematics and Science*, New York: Teachers College Press, pp. 134–46.

KENYON, R.W. (1989) 'Writing *is* problem solving', in CONNOLLY, P. and VILARDI, T. (eds) *Writing to Learn Mathematics and Science*, New York: Teachers College Press, pp. 73–87.

KIERAN, C. (1981) 'Concepts associated with the equality sign', *Educational Studies in Mathematics*, **12**, 3, pp. 317–26.

KINNEAVY, J.L. (1971) *A Theory of Discourse: The Aims of Discourse*, Eaglewood Cliffs NJ: Prentice Hall.

KNUTH, D.E. (1985) 'Algorithmic thinking and mathematical thinking', *American Mathematical Monthly*, **92**, pp. 170–81.

KNUTH, D.E., LARRABEE, T. and ROBERTS, P.M. (1989) *Mathematical Writing*, The Mathematical Association of America.

KONIOR, J. (1993) 'Research into the construction of mathematical texts', *Educational Studies in Mathematics*, **24**, pp. 251–6.

KRESS, G. (1989) *Linguistic Processes in Sociocultural Practice* (2nd ed.), Oxford: Oxford University Press.

KRESS, G. (1990) 'Two kinds of power: Gunther Kress on genre', *The English Magazine*, **24**, pp. 4–7.

KRESS, G. (1993) 'Against arbitrariness: The social production of the sign as a foundational issue in critical discourse analysis', *Discourse and Society*, **4**, 2, pp. 169–91.

KRESS, G. and VAN LEEUWEN, T. (1990) *Reading Images*, Geelong, Victoria: Deakin University Press.

KRESS, G. and VAN LEEUWEN, T. (1996) *Reading Images: The Grammar of Visual Design*, London: Routledge.

LABORDE, C. (1990) 'Language and mathematics', in NESHER, P. and KILPATRICK, J. (eds) *Mathematics and Cognition: A research synthesis by the International Group for the Psychology of Mathematics Education*, Cambridge: Cambridge University Press, pp. 53–69.

LANGER, J.A. (1984) 'The effects of available information on responses to school writing tasks', *Research in the Teaching of English*, **18**, 1, pp. 27–44.

LANGER, J.A. and APPLEBEE, A.N. (1987) *How Writing Shapes Thinking: A Study of Teaching and Learning*, Urbana IL: National Council of Teachers of English.

LAYZER, D. (1989) 'The synergy between writing and mathematics', in CONNOLLY, P. and VILARDI, T. (eds) *Writing to Learn Mathematics and Science*, New York: Teachers College Press, pp. 122–33.

LEAG (1989) *GCSE Syllabuses Mathematics A and B 1991*, London: London East Anglian Group.

LEAG (1991) *Mathematics Coursework Tasks and Performance Indicators (1988–1991)*, London: London East Anglian Group.

LeGERE, A. (1991) 'Collaboration and writing in the mathematics classroom', *Mathematics Teacher*, **84**, 3, pp. 166–71.

LERMAN, S. (1989) 'Investigations: Where to now?' in ERNEST, P. (ed) *Mathematics Teaching: The State of the Art*, London: Falmer Press, pp. 73–80.

LERON, U. (1983) 'Structuring mathematical proofs', *The American Mathematical Monthly*, **90**, 3, pp. 174–84.

LESH, R. and LAMON, S.J. (eds) (1992) *Assessment of Authentic Performance in School Mathematics*, Washington D.C.: American Association for the Advancement of Science.

LESNAK, R.J. (1989) 'Writing to learn: An experiment in remedial algebra', in CONNOLLY, P. and VILARDI, T. (eds) *Writing to Learn Mathematics and Science*, New York: Teachers College Press, pp. 147–56.

LESTER, F.K. and KROLL, D.L. (1990) 'Assessing student growth in mathematical problem solving', in KULM, G. (ed) *Assessing Higher Order Thinking in Mathematics*, Washington D.C.: American Association for the Advancement of Science, pp. 53–70.

LEUNG, F.K.S. (forthcoming) 'The traditional Chinese views on mathematics and education — implications for mathematics education in the new millennium', in HOYLES, C., MORGAN, C. and WOODHOUSE, G. (eds) *Mathematics Education for the 21st Century*, London: Falmer Press.

LINN, R.L., BAKER, E.L. and DUNBAR, S.B. (1991) 'Complex, performance-based assessment: Expectations and validation criteria, *Educational Researcher*, **20**, 8, pp. 15–21.

LMS (1995) *Tackling the Mathematics Problem*: London: London Mathematical Society.

LONG, R.C. (1990) 'The writer's audience: Fact or fiction', in KIRSCH, G. and ROEN, D.H. (eds) *A Sense of Audience in Written Communication*, Newbury Park CA: Sage Publications, pp. 73–84.

LOVE, E. (1981) 'Examinations at 16-plus', *Mathematics Teaching*, **96**, pp. 42–6.

LOVE, E. and SHIU, C. (1992) 'Pupils' perceptions of assessment criteria in an innovative mathematics project', *Proceedings of the 16th International Conference for the Psychology of Mathematics Education*. Durham, NH, pp. 350–57.

MACDONELL, D. (1986) *Theories of Discourse: An Introduction*, Oxford: Basil Blackwell.

MACNAMARA, A. and ROPER, T. (1992a) 'Attainment Target 1 — Is all the evidence there?' *Mathematics Teaching*, **140**, pp. 26–7.

MACNAMARA, A. and ROPER, T. (1992b) 'Unrecorded, unobserved and suppressed attainment: Can our pupils do more than we know?' *Mathematics in School*, **21**, 5, pp. 12–13.

MARKS, G. and MOUSLEY, J. (1990) 'Mathematics, education and genre: Dare we make the process writing mistake again?' *Language and Education*, **4**, 2, pp. 117–35.

MARTIN, J.R. (1989) *Factual Writing: Exploring and Challenging Social Reality* (2nd ed.), Oxford: Oxford University Press.

MARTIN, J.R., CHRISTIE, F. and ROTHERY, J. (1987) 'Social processes in education: A reply to Sawyer and Watson (and others)', in REID, I. (ed) *The Place of Genre in Learning: Current Debates*, Geelong: Centre for Studies in Literary Education, Deakin University.

MARTIN, N., D'ARCY, P., NEWTON, B. and PARKER, R. (1976) *Writing and Learning across the Curriculum 11–16*, London: Ward Lock Educational.

MASON, J.H. (1987) 'What do symbols represent?' in JANVIER, C. (ed) *Problems of Representation in the Teaching and Learning of Mathematics*, London: Lawrence Erlbaum Associates, pp. 73–81.

MASON, J., BURTON, L. and STACEY, K. (1985) *'Thinking Mathematically'* (revised ed.), Wokingham: Addison-Wesley.

MASSEY, A. (1983) 'The effects of handwriting and other incidental variables on GCSE "A" level marks in English literature', *Educational Review*, **35**, 1, pp. 45–50.

MASTER, P. (1991) 'Active verbs with inanimate subjects in scientific prose', *English for Specific Purposes*, **10**, 1, pp. 15–33.

MATHEMATICAL ASSOCIATION. (1987) *Maths Talk*, Cheltenham: Stanley Thornes.

McBRIDE, M. (1989) 'A Foulcauldian analysis of mathematical discourse', *For the Learning of Mathematics*, **9**, 1, pp. 40–6.

McBRIDE, M. (1994) 'The theme of individualism in mathematics education: An examination of mathematics textbooks', *For the Learning of Mathematics*, **14**, 3, pp. 36–42.

McCAFFERTY, D. (1989) 'An Evaluation of Investigative Materials'. Unpublished MSc dissertation, University of Edinburgh.

McINTOSH, M.E. (1991) 'No time for writing in your class?' *Mathematics Teacher*, **84**, 6, pp. 423–33.

McNAMARA, O. (1993) 'Double and add the next', *Mathematics Teaching*, **142**, pp. 23–25.

MEHAN, H. (1979) *Learning Lessons: Social Organisation in the Classroom*, Cambridge MA: Harvard University Press.

MELLIN-OLSEN, S. (1993) 'A critical view of assessment in mathematics education: Where is the student as a subject?' in NISS, M. (ed) *Investigations into Assessment in Mathematics Education: An ICMI Study*, Dordrecht: Kluwer, pp. 143–56.

METT, C.L. (1989) 'Writing in mathematics: Evidence of learning through writing', *The Clearing House*, **62**, pp. 293–6.

MEYER, R.W. (1991) 'A classroom note on integrating literacy activities into the mathematics classroom', *Mathematics and Computer Education*, **25**, 1, pp. 38–41.

MILLER, L.D. (1991) 'Writing to learn mathematics', *Mathematics Teacher*, **84**, 7, pp. 516–21.

MILLER, L.D. (1992a) 'Teacher benefits from using impromptu writing prompts in algebra classes', *Journal for Research in Mathematics Education*, **23**, 4, pp. 329–40.

MILLER, L.D. (1992b) *Writing in Mathematics Classes*, Perth: National Key Centre for School Science and Mathematics, Curtin University of Technology.

MISHLER, E.G. (1986) *Research Interviewing: Context and Narrative*, Cambridge, MA.: Harvard University Press.

MORGAN, C. (1992a) 'Looking at children's writing of mathematics', *Proceedings of the British Society for Research in Mathematics Education*, Milton Keynes: Open University, pp. 9–13.

MORGAN, C. (1992b) 'Written mathematical communication: The child's perspective'. Paper presented at the Sixteenth Conference of the International Group for the Psychology of Mathematics Education, Durham, NH.

MORGAN, C. (1994) 'Writing mathematically', *Mathematics Teaching*, **146**, pp. 18–21.

MORGAN, C. (1995) 'An analysis of the discourse of written reports of investigative work in GCSE mathematics'. Unpublished PhD dissertation, Institute of Education, University of London.

MOUSLEY, J. and MARKS, G. (1991) *Discourses in Mathematics*, Geelong: Deakin University.

MUMME, J. and SHEPHERD, N. (1990) 'Communication in mathematics', *Arithmetic Teacher*, **38**, 1, pp. 18–22.

NATIONAL WRITING PROJECT (1986) *The SCDC National Writing Project Newsletter, About Writing*, **3**.

NATIONAL WRITING PROJECT (1987) *The SCDC National Writing Project Newsletter, About Writing*, **7**.

NATIONAL WRITING PROJECT (1989) *The SCDC National Writing Project Newsletter, About Writing*, **10**.

NCC (1989) *Mathematics Non-Statutory Guidance*, York: National Curriculum Council.

NCTM (1989) *Curriculum and Evaluation Standards for School Mathematics*, Reston, VA: National Council of Teachers of Mathematics.

NCTM (1995) *Assessment Standards for School Mathematics*, Reston VA: National Council of Teachers of Mathematics.

NISS, M. (ed) (1993) *Cases of Assessment in Mathematics Education: An ICMI Study*, Dordrecht: Kluwer Academic Publishers.

O'SHEA, T. (1991) 'A diary of two problem solvers', *Mathematics Teacher*, **84**, 9, pp. 748–53.

OAKS, A. and ROSE, B. (1992) 'Writing as a tool for expanding student conception of mathematics'. Paper presented at the 7th International Congress on Mathematics Education, Working Group 7: Language and Communication in the Classroom, Québec.

ODELL, L. (1985) 'Beyond the text: Relations between writing and social context', in ODELL, L. and GOSWAMI, D. (eds) *Writing in Nonacademic Settings*, New York: Guildford Press, pp. 249–80.

ODELL, L. and GOSWAMI, D. (1982) 'Writing in a non-academic setting', *Research in the Teaching of English*, **16**, 3, pp. 201–23.

OLLERTON, M. (1992) 'Reactions', *Mathematics Teaching*, **140**, p. 28.

OLLERTON, M. and HEWITT, D. (1989) 'Teaching with the ATM/SEG GCSE: A conversation', *Mathematics Teaching*, **127**, pp. 24–6.

OTTERBURN, M.K. and NICHOLSON, A.R. (1976) 'The language of (CSE) mathematics', *Mathematics in School*, **5**, 5, pp. 18–20.

PAECHTER, C. (1995) 'Doing the best for the students: Dilemmas and decisions in carrying out statutory assessment tasks', *Assessment in Education*, **2**, 1, pp. 39–52.

PAGET, M.A. (1983) 'Experience and knowing', *Human Studies*, **8**, pp. 67–90.

PAIK, M.K. and NORRIS, E.M. (1984) 'Writing in mathematics education', *International Journal of Mathematics Education in Science and Technology*, **18**, 2, pp. 245–52.

PEHKONEN, E. (ed) (1997) *Using Open-Ended Problems in Mathematics*, Helsinki: Helsinki University, Department of Teacher Education.

PENNIMAN, V. (1991) *Making Graphs Is a Fun Thing to Do*, Mount Holyoke College, MA: SummerMath for Teachers.

PERKS, P. and PRESTAGE, S. (1992) 'Making choices explicit', *Mathematics in School*, **21**, 3, pp. 46–8.

PIKE, M. and MURRAY, L. (1991) 'Assessing open ended tasks', *Mathematics in School*, **20**, 2, pp. 32–3.

PIMM, D. (1984) 'Who is we?' *Mathematics Teaching*, **107**, pp. 39–42.

PIMM, D. (1987) *Speaking Mathematically: Communication in Mathematics Classrooms*, London: Routledge Kegan and Paul.

PIMM, D. (1991) 'Communicating mathematically', in DURKIN, K. and SHIRE, B. (eds) *Language in Mathematical Education: Research and Practice*, Milton Keynes: Open University Press, pp. 17–23.

PIRIE, S. (1988) *GCSE Coursework: Mathematics — A Teacher's Guide to Organisation and Assessment*, London: Macmillan Education.

POLKINGHORNE, D.E. (1988) *Narrative Knowing and the Human Sciences*, Albany, NY: SUNY Press.

POTTER, J. and WETHERELL, M. (1987) *Discourse and Social Psychology: Beyond Attitudes and Beliefs*, London: Sage Publications.

POWELL, A.B. and RAMNAUTH, M. (1992) 'Beyond questions and answers: Prompting reflections and deepening understandings of mathematics using multiple-entry logs', *For the Learning of Mathematics*, **12**, 2, pp. 12–18.

POWELL, A. and LÓPEZ, J. (1989) 'Writing as a vehicle to learn mathematics: A case study', in CONNOLLY, P. and VILARDI, T. (eds) *Writing to Learn Mathematics and Science*, New York: Teachers College Press, pp. 157–77.

PRENTICE, W.C. (1980) 'The effects of intended audience and feedback on the writings of middle grade students', *Dissertation Abstracts International*, **41A**, p. 934.

PRICE, J.J. (1989) 'Learning mathematics through writing: Some guidelines', *College Mathematics Journal*, **20**, pp. 393–401.

PURVES, A.C. (1984) 'The teacher as reader: An anatomy', *College English*, **46**, 3, pp. 259–65.

QUICK, D.M. (1983) 'Audience awareness and adaptation skills of writers at four different grade levels', *Dissertation Abstracts International*, **44A**, p. 2133.

RADNOR, H. and SHAW, K. (1995) 'Developing a collaborative approach to moderation', in TORRANCE, H. (ed) *Evaluating Authentic Assessment*, Buckingham: Open University Press, pp. 124–43.

RAPAILLE, J.P. (1986) 'Research on assessment process in "natural" conditions', in BEN-PERETZ, M., BROMME, R. and HALKES, R. (eds) *Advances of Research on Teacher Thinking*, Lisse: Swets and Zeitlinger, pp. 122–32.

REDD-BOYD, T.M. and SLATER, W.H. (1989) 'The effects of audience specification on undergraduates' attitudes, strategies and writing', *Research in the Teaching of English*, **23**, 1, pp. 77–108.

REID, I. (1987) *The Place of Genre in Learning: Current Debates*, Geelong: Centre for Studies in Literary Education, Deakin University.

RICHARDS, J. (1991) 'Mathematical discussions', in VON GLASERSFELD, E. (ed) *Radical Constructivism in Mathematics Education*, Dordrecht: Kluwer Academic Publishers, pp. 13–51.

RICHARDS, L. (1990) 'Measuring things with words: Language for learning mathematics', *Language Arts*, **67**, 1, pp. 14–25.

RIDGWAY, J. and SCHOENFELD, A. (1994) 'Balanced assessment: Designing assessment schemes to promote desirable change in mathematics education'. Paper presented at the EARI Email Conference on Assessment.

ROE, P. (1977) *Scientific Text*; Birmingham: University of Birmingham.

ROEN, D.H. and WILLEY, R.J. (1988) 'The effects of audience awareness on drafting and revising', *Research in the Teaching of English*, **22**, 1, pp. 75–88.

ROGERS, A. and MacDONALD, C. (1985) *Teaching Writing for Learning*; The Scottish Council for Research in Education.

ROPER, T. and MacNAMARA, A. (1993) 'Teacher assessment of mathematics: Attainment Target 1 (MA1)', *British Journal of Curriculum and Assessment*, **4**, 1, pp. 16–19.

ROTMAN, B. (1988) 'Towards a semiotics of mathematics', *Semiotica*, **72**, 1/2, pp. 1–35.

ROTMAN, B. (1993) *Ad Infinitum — The Ghost in Turing's Machine: Taking God Out of Mathematics and Putting the Body Back In*, Stanford CA: Stanford University Press.

ROUNDS, P.L. (1987) 'Multifunctional personal pronoun use in an educational setting', *English for Specific Purposes*, **6**, 1, pp. 18–29.

ROWLAND, T. (1992) 'Pointing with pronouns', *For the Learning of Mathematics*, **12**, 2, pp. 44–8.

RUBIN, D.L. and O'LEARY, J. (1990) 'Facilitation of audience awareness: Revision processes of basic writers', in KIRSCH, G. and ROEN, D.H. (eds) *A Sense of Audience in Written Communication*, Newbury Park CA: Sage Publications, pp. 280–92.

RUBIN, D.L. and PICHÉ, G.L. (1979) 'Development in syntactic and strategic aspects of audience adaptation skills in written persuasive communication', *Research in the Teaching of English*, **13**, 4, pp. 293–316.

RUTHVEN, K. (1987) 'Ability stereotyping in mathematics', *Educational Studies in Mathematics*, **18**, pp. 243–53.

RUTHVEN, K. (1994) 'Better judgement: Rethinking assessment in mathematics education', *Educational Studies in Mathematics*, **27**, 4, pp. 433–50.

RUTHVEN, K. (1995) 'Beyond commonsense: Reconceptualising National Curriculum assessment', *The Curriculum Journal*, **6**, 1, pp. 5–28.

SCARDAMALIA, M., BEREITER, C. and GOELMAN, H. (1982) 'The role of production factors in writing ability', in NYSTRAND, M. (ed) *What Writers Know: The Language, Process and Structure of Written Discourse*, London: Academic Press, pp. 173–210.

SCHMIDT, W.H., JORDE, D., COGAN, L.S., BARRIER, E., GONZALO, I., MOSER, U., SHIMIZU, K., SAWADA, T., GILBERT, A.V., McKNIGHT, C., PRAWAT, R.S., WILEY, D.E., RAIZEN, S.A., BRITTON, E.D. and WOLFE, R.G. (1996) *Characterizing Pedagogical Flow: An Investigation of Mathematics and Science Teaching in Six Countries*, Dordrecht: Kluwer Academic Publishers.

SCHOOL MATHEMATICS PROJECT (1989) *Using Investigations: An Introduction to Ways of Working*, Cambridge: Cambridge University Press.

SCHUBAUER-LEONI, M.L., BELL, N., GROSSEN, M. and PERRET-CLERMONT, A.N. (1989) 'Problems in the assessment of learning: The social construction of questions and answers in the scholastic context', *International Journal of Research in Education*, **13**, 6, pp. 671–84.

SCOTT, D. (1991) 'Issues and themes: Coursework and coursework assessment in the GCSE', *Research Papers in Education*, **6**, 1, pp. 3–19.

SEAC (1989) *GCSE Chief Examiners' Conference in Mathematics*, London: School Examinations and Assessment Council.

SEG (1992) *GCSE Syllabuses for 1992 Examinations Section 6: Mathematics and Statistics*, Southern Examining Group.

SEKIGUCHI, Y. (1992) 'Social dimensions of proof in presentation: From an ethnographic inquiry in a high school geometry classroom', *Proceedings of the Sixteenth International Conference for the Psychology of Mathematics Education*, Durham NH, pp. 314–21.

SEKIGUCHI, Y. (1994) 'Mathematical proof as a new discourse: An ethnographic inquiry in a Japanese mathematics classroom', *Proceedings of the 18th International Conference for the Psychology of Mathematics Education*, Lisbon, pp. 233–40.

SHEERAN, Y. and BARNES, D. (1991) *School Writing: Discovering the Ground Rules*, Buckingham: Open University Press.

SHIELD, M. (1994) *Analysis of Student Expository Writing in Mathematics: Coding Manual*, Centre for Mathematics and Science Education, Queensland University of Technology.

SHIELD, M. and SWINSON, K. (1994) 'Stimulating student elaboration of mathematical ideas through writing', *Proceedings of the 18th International Conference for the Psychology of Mathematics Education*, Lisbon, pp. 273–80.

SHUARD, H. and ROTHERY, A. (eds) (1984) *Children Reading Mathematics*, London: Murray.

SINCLAIR, A. (1991) 'Children's production and comprehension of written numerical representations', in DURKIN, K. and SHIRE, B. (eds) *Language in Mathematical Education: Research and Practice*, Buckingham: Open University Press, pp. 59–68.

SINCLAIR, J.M. and COULTHARD, R.M. (1975) *Towards an Analysis of Discourse: The English Used by Teachers and Pupils*, Oxford: Oxford University Press.

SNOW, J.E. (1989) 'The advanced writing requirement at Saint Mary's College', in CONNOLLY, P. and VILARDI, T. (eds) *Writing to Learn Mathematics and Science*, New York: Teachers College Press, pp. 193–7.

SOLOFF, S. (1973) 'Effect of non-content factors on the grading of essays', *Graduate Research in Education and Related Disciplines*, **8**, pp. 44–54.

SPEAR, M.G. (1984) 'Sex bias in science teachers' ratings of work and pupil characteristics', *European Journal of Science Education*, **6**, 4, pp. 369–77.

SPEAR, M.G. (1989) 'Differences between the written work of boys and girls', *British Educational Research Journal*, **15**, 3, pp. 271–7.

SPENCER, E., LANCASTER, J., ROY, J., BENVIE, J. and MCFADYEN, I. (1983) *Written Work in Scottish Secondary Schools: A Descriptive Study*, Edinburgh: The Scottish Council for Research in Education.

STEENROD, N., HALMOS, P.R., SCHIFFER, M.M. and DIEUDONNÉ, J.A. (1973) *How to Write Mathematics*, American Mathematical Society.

STEMPIEN, M. (1990) 'An Analysis of Writing-to-Learn in the Context of a Survey of a Mathematics Course for Students in the Liberal Arts'. Unpublished PhD, State University of New York at Buffalo.

STEMPIEN, M. and BORASI, R. (1985) 'Students' writing in mathematics: Some ideas and experiences', *For the Learning of Mathematics*, **5**, 3.

STEPHENS, M. and MONEY, R. (1993) 'New developments in senior secondary assessment in Australia', in NISS, M. (ed) *Cases of Assessment in Mathematics Education: An ICMI Study*, Dordrecht: Kluwer Academic Publishers, pp. 155–71.

STEWARD, D. (1989) 'Prerequisites', *Mathematics in School*, **18**, 1, pp. 12–13.

STEWART, M. and GROBE, C. (1979) 'Syntactic maturity, maturity of writing and teachers' quality ratings', *Research in the Teaching of English*, **13**, 3, pp. 207–15.

STEWART, M. and LEAMAN, H.L. (1983) 'Teachers' writing assessments across the high school curriculum', *Research in the Teaching of English*, **17**, 2, pp. 113–25.

STRUBE, P. (1989) 'The notion of style in Physics textbooks', *Journal of Research in Science Teaching*, **26**, 4, pp. 291–9.

SULKE, F. (1990) 'A-Level mathematics through in-course assessment: Broadening experiences and assessment procedures', *Teaching Mathematics and Its Applications*, **9**, 3, pp. 108–10.

SUTTON, C. (1989) 'Writing and reading in science', in MILLAR, R. (ed) *Doing Science: Images of Science in Science Education*, London: Falmer Press, pp. 137–59.

SWALES, J. (1985) *Episodes in ESP*, Oxford: Pergamon Press.

SWATTON, P. (1992) 'Children's language and assessing their skill in formulating testable hypotheses', *British Educational Research Journal*, **18**, 1, pp. 73–85.

SWINSON, K.V. and PARTRIDGE, B.D. (1992a) 'An investigation of the extent to which writing activities are used in mathematics classrooms'. Paper presented at the Sixteenth Conference of the International Group for the Psychology of Mathematics Education, Durham, NH.

SWINSON, K.V. and PARTRIDGE, B.D. (1992b) 'Writing in mathematics — is it always beneficial?' Paper presented at the 16th Conference of the International Group for the Psychology of Mathematics Education, Durham NH.

TALL, D. (1990) 'Misguided discovery', *Mathematics Teaching*, **132**, pp. 27–9.

TANNER, H. and JONES, S. (1994) 'Using peer and self-assessment to develop modelling skills with students aged 11 to 16: A socio-constructivist view', *Educational Studies in Mathematics*, **27**, 4, pp. 413–31.

TARONE, E., DWYER, S., GILLETTE, S. and ICKE, V. (1981) 'On the use of the passive in two astrophysics journal papers', *The English for Specific Purposes Journal*, **1**, 2, pp. 123–40.

THOMSON, M. (1991) 'Mathematics and dyslexia', in DURKIN, K. and SHIRE, B. (eds) *Language in Mathematical Education: Research and Practice*, Buckingham: Open University Press, pp. 188–97.

TOBIAS, S. (1989) 'Writing to learn science and mathematics', in CONNOLLY, P. and VILARDI, T. (eds) *Writing to Learn Mathematics and Science*, New York, NY: Teachers College Press, pp. 48–55.

TOMLINSON, B. (1990) 'One may be wrong: Negotiating with nonfictional readers', in KIRSCH, G. and ROEN, D.H. (eds) *A Sense of Audience in Written Communication*, Newbury Park CA: Sage Publications, pp. 85–98.

TORRANCE, H. (1992) 'Research in assessment: A response to Caroline Gipps', *British Educational Research Journal*, **18**, 4, pp. 343–9.

TORRANCE, H. (1995) 'Teacher involvement in new approaches to assessment', in TORRANCE, H. (ed) *Evaluating Authentic Assessment*, Buckingham: Open University Press, pp. 44–56.

ULEAC (1993) *Coursework Assessment 1993: Mathematics A*, London: University of London Examinations and Assessment Council.

ULEAC (1994) *GCSE Mathematics 1384: Coursework Assessment 1995/6*, London: University of London Examinations and Assessment Council.

VAN DORMOLEN, J. (1986) 'Textual analysis', in CHRISTIANSEN, B., HOWSON, A.G. and OTTE, M. (eds) *Perspectives on Mathematical Education*, Dordrecht: Reidel, pp. 141–71.

VAN DEN HEUVEL-PANHUIZEN, M. (1996) *Assessment and Realistic Mathematics Education*, den Haag: Koninklijke Bibliotheek.

VANDE KOPPLE, W.J. (1991) 'Themes, thematic progressions, and some implications for understanding discourse', *Written Communication*, **8**, 3, pp. 311–47.

VILE, A. and LERMAN, S. (1996) 'Semiotics as a descriptive framework in mathematical domains', in PUIG, L. and GUTIÉRREZ, A. (eds) *Proceedings of the 20th Conference for the Psychology of Mathematics Education* (vol. 4), Valencia, pp. 395–402.

WADE, B. and WOOD, A. (1979) 'Assessing writing in science', *Language for Learning*, **1**, 3, pp. 131–8.

WALKERDINE, V. (1988) *The Mastery of Reason: Cognitive Development and the Production of Rationality*, London: Routledge.

WATSON, A. (1986) 'Opening-up', *Mathematics Teaching*, **115**, pp. 16–18.

WAYWOOD, A. (1992a) 'Analysis of lexical-count data from writing-to-learn mathematics'. Paper presented at the MERGA, Armadale, New South Wales.

WAYWOOD, A. (1992b) 'Journal writing and learning mathematics', *For the Learning of Mathematics*, **12**, 2, pp. 34–43.

WAYWOOD, A. (1994) 'Informal writing-to-learn as a dimension of a student profile', *Educational Studies in Mathematics*, **27**, 4, pp. 321–40.

WELLS, D. (1993) *Problem Solving and Investigations* (3rd (enlarged) ed.), Bristol: Rain Press.

WHITE, J. (1991) *Changing Practice: A History of the National Writing Project*, National Curriculum Council.

WHITWORTH, R. (1988) 'Mechanics: Advanced Level coursework investigations', *Teaching Mathematics and its Applications*, **7**, 4, pp. 169–77.

WILDE, S. (1991) 'Learning to write about mathematics', *Arithmetic Teacher*, **38**, 6, pp. 38–43.

WILIAM, D. (1993) 'Paradise postponed', *Mathematics Teaching*, **144**, pp. 20–2.

WILIAM, D. (1994) 'Assessing authentic tasks: Alternatives to mark-schemes', *Nordic Studies in Mathematics Education*, **2**, 1, pp. 48–68.

WILLEY, R.J. (1990) 'The pre-classical roots of the addressed/invoked dichotomy of audience', in KIRSCH, G. and ROEN, D.H. (eds) *A Sense of Audience in Written Communication*, Newbury Park CA: Sage Publications, pp. 25–39.

WILLIAMS, J. (1977) *Learning to Write, or Writing to Learn*, Windsor: NFER.

WING, T. (1985) 'Reading Children Reading Mathematics, *Mathematics Teaching*, **111**, pp. 62–3.

WOLF, A. (1990) 'Testing investigations', in DOWLING, P. and NOSS, R. (eds) *Mathematics versus the National Curriculum*, London: Falmer Press, pp. 137–53.

WOODROW, D. (1982) 'Mathematical symbolism', *Visible Language*, **16**, 3, pp. 289–302.

Index